TOMMY AND JIMMY:

The Dorsey Years

TOMMY

AND

The
Dorsey
Years

JIMMY

HERB SANFORD

ARLINGTON HOUSE

NEW ROCHELLE, N.Y.

Library of Congress Catalog Card Number: 72–78483

ISBN 0–87000–146–9

MANUFACTURED IN THE UNITED STATES OF AMERICA

Author's Note

FOR a long time, I wanted to do a book about Tommy and Jimmy Dorsey. I loved the music and the people. I had witnessed at first hand the development that took place in the jazz of the thirties, and I was lucky to have had as friends and associates Tommy and Jimmy and others who helped make it all happen. I felt that getting in touch with friends who also remembered those times would be a joy, and I felt that setting down the result might be interesting to others.

For years, I could not find the time. Later on, I didn't get around to it. Then Hank O'Neal introduced me to Neil McCaffrey. And it was Neil McCaffrey who gave me the opportunity to write the book. Neil's interest in and knowledge of the subject impressed me. His faith and encouragement got me started and kept me going.

I needed help, and it came—from Cork O'Keefe, Bill Challis, and Jack Egan, who played such key roles in the story. Henry Butler remembered some of the early years, and Ed Kirkeby recalled the formative years. Several old friends—Randy Hall, Squirrel Ashcraft, and Bill Priestley—who were fellow college musicians, continued their participation in jazz and were in touch with the Dorseys to the end. Bing Crosby, Hoagy Carmichael, and Johnny Mercer were close friends of Tommy and Jimmy, and were generous with their understanding and help. One of the most heartwarming things that ever happened was the response of former members of both bands—Kay Weber, Bob Eberly, Jack Leonard, Yank Lawson, Paul Weston, Deane Kincaide, Bobby Byrne, Charlie Frazier, Carmen Mastren, Johnny Mince, Gene Traxler, Bobby Burns, Cliff Leeman, Lee Castle, Sy Oliver. To all of these friends; to those others who contributed valuable quotes; and to those who gave their encouragement and lent priceless photographs—Marian McPartland, Lee Wiley, Mercedes and Chan Kibbee, Dorothy and Bill Demling, Joe Bryan, Frank Driggs, Walter E. Jones, Kenny Davern, Eddie Condon, Lynn Hutchinson, Hay McClinton, and Garry Moore—I am grateful. And I am thankful that Tommy and Jimmy were my friends.

HERB SANFORD

March, 1972

Tommy and Jimmy Dorsey were in the vanguard of the Big Band Era, in the front line. They made music that made them landmarks all the way through that wonderful time. Some of the things that happened along the way— personal recollections and those of their friends —are recounted here. Sometimes tempestuous, always vital, with great warmth, and with a sharp sense of humor, the Dorseys are remembered both for their musical genius and as two extraordinary human beings.

Contents

Introduction

I can't think of anyone more qualified to write the saga of the fabulous Dorseys than Herb Sanford. This fella was there. He was an integral part of everything that went on.

Tommy and Jimmy were two of my very best friends in the music business. Tommy, mercurial, explosive, loaded with talent and an unforgettable personality. You always knew when Tommy was around. He took a position on every issue, and you knew where he stood. You had to like him, and you had to respect him. Not only for his immense talent, but for his uncompromising integrity. Tommy was pretty frank, all right.

Now Jimmy—Jimmy was a different type fella. Something of a dandy, very modish, soft-spoken. He had good taste in the things life afforded, as well as in music. He was an inveterate punster. He collected them. I can still hear him at rehearsals, cracking some particularly odious pun, and then beaming at the derisive howls it evoked. He was especially proud if the bandsmen pelted him with mutes, drumsticks, and other impedimenta of the tour.

About most things, other than music, Jimmy was rather shy and self-effacing. Sometimes on the Kraft Music Hall, he'd have some announcements to make—introductions of a guest, and such like. This was a chore which literally terrorized him, and led to some amusing malaprops.

Like the evening one of our guests was a famous baritone from the Metropolitan Opera. Jimmy presented him as follows: "And now, ladies and gentlemen, allow me to introduce a famous opera steer."

This was a particularly appropriate description to the folks in the studio audience, since the singer was of more than ample girth. The band broke up, of course.

Tommy, to be sure, was more articulate. I recall one day with the Whiteman band in Baltimore. Tommy had missed a rehearsal, and Pops had fined him $50.

Tommy was irked because he claimed he had a legitimate excuse. Before the matinee, he brooded a bit in a nearby pub (there always seemed to be one near the stage door), and when the band took their places on stage in back of the curtain, he was pretty well pumped up.

Pops was standing on the podium, baton poised, waiting for the signal for the curtain to open and to give the downbeat for the opening strains of *Rhapsody in Blue*.

Tommy arose from his seat, trombone in hand, and announced in a loud voice, "Pops, unless you forgive the fine, when the curtains open, I'm going to play *Come to Jesus* in whole notes."

"You wouldn't," hissed Pops.

"Wait till you hear me," barked Tommy, with mouthpiece to his lips.

At this moment, the curtains started to open. "Forgiven," said Pops, in abject surrender, with a downbeat that more resembled a Sign of the Cross.

I often wondered how Tommy's choice of an opening selection would have gone over.

Yes, this was a colorful and appealing pair of brothers.

It's curious in our business how you work with people and become inseparable companions and then their work takes them in one direction and yours in another. The years go by and you hardly ever see them any more.

Of course, I followed their careers, and was immensely proud of their progress. It's interesting to speculate on what innovative and creative things they might have achieved if they had lived.

Tommy and Jimmy were genuine geniuses.

Bing Crosby

I

REHEARSAL

1

Jazz at the Ramblers Inn

WE listen hard. We tune in 1937 and hear Dave Tough's drumbeats cue the band for the introduction. In the second bar, we know it is leading to the sound of Tommy Dorsey's trombone on *Song of India*. We push on to 1941, and we hear the sound of Jimmy Dorsey's alto sax on *Amapola*.

We listen harder, and it comes back loud and clear . . . a spring night at Princeton in 1925. We were college musicians, and we knew where to go to hear some of the best jazz of the time. We drove straight to the Ramblers Inn, on Pelham Parkway, in the north Bronx, where the California Ramblers were playing.

First stop was Harvey Bergen's Stables, where we rented a Model T Ford. There were probably four or five of us; a given expedition, recalled at random, might have included Randy Hall, Dave Danforth, Frank Orvis, and Ave Sherry. Any number could pile in.

We headed north on the Lincoln Highway. The trip was something of an obstacle race. There was as yet no Holland Tunnel or Lincoln Tunnel to speed us under the Hudson River from New Jersey to

Manhattan. We boarded the ferry at Weehawken, and landed in New York on Forty-second Street.

Things were a lot different in 1925. An advertisement in the *New York Times* announced, "Ford Touring Car—$290." But it wasn't all so different. The *Times* ran one of its very own special kind of editorial, which could well be reprinted today with a contemporary usage of the title word, "Bread." It read, "Bread, according to recent investigation, supplies one quarter of the entire motive power for modern human society . . . While man cannot live by bread alone, neither can he live without it." This is as true in 1972 as it was in 1925, whether we mean the staff of life or a medium of exchange.

Forty-second Street in 1925 was certainly different. It was safe. It was enchanting. It was the heart of the theatre district. We drove past the New Amsterdam, which housed Ziegfeld productions, the marquee proclaiming Marilyn Miller in "Sunny" (song hit: *Who*). At the 46th Street Theatre, it was Al Jolson in "Big Boy" *(Rainbow 'Round My Shoulder)*. "Abie's Irish Rose" was in its fourth year. "No, No, Nanette," starring Louise Groody, was the big hit. *Tea for Two* and *I Want to Be Happy* were heard everywhere.

We sped through Harlem, past Connie's Inn and the famous Cotton Club, soon to become Duke Ellington's base, on up the Grand Concourse, through the Bronx, and, finally, onto Pelham Parkway, arriving at the Ramblers Inn on Pelham Bay.

We came equipped with our own "fresh gin." We entered to the tune of *Sweet Georgia Brown*, ordered set-ups to the tune of *Five Foot Two, Eyes of Blue*, and listened to the tune of *Copenhagen*.

The Ramblers Inn was filled with devotees, including college students, young marrieds, and musicians, who, on a night off, came to listen. In the band were Red Nichols and Bill Moore on trumpets (Red actually played cornet most of the time, as did Bix Beiderbecke); Tommy Dorsey on trombone; Jimmy Dorsey, Bobby Davis, and Arnold Brilhart on reeds; Adrian Rollini on bass sax; Tom Fellini, banjo; Irving Brodsky, piano; Stan King, drums. Bobby Davis, beside playing sax, drew attention with his solos on the mellophone, a brass instrument which, on first glance, might be mistaken for a French horn.

They were all young, some of them our age, some a little older. As individuals, they were not known to the public, but they were making jazz history. Every one of them was a remarkable musician; four were shortly to become big stars and, not long afterward, famous bandleaders: the Dorseys, Nichols, Rollini.

One of our number was Randy Hall, who played a fine sax in our college band. If there had been a crystal ball handy, we might have looked and seen Randy, in the far-off year of 1960, managing Red Nichols and his band on a State Department tour of Asia and the Middle East. We might also have seen that, eleven years later, in 1936, I would become Tommy Dorsey's radio producer. But we would have thought it incredible.

The California Ramblers heralded the Big Band Era, then about ten years off. Along with the Jean Goldkette band in Detroit, they were developing the kind of jazz that ushered in the Swing Era. A few years later, swing-band jazz was being played by the Casa Loma, Ben Pollack, and the Dorsey Brothers, and Benny Goodman raised the curtain in 1935 on what we know as the Big Band Era.

Certainly the California Ramblers were precursors. To the followers who crowded into the Ramblers Inn, they were something new: a big band, with an irresistible beat, presenting exciting jazz soloists. There were no special arrangements. They used stock orchestrations for backgrounds, adding their own touches and superimposing solos. Many of their renditions were "head" arrangements—that is, effects improvised in rehearsal without the aid of specially-written arrangements. The end result was very special indeed. Categorically, the Ramblers were a dance band. For those who wanted to dance, the beat was right. But there were many who just wanted to listen.

And listen they did—and watch. They were fascinated as they watched Adrian Rollini play the couenaphone, a specialty instrument developed by Adrian. It looked like a small saxophone, and had valves arranged like notes of the keyboard. The bell, which gave it the appearance of a sax, was fake; the sound, somewhat like a harmonica, came from the valves. When people asked what it was called, "couenaphone" was too puzzling, so they changed it, simply, to "goofus." Adrian, combining his knowledge of vibes with his bass sax technique, produced some lively jazz on the goofus.

Another sound with a visual counterpart was the slapstick, featured by Stan King, the drummer. It was a small wooden plank, split and hinged. It was waved so that one part would fly open and back, the sound timed to coincide with the afterbeat. Stan used it most effectively, to the delight of the customers.

Among those who came to listen was Spencer Clark, a young reed musician whose attention focused mainly on Adrian Rollini and his bass sax. Before long, Spence was subbing for Adrian, and a year or so later, when Adrian moved on, Spence joined the California Ramblers. Spence and the late Joe Rushton are two of the few who can be compared to Rollini on the bass sax. Rollini was the prototype.

Spence recalls first meeting Tommy and Jimmy at the Ramblers Inn in 1925. "Jimmy, being a reed man, made the bigger impression on my memory. His playing ability and thinking were far beyond any other reed player of my knowledge and I listened with a feeling akin to awe. He was quiet, almost shy, compared to Tommy, but had a fine sense of humor."

Spence remembers a trick Jimmy employed "usually when loaded, of taking a part of his sax stand, a metal rod about two feet long and a quarter inch diameter, with a sort of shepherd's crook at the top, placing a cornet mouthpiece on the crook end and playing licks in the mouthpiece. The effect was great to the public and looked like some kind of strange instrument.

"Tommy's forte," says Spence, "was conversation—sharp, cutting, and very humorous. His playing at that time was acceptable. No one cared about straight playing and his jazz was as good as any other trombonist. He did not show off his breath control, along with the beautiful pure tone which helped identify him later, probably because appreciation for it did not as yet exist in the jazz environment of that day."

Spence lives in Chicago, and he still plays—not only bass sax, but vibes, clarinet, alto and tenor sax, guitar, string bass, and piano.

Another early admirer of the California Ramblers was Herb Weil, drummer, now an executive at Local 802 of the Musicians Union in New York. He did occasional recordings with the Ramblers in 1925, and joined a year later, replacing Stan King. Herb says, "The biggest musical kick I ever had was playing with Adrian Rollini. He made you *want* to play. His tone, intonation, attack, and creative ideas were inspiring."

The emergence of the California Ramblers was no accident. It was the work of Ed Kirkeby—leader, vocalist, manager, broker, mentor, entrepreneur. Before the Ramblers met Ed in 1921, they were a barnstorming group of young musicians, recently out of school. They were from Ohio and Pennsylvania, but called themselves the California Ramblers because, as Ray Kitchingman, the banjo player, said, "It sounds good."

Kirkeby, then a record producer and talent booker, arranged an audition with the B. F. Keith Circuit. As if Ed had written the script, the band was booked into the spot usually requiring years to reach —the Palace Theatre. And they were on the bill with Singer's Midgets, too!

After a season at the Post Lodge in Larchmont, New York, Ed looked for a place they could call their own. He found the Pell Tree Inn, on Pelham Bay, operated by Pete Shanley, of the famous old New York restaurant family. It became the California Ramblers Inn.

Doing what came naturally, Ed was scouting talent. He went to the St. Nicholas Rink, near what is now Lincoln Center, to hear a band called the Scranton Sirens. It was a small jazz band from the Scranton/Wilkes-Barre district of Pennsylvania. It was later considered a milestone in the developing jazz of the period. It had a sixteen-year-old trombone player named Tommy Dorsey and an eighteen-year-old sax and clarinet player named Jimmy Dorsey.

Jimmy joined the California Ramblers in the summer of 1924, followed by Tommy and Red Nichols. Four of the original members were still there: Adrian Rollini, Stan King, Irving Brodsky, and Bill Moore. With this personnel, the California Ramblers entered their finest period. The first record made with this combination was *Sweet Georgia Brown* and *Everything Is Hotsy Totsy Now*, which remains a collector's item.

Bill Moore was a Negro, but so light-skinned that most customers didn't know they were listening to a "mixed" band, probably the first. In those frontier days, this was a hazard. Some of the spots where the band played publicized Bill as an Indian or a Hawaiian. Presumably, they felt that it was safer public relations. In addition to playing a fine trumpet, Bill was an entertainer. When he got in front of the band and did the strut, they howled.

It was the music that drew us from Princeton to Pelham Bay. But there was more. The inn served a stupendous shore dinner, with plenty of steamed clams, lobster, broiled chicken, salad, and dessert. The price: one dollar and fifty cents. Randy Hall reminded me of this, then added, "Maybe you'd better say a dollar seventy-five, they won't believe a dollar fifty." But there is documentary evidence. In Ed Kirkeby's scrapbook, there is a newspaper ad mentioning the dinner, and the price was $1.50.

This was during Prohibition, when hotels were in trouble because they had no bar business to cover restaurant costs. I asked Ed how he managed to break even at the Ramblers Inn—and I know they never allowed any undercover liquor sale. Apparently the nominal cover charge paid for the band. The rest of the answer, I think, was good management on the part of Ed Kirkeby.

As the stars left for various assignments and to form their own bands, the California Ramblers, as we knew the band, eventually came to an end. Ed took over management of Fats Waller in 1938, and the relationship lasted until Fats's death in 1943. Ed is active today; in 1970, the Deep River Boys, managed by Ed for thirty years, toured East Africa as part of the Cultural Exchange Program.

The Ramblers Inn has a history. It was a handsome mansion in the 1800's. In the 1890's it was a roadside tavern known as the Knicker-bocker Inn. After the tenure of the California Ramblers, it became the Pelham Heath Inn. It was destroyed by fire in 1947. The site is now occupied by the Mother Butler High School.

If the school's curriculum includes the history of the spot, and I hope it does, I am sure the students and their teachers will, inevita-bly, hear the Sound of Music, the music made by the California Ramblers.

Tommy and Jimmy moved on to become stars in the historic Gold-kette band. After that, they were part of Paul Whiteman's grand array of talent. The story of their rise to fame begins in the coal-mine district of Pennsylvania . . .

2

꧁ ꧂

Mention the Name
in Lansford

JAZZ emerged from inner America. King Oliver and Louis Armstrong came to Chicago from New Orleans. Chicago produced the Austin High Gang, which included Jimmy McPartland, Bud Freeman, Frank Teschmaker, and Jim Lanigan, plus Eddie Condon, Dave Tough, Benny Goodman, Joe Sullivan, George Wettling, and Gene Krupa. Indiana was a proving ground, with Hoagy Carmichael as catalyst for jazz gatherings which included Bix Beiderbecke, who came from Davenport, Iowa, by way of Chicago. Recording sessions at the Gennett studios in Richmond, Indiana, resulted in collector's items. Detroit was the emanating center for the Goldkette and Casa Loma bands. Texas gave us Jack Teagarden; Kansas City, Count Basie; St. Louis, Frank Trumbauer; Kentucky, McKinney's Cotton Pickers. The coal-mine district of Pennsylvania gave us the Dorsey brothers.

We are told of Jimmy Dorsey, at the age of twelve, playing the time-honored cornet solo, *Carnival of Venice*, in the town pavilion, before a large crowd. It is easy to imagine the twelve-year-old Jimmy attacking it with assurance, even bringing off the triple-tongueing safely.

It happened in Lansford, Pennsylvania, where Tommy and Jimmy grew up and learned their notes. Their birthplace was Shenandoah, in the coal-mining Alleghenies, forty-five miles south of Scranton. The family moved twelve miles east to Lansford, where Thomas F. Dorsey became leader of the Lansford Band. Henry Butler, Indianapolis journalist, whose home town was Mauch Chunk, seven miles from Lansford, recalls the band as a "darn good marching and concert outfit."

The elder Dorsey was also a teacher. Two of his pupils were venturesome enough to keep any music school alive and audible. There is the widely-circulated story that Mr. Dorsey hid the boys' shoes, so that they would have to stay inside and practice. This is undoubtedly true, but it is also true that Tommy and Jimmy really *liked* to play. They learned just about every instrument in the band, starting with cornet. Tommy settled on trombone, Jimmy on sax and clarinet. But they never let go of the cornet. Throughout their careers as bandleaders, each would seize any opportunity for a little cornet playing on the side. Another pupil was Tommy's and Jimmy's sister Mary. A feature of practice sessions was the quartet: Thomas, Sr., baritone sax and cornet; Tommy, tenor sax and euphonium; Jimmy, cornet and alto sax; Mary, E flat ballet horn.

Henry Butler remembers playing piano with the Dorseys when he and they were in their teens. At that time, suffragettes were demonstrating in front of the White House, Al Jolson was playing on Broadway in "Sinbad," singing the George Gershwin-Irving Caesar song hit, *Swanee*, but in Lansford and Mauch Chunk it was jazz and combos and gigs and barnstorming. Henry calls it "that forgotten era of ubiquitous dance pavilions."

One of the combos was the Syncopaters, organized by Vollmer Miller in 1919, when Jimmy was fifteen, Tommy not yet fourteen. Henry Butler recalls rehearsing at his family's home in Mauch Chunk before playing at the Flagstaff dance hall—pavilion, that is. There were six of them: Vollmer Miller, C melody sax; Henry Butler, piano; Henry's brother, Will, banjo; Haman Miller, drums; Tommy Dorsey, trombone; Jimmy Dorsey, sax and cornet. Jimmy played sax on one side of his mouth, switching to the other side for the cornet—this, according to Henry, to develop both embouchures.

Young Jimmy

Young Tommy

Recalling this early association, Henry says, "I couldn't dig Tommy's tromboning then, it was experimental . . ." This is understandable; the trombone took longer to develop as a solo jazz instrument than the trumpet and clarinet. Miff Mole was the one who, perhaps more than any other, made the trombone a *solo* jazz instrument.

Going on, Henry says, "But I could dig Jimmy's expertise on both cornet and sax. On cornet, Jimmy had extraordinary facility. We went through the Liszt *Second Rhapsody,* Jimmy playing notes way out of orbit, almost to the top of the piano scale."

Tommy and Jimmy played with many regional outfits in those barnstorming days. In addition to the Syncopaters, there were the Scranton Serenaders and the Wild Canaries. Then, in 1921, at the ages of fifteen and seventeen, they joined the Scranton Sirens, organized in 1919 with Billy Lustig as violinist-leader. When Tommy and Jimmy joined, they played with Fuzzy Farrar, trumpet; Sid Trucker, sax; Irving Riskin, piano; Joe Settler, drums; Tom Edwards, banjo. Also with the Scranton Sirens during this period was the future bandleader, Russ Morgan, who played both piano and trombone.

For Tommy and Jimmy, joining the Scranton Sirens was an important move. It exposed them to more people in more places, and it put them on the road that led to star spots in big bands and fame as leaders of their own bands.

An early admirer of the Sirens was Bob Stephens, a young Scranton trumpet player, destined to become the first A & R man (artists and repertoire) at Decca Records, when the company was organized in 1934. At Decca, Bob recorded the Dorsey Brothers and the subsequent Jimmy Dorsey band. He remembers the early days, even recalling that the Scranton Sirens drummer, Joe Settler, blazed a trail by beating four to the bar.

Another early follower was Bill Challis, then a Wilkes-Barre high school student, who played C melody sax and who, a few years later, would make jazz history as arranger with Jean Goldkette and Paul Whiteman. Ludwig's Music Store, like the proverbial candy store, was the Wilkes-Barre center for information and talk: "You should hear this sax." . . . "Have you heard the Dorsey brothers?" . . . "They're playing tonight . . ." It was two members of the Scranton Sirens, Russ Morgan and Fuzzy Farrar, who told Challis about the Dorseys before he had heard them play.

Famous bands of the time—the Original Dixieland Jazz Band, Paul Whiteman—came to play at the huge Armory in Scranton. "Scranton was the center and heart of the coal region," says Bill. "It was a good business district and could support a dance every night of the week." Bill was a young fellow who liked music, and so he bought a horn and looked for a place to play. He started with Guy Hall, the provincial Meyer Davis. Hall was composer of *Johnson Rag*, which, some of us will remember, was later played by Jimmy Dorsey and Glenn Miller.

Another job was with Freddie Smalls, local bandleader and piano player, who arranged for Bill to sit in and play with the Scranton Sirens when they played a date at the Elks Hall in Wilkes-Barre. As a result Bill was invited to play with the Sirens on weekends while he was still in school. This was good experience, but Bill's interest was in arranging, and that meant looking for an opportunity with a bigger band.

The Scranton Sirens expanded their horizons and ventured out of their neighborhood-regional orbit and took to the road. In New York, they played at the St. Nicholas Rink, across from what is now Lincoln Center. St. Nick's, pre-dating the old Madison Square Garden, accommodated all kinds of activities, including fights, skating, and jazz. It was where Tommy and Jimmy were spotted by Ed Kirkeby, when he was developing the California Ramblers.

The Scranton Sirens turned out to be a source of supply for the developing big bands. Fuzzy Farrar, Russ Morgan, and Irving Riskin became part of the Jean Goldkette band when it sprang up and grew in Detroit—Morgan as arranger and conductor, Farrar as first trumpet, Riskin as pianist. Jimmy, followed by Tommy, moved on to the California Ramblers and the Goldkette band. Bill Challis joined Goldkette, then moved on to Whiteman's organization, where he was with the Dorseys, Bing Crosby, Bix Beiderbecke, Frank Trumbauer, and Hoagy Carmichael.

3

Muttings-on-the-Crow

IN the spring of 1926, Bill Challis journeyed to Southboro, Massachusetts, near Boston, to deliver his arrangement of *Blue Room* to Charlie Horvath, the Goldkette band's drummer and manager. The band was doing one of those "battle of music" dates, playing alternately with Mal Hallett at a nearby ballroom.

They needed a trombone player in a hurry. Bix, Don Murray, and Jimmy Dorsey suggested Tommy. Horvath telephoned Tommy, and Tommy boarded a train. The train was on time, but Tommy was late. It began to look as if the music battle would be won or lost with one less trombone.

Tommy finally got there in a cab with a bewildered driver. The driver had located the ballroom, "Nuttings-on-the-Charles," in spite of Tommy's insistence that the name was "Muttings-on-the-Crow."

It was a big laugh with the band. And it became one of those stories that stuck. I have heard it from Bill Challis, Cork O'Keefe, Bill Rank, and others. I feel sure that the staying power of the story is due, not just to amusement at the sound of the wrong name, but to Tommy's delivery of the story, as remembered by those who were there. The years would show Tommy to be an accomplished raconteur, with his own special style, and with the right kind and amount of embellishment.

Bill showed up with his three saxophones and his *Blue Room* arrangement. The Goldkette band had come to Wilkes-Barre periodically, and Bill had done an arrangement of *Baby Face*, which worked so well that it was played repeatedly. Horvath had said, "Do some more." *Blue Room* worked even better. It brought Bill $125 plus an offer to stay on as arranger. Bill put his saxophones away.

Horvath told Challis, "Sax players are a dime a dozen, but we need arrangements." He was wrong about sax players—good ones, that is —but he was right about arrangements. They were much needed, and arrangers were less numerous than they became ten years later. There had been no arrangements with the Scranton Sirens, other than the "head" arrangements they created as they played. But, for several years, bands had been getting bigger, increasing from six to ten players, with three saxes, two trumpets, trombone—and this brought with it the need for arrangements. Skillful arrangers, in turn, may have been partly responsible for the advent of the big bands, with larger sections and their four- and five-part harmony.

Jean Goldkette was a phenomenon. Not a bandleader in the usual sense, he was a concert pianist, real estate operator, and booker turned entrepreneur, with a special sense for assembling the right musicians. Goldkette musicians included—beside the Dorseys—Bix Beiderbecke, Frank Trumbauer, Joe Venuti, Eddie Lang, Pee Wee Russell, Don Murray, Bill Rank, Russ Morgan, Steve Brown, Fred ("Fuzzy") Farrar, Paul Mertz, Spiegel Wilcox, Doc Ryker, Irving Riskin, Chauncey Morehouse, and others.

Goldkette had help from Charlie Horvath. It was Horvath who got hold of Bix and Trumbauer in St. Louis and brought them to Detroit. Goldkette booked bands in three spots—the Book-Cadillac Hotel, the Detroit Athletic Club, and the Greystone Ballroom, which he owned.

The Goldkette office was a wild place, located in a building on Woodward Avenue, at a corner where the street sounds were the noisiest in town. The sounds inside the office were noisy, too. Goldkette, an accomplished salesman, spoke softly. Horvath was more volatile and voiced his points with more volume. Their arguments reached high intensity. One time, during one of these arguments, Goldkette said, "Excuse me," and started to open the window.

"Are you crazy?" Horvath cried. "Why are you opening the window?"

"To let some of the noise out."

Keeping peace between the two Dorseys was a Horvath chore that did not appear on the organization sheet. It was a task that had to be handled adroitly, and could rarely be accomplished with impunity, as Charlie sadly discovered. Bill Rank, trombonist when Tommy and Jimmy were both in the band, recalls, "Jimmy was always the level-headed one. Tommy was impulsive and aggressive. They used to fight like cats and dogs, but no one had better say anything about either one of them, because, down deep, they loved each other. One time in Hazleton, Pennsylvania, Tom and Jim got into it in a room at the Hazel Hotel. Jim had a new sax, gold-plated on the bell. Tommy picked it up and threw it on the floor and jumped on it. You can guess what happened after that."

Bill Rank was best man at Tommy's wedding, when Tommy and Mildred Kraft, remembered by all as "Toots," were married a year or so before. Jimmy broke down and cried on Bill's shoulder, lamenting the fact that he had lost his roommate.

Bix was hired for a recording date at the Gennett studios in Richmond, Indiana. He took with him Tommy Dorsey on trombone; Don Murray on clarinet; Howdy Quicksell, piano; Paul Mertz, banjo; Tommy Gargano, drums. Bix asked Hoagy to come along; it might turn out to be a good session. During a break, Bix ad-libbed a theme that caught everyone's ear. As Bix played on, developing the theme, the others went along as naturally as if it were something they knew. They recorded it, and there it was—a great tune with no title. They started brainstorming. It was Bix's tune . . . Bix's home town was . . . Tommy hollered out the title, *"Davenport Blues!"* The record was issued under the name of Bix's Rhythm Jugglers.

According to Hoagy Carmichael, the first recording of a jazz session to be released to the public was done at Gennett. It was *Dipper Mouth Blues*, by King Oliver and the Creole Jazz Band, with Louis Armstrong, around 1923.

The Goldkette dates east of Detroit were booked by Cork O'Keefe, a young Lehigh graduate, who was to become an important figure in the growing band business. In the fall of 1926, when Charlie Horvath left to open his own office, Cork went to Detroit to manage the Goldkette operation. The relationship was immediately productive. Cork arranged bookings at New York's Roseland; during these periods, there were recording sessions at Victor.

Cork had problems, of course. One day, the manager of the Book-Cadillac notified him that Tommy Dorsey was to be fired immediately. Cork got on the phone and asked what had happened. The manager refused to discuss it—just fire him, that's all. After another telephone call or two, Cork finally persuaded the manager to say what had happened. It seemed the band was running a gauntlet of request numbers. A gentleman asked for *Missouri Waltz*—in fact, he asked for it several times without its being played. (Other reports later indicated that the gentleman asked for *Missouri Waltz* not several times but continuously—admittedly, without results.) Finally, Tommy (who was not the leader) told him, flatly, "No!" and added some advice that would come through on television as blips. What made the incident such a crisis was that the gentleman was one of the Fisher Brothers family, and, in General Motors land, one does not turn down a Fisher request so unequivocally. Tommy was removed from the Book-Cadillac to play another Goldkette assignment.

Bill Rank, while reminiscing, recalled a happening when the band played at the University of Pennsylvania. After the job, they all went to Longo's Italian restaurant for spaghetti. Bill and Jimmy noticed a private dining room with the door open, empty except for a girl lying face down on a couch, out cold. After a fast exploratory look, Jimmy took his pen, lifted her skirt, and signed his autograph, "Jimmy Dorsey."

In January of 1927, in an engagement at Roseland, the Goldkette band was in its finest period. They played *Hoosier Sweetheart, My Pretty Girl, Sunday, Blue Room, Clementine.* They are Challis arrangements, but Bill likes to credit some of those who helped with ideas. *Pretty Girl* is Jimmy Dorsey's arrangement, according to Bill. "I only annotated it," he says. "I didn't want good ideas to be wasted." Jimmy was a creative musician, and he did originate ideas; but, in my opinion, it is a credit to Bill Challis that he wrote arrangements which made use of the talents of the musicians who played them. *Sunday* is an example. Much of the ensemble is the voicing of Bix's variations on the melody. Bill also refers to Joe Venuti and Eddie Lang, who, he says, were most helpful.

One of my favorite renditions by the Goldkette group is *Clementine.* Bill says it wasn't really an arrangement. Howdy Quicksell supplied the introduction and ending. The rest was a head arrangement, the ensemble following the melody line, Bix doing the fill and giving us one of his most appealing solos.

It couldn't last. The payroll for this collection of stars was too high. And, even though they were engaging personalities individually, they were not always easy to handle as a group. They and the record company could not agree on the selection of material to be recorded. The band's following was chiefly college students, plus musicians, jazz buffs, and a musically aware segment of the public. Whiteman had a higher payroll, but he was reaching a public that supported it.

And so came the inevitable break-up, in the fall of 1927. The Jean Goldkette band left a trail that pointed the way to good things in the future. The trail was marked by virtuoso performance, innovation, advancement in enlarging jazz horizons. It was a harbinger of the big bands that were to have such a commanding presence in the mid-thirties.

Bill Challis, star arranger for Jean Goldkette and Paul Whiteman

4

Happening at Million Dollar Pier

IN August of 1927, Cork O'Keefe booked the Goldkette band at the Million Dollar Pier in Atlantic City. At the same time, Paul Whiteman, on a Paramount-Publix tour, was appearing in Philadelphia. Jimmy and Tommy had joined Whiteman by this time. Also with Whiteman on the tour were Red Nichols, Miff Mole, and Bing Crosby.

There were rumors that the Goldkette band was breaking up. There was speculation that Jimmy Dorsey was promoting the rumors. Promoting, not starting. The break-up was a virtual certainty. The supposition was that Jimmy wanted Whiteman to hire some of the Goldkette personnel and was maneuvering.

On a night off, Jimmy and others in the Whiteman band, including the maestro, journeyed from Philadelphia to Atlantic City to hear the Goldkette band. It was a big night, a capacity crowd at the Million Dollar Pier. And this particular night was an event. "Pops" Whiteman came to call.

Bix and Bill Challis suggested to Whiteman that he conduct a set.
"But I don't know the arrangements," Whiteman began.

"That won't matter," was the reply. "Just beat it off . . ."

Whiteman turned to the audience. "What do you want to hear?"
Suggestions were shouted from all directions. There were lots of
titles.

Whiteman turned to the band. "*St. Louis Blues.* One and two and
. . ." Bill Challis remembers it well. Some adjustment was required
to stay together in the first sixteen bars. After that, it was positively
inspired. The crowd went wild. When *St. Louis Blues* ended, they
cried for more. The band had never been accorded an ovation such
as this. It was a new experience.

Whiteman's showmanship had won the audience. The Goldkette
band, with all its stars, had never made it as a stage attraction. The
response of the audience there at Atlantic City must have had its
effect on Whiteman. He undoubtedly was thinking about what these
stars could do if they were presented in a proper setting. More
numbers followed *St. Louis Blues,* and the set ended with a triumphant *Tiger Rag.*

Bill Challis remembers glancing across the auditorium, during the
applause at the end of the set. A forlorn figure stood in the doorway,
watching. It was Jean Goldkette.

After the break-up of the Goldkette band in September, the migra-
tion began. Bill Challis joined Whiteman. Bix, Trumbauer, Bill Rank,
Venuti and Lang, Don Murray, and Chauncey Morehouse moved to
Adrian Rollini's new band, The New Yorkers, named for the New
York night club where they played. It was an excellent band, but
neither the club nor the band lasted for long.

Fuzzy Farrar, who, after the Scranton Sirens, became the indis-
pensable first trumpeter in the Goldkette band, began a long and
successful career in radio and recording, working with Nat Shilkret,
Don Voorhees, and other leading conductors.

Cork O'Keefe went on to pursue a distinguished management
career, which included organizing the Casa Loma band, developing it from what had been a relief band in the Goldkette stable;
cofounding Rockwell-O'Keefe, famous talent agency, now General
Artists; and managing the Dorsey Brothers and the Jimmy Dorsey
band.

Paul Whiteman continued the Paramount-Publix tour—Boston,
Buffalo, Cincinnati, Detroit, Indianapolis. Bix and Trumbauer, on

tour with Rollini, showed up in Indianapolis, and it was there that they joined Whiteman.

The hiring was not unexpected. It seemed logical, almost inevitable. Whiteman had helped usher in the twenties with a new kind of music. Always an innovator, he commissioned George Gershwin to compose an orchestral work in the jazz idiom: *Rhapsody in Blue*, introduced in 1924. Now, in 1927, Bix Beiderbecke and Frank Trumbauer, along with Tommy and Jimmy Dorsey, Bill Challis, and Bing Crosby and the Rhythm Boys, added a new dimension.

The tour continued. Tommy brought with him a little C cornet. Between shows, he entertained the band by playing Louis Armstrong's record choruses. Bill Challis says, "He seemed to know everything Louis ever did, as well as—on trombone—everything Miff ever did."

Jimmy Dorsey and Bill Challis roomed together on the tour. Bill tells of a night in Indianapolis at the Indiana Hotel. Bill had a hand organ in the room; he worked on arrangements in the evenings, while the band was performing.

On this particular evening, Bill was working far into the night. About 2:00 A.M., there came a knock at the door. It was Jimmy, and with him were Paul Whiteman and Hoagy Carmichael. Hoagy headed straight for the organ and played his *Washboard Blues*. It was beautiful—and it wasn't the glow from the pubs that made it sound that way. It was the evocative quality of the music.

Whiteman turned to Challis. "Get this down. We'll do it in Chicago."

And so they did—a twelve-inch record, with Hoagy at the piano. Hoagy also did the vocal . . . "Mornin' comes with cloudy skies and rain / My poor back am broke with pain . . . Oh Lordy, won't you hear my song?" The arrangement had changes of mood and tempo. Jimmy and Tommy and Bix did the jazz interludes. It was recorded on November 18, 1927.

A few days later, while still in Chicago, Whiteman recorded another Challis arrangement, *Changes*. Challis and Grofe arrangements were usually done on different dates with different personnel. But Challis remembered that Whiteman once told him he could use anyone he wanted. This he did when *Changes* was recorded. He used the works, about forty people, including two vocal groups—the Rhythm Boys, in a characteristic passage, and the "sweet" trio (trombonist Jack Fulton, violinist Charlie Gaylord, and guitarist "Skin"

Young) as background for Bix's memorable solo.

The Whiteman recording of *San* included a three-trumpet jazz chorus, voiced for second and third to fit Bix's lead. The other two trumpets where played by Jimmy Dorsey and Charlie Margulis. Bill Challis was the arranger—and, on this one, he also played piano.

Being Jimmy's roommate could present problems. Bill Challis recalls one morning when he somehow managed to get into the bathroom first. When he was dressed and starting to go for breakfast, Jimmy called, "Come back and wake me."

After breakfast, Bill stopped in at the theatre for the first show of the day. The introduction of the opening number was written for Jimmy on clarinet, but, when the show started, there was no clarinet to be heard, only the orchestral background. The show ended, minus one sax-and-clarinet player.

"Fifty bucks!" This was Whiteman's greeting when Jimmy arrived backstage after the show. Immediately, before there was an opportunity for Jimmy and Tommy to say anything to each other, Tommy approached Bill and asked, "How come you didn't wake up the brother?" Bill offered to pay the fine, but Whiteman relented.

Soon afterward, Jimmy married Jane Porter, whom he had met several years before in Detroit, and who was the Miss Detroit of 1927. Jimmy decided it was time to move on from the Whiteman band. He felt he was not getting enough recordings; he was being used only on the Challis arrangements. Tommy had already left. They were both headed for a non-stop work schedule in the radio and recording studios in New York.

The Dorsey boys had come a long way from Mauch Chunk and Muttings-on-the-Crow. There was a long, eventful road ahead.

5

"Just Call Plunkett's..."

PLUNKETT'S was a way station for musicians, a New York speakeasy on West Fifty-third Street, under the elevated. It was a point, between any two other points, where it was a good idea to stop. If Jimmy Plunkett had kept a log, it would have documented the movements and whereabouts of the top jazz musicians during the late twenties and early thirties. A random check of those present at any time might have found Jimmy McPartland, Jack Teagarden, Eddie Condon, Red McKenzie, Tommy Dorsey, Benny Goodman, Jimmy Dorsey, Glenn Miller . . .

Plunkett's was General Headquarters. When a conductor or contractor wanted a certain musician for a radio or recording date, the direct line of communication was Plunkett's call board, which occupied a prominent position near the front door. It was covered with messages; the phone rang constantly.

The place was listed in the telephone directory as the "Trombone Club"—in honor of Tommy, according to Eddie Condon. Bill Priestley says it was aptly named, recalling that ". . . someone looked down the bar one day, and *every* customer was holding a trombone case."

Eddie was a regular; he tells of what he calls the "communal system" of buying drinks. If you were broke, there was always someone who would buy. Another time, it would be you who would buy.

Plunkett's was a source of instant bands. Bill Priestley remembers attending a cocktail party which was sagging. He knew that the remedy was music. He wanted to help out the hostess, and he knew where to call. When Plunkett's telephone answered, Bill asked, "Who's there?" In about fifteen minutes, Benny Goodman and the Mound City Blue Blowers, which included Eddie Condon and Red McKenzie, showed up. The party started to swing.

There were times when Plunkett's was the eye of the storm. One of them occurred when Jimmy McPartland was reckless enough to step in to separate the Dorseys when they were staging one of their jousts. The result was predictable. McPartland is a tough guy, but the role of peacemaker was too tough.

There was a real need for the call board. The demand for expert musicians in radio was increasing steadily. Most of the early programs were musical, featuring studio orchestras. The Depression did not stand in the way; the rise of radio as a mass medium took place during the Depression. On the hour and half hour, corridors in the buildings where radio networks and stations were located resembled railroad junctions; musicians changed from one studio to another, one program to another. There was a period when Benny Goodman and Jimmy Dorsey were sharing an apartment. Both were doing much studio work. For no reason in particular, when one got a call, he sent the other to sub for him. Either way, there was no cause for complaint on the hiring end.

There were some excellent studio orchestras conducted by recording veterans, such as Nat Shilkret. One of the early musical "strips," a quarter-hour across the board, had Shilkret as conductor and alternated Ruth Etting and the Boswell Sisters. Bill Challis was arranger, and the Dorseys were among those in the orchestra. Lennie Hayton, Victor Young, and Don Voorhees used the talents of leading jazz men in their orchestras. Hayton was a Whiteman alumnus. A memorable part of the Whiteman record of *Sweet Sue* is Lennie's celeste in back of Jack Fulton's vocal. Young and Voorhees were successive conductors of the Atwater Kent Dance Hour in 1929. The band was, ostensibly, Goldkette's. It had been two years since the break-up, but Jean was still active in the business and the name had carryover value. The studio band was much larger—about thirty men. There were reminders of the original Goldkette band—Fuzzy Farrar was among those present, and the studio band was booked by Cork O'Keefe. Another musician in that studio band was Arnold Brilhart, who had been in the California Ramblers. It seemed that Arnold was in almost every studio band; he was that good.

There was one studio band which stood out from the rest. It seemed bigger and louder than all of them. This was the fifty-five-piece band in the Lucky Strike Hour, conducted by B. A. Rolfe. It thundered along with the inexorable force of a juggernaut. Opening the studio door, during a rehearsal, was like entering a foundry, especially if you came in near the percussion.

But the program was a full hour and it had many hours of rehearsal. It was a source of income for musicians, and the band was large enough to accommodate a lot of them. The layout was so vast, it was impossible for Rolfe to keep an eye on everything that was going on. For a bit of diversion, during the long hours of rehearsal, Tommy Dorsey occasionally played a half tone off. There was so much sound and volume that the dissonance created by Tommy never reached Rolfe. The recipient, the one who bore the brunt, was Phil Napoleon, who played trumpet and sat directly in front of Tommy.

Joe Venuti and Tommy Dorsey were together in a number of studio bands. There were times when some sort of antidote was needed to counter a low music quotient. At such times, Venuti and Dorsey thought alike. Bill Priestley recalls a New Year's Eve broadcast. "The leader," says Bill, "made the unwise move of angering Tommy and Venuti at rehearsal. So they sneaked back to the studio, before anyone returned for the program, and in the big stand-up chimes inserted a piece of paper, rolled up in the bottom of each pipe, so that, when released, the paper expanded and deadened the note completely. The result was that, when the old year went out, the leader signalled for the chimes and got 'tick'—'tick,' a little louder—'TICK,' really hard blow, but no note—and finally the chimes player, realizing he'd been had and the leader having a change of life, gave a full golf swing on the last note, which over-turned the whole chimes set. It sounded like they were taking the annual inventory at Hammacher Schlemmer's." The incident was duly reported by Tommy and Joe at Plunkett's after the show.

A musician who doubles—plays more than one instrument in a broadcast—is paid extra for each additional instrument. A sax player is paid extra if he plays the clarinet in the same broadcast, and he is

The Dorseys often backed Connee Boswell and her sisters on their
early records

Great songsmith and singer Johnny Mercer

paid still more if he plays flute. One of those who fared well under this rule was Ross Gorman. He had a head start: when he was with Whiteman, he played twelve different reed instruments, including the musette. To Gorman, these were not sufficient to take care of all the studio work properly. So he invented new instruments. His work room at home, stacked with an inexhaustible supply of instruments for doubling, was the equivalent of a blank check drawn to his order.

The radio work alone was enough for a full schedule. But there were recording dates, too. There were many Dorsey Brothers recordings with familiar names—Fuzzy Farrar, Arnold Brilhart, Frank Teschmaker, Arthur Schutt, Eddie Lang, Ray Bauduc, Glenn Miller, Bunny Berigan. Tommy and Jimmy recorded with Bing Crosby, Mildred Bailey, and Connee Boswell. They did many records with Red Nichols. And they were part of a group assembled by Hoagy Carmichael for some dates at Victor, a group that also included Jack Teagarden, Gene Krupa, Benny Goodman, Bud Freeman, Joe Venuti, and Bix Beiderbecke.

A few of the gang—Jimmy Dorsey, Joe Venuti, Eddie Lang, and Frank Signorelli—strayed from radio and recording to play in the pit orchestra of Joe Cook's Broadway show, "Rain or Shine," conducted by Don Voorhees. Dave Chasen, the Hollywood restaurateur, rode a ferris wheel on stage. Joe Cook's home in Lake Hopatcong, New Jersey, was as much fun as "Rain or Shine." Among the memorabilia was a baseball, exhibited in a glass case, with the inscription, "The only baseball not autographed by Babe Ruth."

Campuses were good territory for jazz musicians. The students understood and appreciated the music, and the musicians liked to play for them. When Jimmy Dorsey and Benny Goodman were playing at Princeton during a house party weekend in 1928, they sat in with the undergraduate band of Bill Priestley and Squirrel Ashcraft. Bill remembers that, when they played *Tiger Rag*, Jimmy borrowed Brainard Kremer's alto sax and played his famous chorus just the way he had recorded it. Jimmy handed back the alto sax to Kremer, who "promptly played the chorus right back at him, note for note, which brought down the house and fractured Benny and Jimmy, as well as all of us . . . Benny Goodman and Jimmy Dorsey then did a 'question and answer' chorus on the blues, playing some very amusing a la Ted Lewis type of corn, holding the instruments up in the air, playing on one knee."

It was late, one night at Plunkett's, when Randy Hall and Bill

Priestley escorted Tommy home, back to the apartment he and
Jimmy were sharing. This was one of the infrequent periods when
Jimmy was on the wagon. He and Tommy seemed to alternate: when
one was on the wagon, the other was on the booze. It was a problem.
The one who was on the wagon was impatient with the one who was
not.

Jimmy opened the door and confronted the three of them, Randy
and Bill supporting Tommy. Jimmy was angry, but not at Tommy. He
exploded at Randy and Bill. It was their fault. They had got Tommy
drunk. They should have had more consideration.

It was confusing. No one knew better than Jimmy that Tommy
needed no help when he was in the mood to have a few drinks.
Maybe it was that protective thing that went on between them. Soon
Jimmy would be off the wagon; everything would be normal again.

On another occasion, Tommy was carried out of Plunkett's, and
not because he was drunk. He was taken to the hospital; it was
appendicitis, and there was an emergency operation. When he
recovered, Tommy went on the wagon. He stayed on for many years.
When he did start drinking, it wasn't for long. He went back on the
wagon and stayed on for most of the rest of his life.

Along about 1933, there was a new boy in town. Bill Priestley
recalls meeting up with Red McKenzie that summer. "Red mentioned a 'new kid, Johnny Mercer,' who was very nervous at finding
himself in the fast company of the Whiteman organization and how
he and Jack Teagarden had reassured Mercer to help him over his
stage fright." That was the year Johnny sang with Teagarden and the
Whiteman "Swing Wing." It was the year he wrote *Lazy Bones* with
Hoagy Carmichael. In another two years, he would be on his way to
fame in Hollywood.

The decade was getting older. Repeal came along to make it easier
for the operators of some of those places where the bands played. We
were on the eve of the Big Band Era.

II

PERFORMANCE

6

The Brothers:
Mac and Lad

IT was spring, 1934. For five years, the Dorsey brothers had played anonymously in the studio orchestras of top radio programs. They had made many distinguished recordings under their own name, featuring the best musicians. Now they decided to assemble an organized band and appear in person.

It was a great band. It was an augury of things to come.

George Simon, author of *The Big Bands*, heard the Dorsey Brothers when their band was only a few weeks old. It was near Boston, at Nuttings-on-the-Charles, the place Tommy thought was Muttings-on-the-Crow eight years before. In his book, George tells how he and several fellow college musicians "stood transfixed in front of the bandstand . . . listening to a band we'd never heard of before and the likes of which we hadn't known until then even existed . . . one of the slickest, most exciting musical aggregations ever to enter our musical lives . . . it was a stupendously, solidly swinging band that impressed us that night . . ."

This is exactly what I thought when I first heard the Dorsey Brothers a month or so later, and I can't say it any better. It was indeed a swinging band. In both concept and execution, there were characteristics which were developed to a high degree in the later work of both Dorseys. The music reached out and communicated with the audience.

Glenn Miller and Ray McKinley were in the band. Their talent and experience, added to that of the Dorseys, helped explain the immediate acceptance of the band. Beside playing trombone, Glenn was arranger. Ray McKinley was a great asset, both for his impeccable drumming and his showmanship. The instrumentation was unusual, in that there were three trombones and one trumpet.

Glenn helped organize the band. He and Ray were on a western tour with the Smith Ballew band. When Glenn learned that Tommy and Jimmy were about to organize a band, he called Tommy and told him that Ballew was giving up his band. Glenn and Ray joined the Dorseys, along with four others from the Ballew band—saxist Skeets Herfurt, trombonist Don Matteson, guitarist Roc Hillman, and the band's first vocalist, Kay Weber.

On scene was a former associate, Cork O'Keefe, who had managed the Goldkette band and organized the Casa Loma Orchestra. Cork was a partner in Rockwell-O'Keefe, the talent agency which handled Bing Crosby and Connee Boswell, and launched the Dorsey Brothers band.

Cork and Kay Weber still remember vividly the long hours of rehearsal put in at the Rockwell-O'Keefe offices, when the band first got together. The Dorseys and Miller were perfectionists—to a degree which, in retrospect, was prophetic. At first, there was the question of who would be leader. Jimmy was scared. Tommy, it was agreed, would be the one to stand in front. This was the practical decision. Jimmy was not always diplomatic with customers, whereas Tommy didn't mind taking care of a few happy birthdays.

The band signed with the newly-organized Decca Records and found their recording director to be Bob Stephens, the trumpet player from Scranton, who remembers Tommy and Jimmy in the Scranton Sirens. Some of those Dorsey Brothers records are collector's items—*Honeysuckle Rose* (two sides), *Stop, Look and Listen*, *Milenberg Joys*, *Dinah*.

The band played all of that first summer at the Sands Point Bath Club on Long Island. Bob Crosby had joined the band to share the

The Dorsey Brothers Orchestra rehearsing at NBC, spring 1934. Front: Bob Crosby, Kay Weber, TD. Second row: Skeets Herfurt, Jack Stacey, JD, Roc Hillman. Back: Don Matteson, Ray McKinley, George Thow, Glenn Miller, Bobby Van Eps, Delmar Kaplan

vocal department with Kay Weber. Sands Point meant air time, which was increasingly important. Skeets Herfurt recalls the night of the big storm. Thunder, lightning, wind, rain—and lights out. The band continued playing, at first trying valiantly to play the arrangements from memory, then switching to choruses of old favorites. At the end of the set, Jimmy said, "Mac, how are we going to do the broadcast without any lights?"

It was a terrifying question. This was to be the very first network broadcast of the new Dorsey Brothers band. And no lights. Tommy disappeared and returned with enough candles to light all the stands. The candles were hard to come by; they had to be grabbed from waiters trying to get them to screaming customers. According to Skeets, the panic button produced a good result: the broadcast came off without a mishap.

After the summer at Sands Point came more one-nighters. As with all bands, the one-nighters were necessary, financially and as a proving ground. They were strenuous, and there were strains—especially between Mac and Lad—Tommy and Jimmy, that is. Jimmy called Tommy "Mac," Tommy called Jimmy "Lad." Separately, they each referred to the other as "the brother."

Their differences were not in music philosophy or approach. They liked the same kind of music, and they played in the same general groove, although with individual characteristics. Their differences were over details, and sometimes the details were blown up.

There were welcome interludes whenever the band was in Pennsylvania within any sort of reasonable distance from the Dorsey home in Lansford. "Mom" Dorsey always had the band come for dinner. Mrs. Thomas F. Dorsey, mother of the brothers, was affectionately called "Mom." And the dinners were something to be enjoyed and remembered. I am glad this excellent custom continued, for I was to experience it a few years later.

In the spring of 1935, the band played for a police ball in the Armory in Troy, New York. Present was a local boy, from nearby Hoosick Falls, who was getting attention for having recently won Fred Allen's Amateur Contest. It was discovered that the local boy knew how to sing. He was Bob Eberly. Bob Crosby was leaving to lead the new Bob Crosby band. Tommy asked Bob Eberly to come to North Adams, Massachusetts, where they were scheduled for another one-nighter, and join the Dorsey Brothers.

About a year after the band played its first engagement, the Dorsey Brothers opened at Glen Island Casino, in New Rochelle, New York. This was the most popular and sought-after of all the band spots in the east. For the previous two seasons, Casa Loma had played to enthusiastic crowds at this attractive spot on Long Island Sound.

Opening night was a grand affair. Pals and devotees came from all directions. Kay Weber remembers some of them. "Franklin D. Roosevelt, Jr.—I think he was in college then. I recall his white shoes were smudged . . . Naturally, all the great musicians—Jack Teagarden, Jack Jenney—Tommy literally busting a gut to impress them—Jerry Colonna, who often came in and sang his robusto renditions of *You're My Everything* and *Vesti la Giubba* . . . John Barrymore and his young love, Elaine Barrie . . . Lena Horne with Lennie Hayton . . . most of the Yankee baseball team—they were soon to be the world champions—Red Ruffing, Lou Gehrig . . . Connee Boswell was there . . ."

It was a big night. It looked like a good summer. The time was right and the Dorsey Brothers were ready. But resentment was building between Tommy and Jimmy. Jimmy resented Tommy being in front, presumably taking all the credit while taking care of the happy birthdays and anniversaries. Tommy resented Jimmy sitting there, criticizing him "with his eyes," as he once put it to Bob Eberly. And there was the fateful question of tempo.

One night, about two weeks later, Tommy called for *I'll Never Say 'Never Again' Again* and counted off the tempo. In this number, Jimmy and Jack Stacey switched from saxes to cornets to join George Thow for a three-cornet chorus. Jimmy felt that the tempo was too fast for the cornet chorus. He looked up and remarked:

"Mac, that's a little fast, isn't it?"

Tommy's reaction was instant. He walked out, straight out and away. No big scene, just a swift exit into the night.

Ed Dorn, manager of Glen Island Casino, telephoned Cork O'Keefe, who was having dinner at nearby Wykagyl Country Club. "You better get over here."

Cork sped to Glen Island, found Jimmy looking off in the distance, nonchalantly smoking a cigarette as if nothing had happened.

"Where's Tommy?"

"He's gone."

"Why?"

A rare picture of the Dorsey Brothers Orchestra at New York's Palais Royal, January 1935: Jack Stacey, Kay Weber, Jimmy, Tommy, Skeets Herfurt, Bob Crosby

"You know how Mac is. It's the problem we've always had. I was playing baritone, the tempo was too fast for the cornets, so I told him, 'Mac, the tempo stinks.' "

It happened on Decoration Day. "Separation Day," they later called it.

While Jimmy carried on and Tommy remained incommunicado, radio stars and program executives were figuring out plans for the upcoming season. Kraft wanted to buy Bing Crosby. Along with Bing, the Rockwell-O'Keefe office wanted to sell Jimmy and the Dorsey Brothers band, which was, de facto, the Jimmy Dorsey band. Before the band could be sold to the advertising agency and sponsor, it was necessary to sell it to Bing.

Bing had not heard the band, because, in those days, the "remotes" —i.e., the broadcasts from hotels and clubs—did not reach California. But the horses were running at Saratoga in August and Bing would be there. He didn't want to go to Glen Island—he didn't want to get into crowds and, besides, he would have to wear the hairpiece.

Cork O'Keefe suggested they do a record date. This would give Bing a chance to hear the band. This was okay with Bing. He would come to New York from Saratoga. In the aftermath of "Separation Day," Bing was impartial. He wanted to hear the band with both Tommy and Jimmy. The situation had to be handled adroitly. Every band in the business was hustling the job, wanting to work with Bing.

Cork located Tommy and persuaded him to do the record date. "For you I'll do it," Tommy said, "and for Bing, but not for that_____."

It was a hot August day when they assembled at Decca. Bing listened to the band, liked it. Then Decca's boss, Jack Kapp, entered, and a most confusing scene unfolded. Kapp asked what song was being recorded. No one seemed quite sure. It appeared the song was *I Wished on the Moon.* Lou Diamond, representing the publisher, Famous Music, embarked on a sales talk. Jimmy interrupted, saying, "Let's make *Dipper Mouth*." Bing couldn't care less. He just wanted to hear the band and find out how he sounded with it. Furthermore, he would do only one vocal chorus, which seemed highly irregular.

Finally, Kapp said, "Are you going to make it or aren't you?"

Bing replied, "I can't sing more than one chorus and do it well."

"It's up to you. I can't argue if your mind's made up."

For Jack Kapp, this was, alas, not the day. No record was made. Bing heard the band and departed.

Bing told Cork he wanted the band. He liked both Tommy and

Jimmy, but would take either one. Jimmy, of course, wanted the job, but would back off if Tommy got it.

This was Cork's cue for one last effort at reconciliation. He arranged for a meeting in his office. Tommy agreed to attend, stating that he would not budge. It was grim. The question was put to Tommy: would he come back?

Tommy rose from his chair, walked slowly toward the door, turned and said, "I wouldn't go back with that_____if I had to drop dead." Then he turned to Cork and said, "And *you*—what I won't do to *you!*" Then he left.

Jimmy had been looking out the window. He turned to Cork, tears in his eyes.

"What'll I do?"

"From now on, you're the boss."

It was the end of the Dorsey Brothers band, little more than a year from its beginning. But it was not the end for the Dorsey brothers. It was a new beginning.

7

Transition: Two Bands for One

THE walkout was fateful. Tommy stuck to it, but not because he was too stubborn to backtrack. I feel sure that, having taken the step, he knew, intuitively, that the separation was right. To be sure, he was catapulted by the emotion of the moment. And his curtain line at the meeting in Cork's office hardly seemed a wise conclusion thoughtfully arrived at. But events would show that the move was right.

Between Tommy and Jimmy there were similarities—and some differences. Each had a temper, but showed it differently. As Cork O'Keefe explains it, "Tommy would raise hell, Jimmy would insinuate it." They were alike in that their tempers were balanced by compassion.

Tommy was outgoing and demonstrative, Jimmy was easygoing and reticent. In Jack Egan's words, "Tommy was the politician, but, with Jimmy, you had to know him." A sense of humor was an asset shared equally and abundantly.

In music, it was mostly similarities. There was great expertise on the instruments. Both were creative musicians. Each was a perfectionist. They both played with taste. There were those who said Tommy was more "commercial." This was a vote of confidence or a dismissal, depending on who said it. Tommy, it is true, used a wider range of material. And the sound of that trombone sometimes gave an undistinguished ballad much appeal. Both were knowing judges of material, although, on the whole, Tommy's choice appealed to a wider public.

There were no differences that made Tommy and Jimmy incompatible as people, as friends, or as musicians. But they were not compatible as co-leaders, especially when each one was a virtuoso. Tommy stood in front and conducted, but it was a joint venture. Each has his say, and they didn't always agree. There had to be one leader.

Jimmy set about finding a trombone player to play Tommy's parts in the Jimmy Dorsey band, while Tommy set about finding himself a band.

For a time, Jimmy presided over what Cork O'Keefe calls a "parade of trombone players." What this means is that old friends helped out in the pinch. Among them were Jack Jenney, Will Bradley, and Jerry Colonna; they came to Glen Island after playing radio shows, and played the rest of the evening with Jimmy's band. But they were not available for the job. Finding a trombonist who could play Tommy's book wasn't easy. Glenn Miller had moved on months before to help organize the Ray Noble band.

Jimmy remembered a young trombone player he and Tommy had heard the previous winter in Detroit, where the Dorsey Brothers were appearing at the Fox Theatre. While in Detroit the band, with Kay Weber and Bob Crosby, was invited to Cass Technical High School. They were welcomed in a mass meeting in the auditorium. Tommy played with the school band, whose leader and trombone player was sixteen-year-old Bobby Byrne.

Bobby was invited to come to the theatre and see the show. As if for indoctrination, he arrived backstage at the very moment when Tommy and Jimmy were in the midst of a fight. Then he moved out front and saw the show. He still recalls a Duke Ellington medley with Kay Weber's sympathetic singing of *Solitude*.

There were some sideshows, too. Joe Yukl, Glenn Miller's replacement, agreed to allow the band members, for one dollar apiece, to

Song publisher Jack Bregman with Mac and Lad

Kay Weber sings *Solitude* with Jimmy's band in autumn 1935

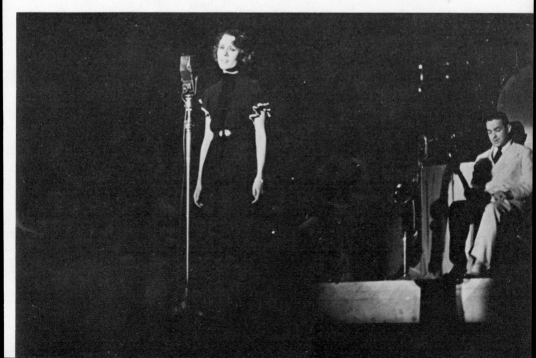

watch Bob Crosby toss a pie in his face. Joe also jumped into icy Lake
St. Claire—in return, of course, for one dollar apiece. And for Joe
there were no ill effects. It was pianist Bobby Van Epps who caught
cold as he paid his dollar and watched from dry land.

While the band was still in the area, Tommy and Jimmy asked
Bobby Byrne to play a one-nighter with them at a nearby Air Corps
base. Bobby played the date, said goodbye, and thought it was the
end of a pleasant encounter. It was not long afterward, only a few
months, when Bobby received a wire from Jimmy: come to Glen
Island.

Bobby brought his harp along, just in case. He could play it, too,
also piano and flute. But the important thing was the way he played
trombone. He was the answer to the problem. He could play Tommy's book, and he made a beautiful sound. Bobby also found time for
various other activities. He was a camera buff. He liked fencing, and
brought along his swords. Bob Eberly was awakened at 4:00 A.M. one
morning by Bobby, who was looking for someone who would join
him for fencing practice. Bobby bought a motorcycle for thirty-five
dollars. Bob Eberly, who roomed with Bobby, well remembers the
sound which heralded Bobby's arrivals and departures.

In September of 1935, Tommy took over the Joe Haymes band and
began building the Tommy Dorsey band. From the Haymes personnel he acquired a talented young arranger, Paul Weston, who was to
be an asset as Tommy's band developed. Paul was a Dartmouth
graduate and, incidentally, a Phi Beta Kappa. Gene Traxler, the
bassist, stayed with Tommy steadily for four and a half years. Noni
Bernardi, one of the alto sax players, made the arrangement of Tommy's theme, *Getting Sentimental Over You*. Noni is today a Los
Angeles city councilman.

Tommy got started recording with Victor that same month. Ed
Kirkeby, who had scouted Tommy and Jimmy for the California
Ramblers, was recording director at Victor. He signed Tommy, and
Tommy asked if he could get an advance. "Sure," replied Ed, "but
better yet, let's record right away—next week." The band's first
recording was *Take Me Back to My Boots and Saddle*.

The band's first steady job in New York was at the French Casino.
"We were strictly the dance music," says Gene Traxler, "and had the
dubious honor of finishing each night at 3:00 A.M. But Tommy, want-

ing to make good, always played ten or twelve minutes overtime.
One night Sam Weiss, the drummer, set an alarm clock under the
bandstand where no one could get to it to turn it off, and sure
enough, at 3:00 A.M. on the button, we were in the midst of *The Very
Thought of You* and it started ringing and continued for at least five
minutes, sounding like a fire alarm."

Tommy set out to build up the band personnel. In at least one
instance, he made a decision on impulse. He listened to Bert Block's
band, broadcasting from the Roadside Rest in Oceanside, Long Island. He liked the work of the vocalist and decided immediately to
hire him, without meeting him and hearing him in person. The
impulse was right. The vocalist was Jack Leonard.

"My first meeting with Tommy," recalls Jack, "was the night I
went to work for him at the Shrine Mosque Theatre in Newark." A
network broadcast was scheduled, and there was no time for Jack to
rehearse or check keys, which had been set for the previous vocalist.
"I was petrified thinking I would sound badly on coast-to-coast radio
due to improper keys, and I mentioned this to Tommy before going
on. His reply was, 'Don't worry about it, they'll love you.' That was
the start of a truly exciting experience for me."

Two others from the Block band joined Tommy, along with Jack
—Axel Stordahl, arranger and trumpet player, and Joe Bauer, trumpet player. Jack, Axel, and Joe sang vocal choruses as the Three
Esquires. Jack says, "In a three-man package, the astute TD had a
vocal trio, two trumpet players, an arranger, and in me a solo vocalist
plus lead singer in the trio."

Carmen Mastren recalls, "I was working with Wingy Manone
when I joined. Tommy also asked Joe Marsala to join. Joe said, 'I can't
read music,' and Tommy said, 'I'll teach you,' but Joe stayed with
Wingy. I remember Tommy coming to the Hickory House before I
joined, and he heard us playing *Panama* and liked it. Later, he asked
me to make an arrangement, which I did. I left it in New York to be
copied and mailed to the Avery Hotel in Boston. I never received it.
For years after I left the band, every time I saw Tommy he'd say,
'Where's that arrangement of *Panama*?' "

Tommy featured a small jazz band within the big band—the Clambake Seven, with vocals by Edythe Wright. Their first recording late
in 1935 was the hit of the season, *The Music Goes 'Round and
Around.*

Jimmy's band was signed for the Kraft Music Hall, starring Bing Crosby. Jimmy decided to take the entire personnel to California. He could have handled the radio assignment and the collateral work with some local replacements. But he insisted on taking everyone, including Kay Weber and Bob Eberly, neither of whom were to appear on the radio program. Bob recalls this affectionately, saying, "I was not needed." But he *was* needed—for bookings other than radio, and for the future. There was camaraderie in that band. I have talked with a number of those who were there. Not one has failed to mention it.

The pilgrimage from New York to Hollywood was made in the cars of various band members. Bob Eberly drove with Ray McKinley. They all converged on Houston, Texas, for a stay of several weeks. Bobby Byrne had spent all his money for a new car and arrived in Houston flat broke. He found a room at the Y.M.C.A. and looked around for his friends. He must have been the first to arrive, for he could find no one. For a day and a half, the food he saw through restaurant windows looked awfully good.

After Houston, the cavalcade moved on to California. Cork came out from New York in December to make sure all was ready for that January start. Paul Whiteman was still doing the Kraft show from the east. To promote the new Bing Crosby show, Bing and Jimmy did "cut-ins" from Hollywood during December.

Christmas was approaching. Cork was preparing to go home to be with his wife, Marge. Bing didn't want Cork to leave.

"Why go back to New York?"

"To be with my wife for Christmas."

"What's the phone number?"

Bing called Marge and persuaded her to come to Hollywood. The O'Keefes enjoyed a jolly Christmas with the Crosbys.

In January, Bing Crosby began his tenure of the Kraft Music Hall with the help of Jimmy Dorsey and his band. In the same month, the band played the Los Angeles Palomar, the most important ballroom spot for bands on the west coast. And, in the same month, Cork O'Keefe returned east to see if his New York office was still there. For Jimmy and the band, Hollywood was home base for the next year and a half.

To my old friend
Herb —
Warmest Regards
Bing
Crosby

Bing was close to the Dorseys since the Whiteman days

1936 was the year swing moved in everywhere. Swing was not new, but Benny Goodman's smashing success the year before pointed the way for a whole new wave. Listening and dancing to the music of popular swing bands was pursued with vigor by just about everybody, with the young crowd in the vanguard. It was a spectator sport, a pervasive part of the American Scene.

It was not an easy year for Tommy, but it was an important one. It was a year of development. The New York opening was at the Lincoln Hotel, now the Manhattan. It was attended, like all such openings, by many professional people, including the usual quota of music publishers and song pluggers. Jack Bregman and Rocco Vocco, two leading publishers, asked Cork O'Keefe to come and sit at their table.

Cork agreed, but remembering the last time he had seen Tommy, asked, "Who'll get the police protection?" He got there while Tommy and the band were on the air. Cork decided he would make the try. As Tommy came off the bandstand, at the conclusion of the broadcast, Cork was standing there, alert, ready for the confrontation. Tommy was struck dumb. Cork laughed. Tommy threw his arms around Cork, accompanied him back to the table, and joined in an uproarious ribbing session. All was well.

After the Lincoln Hotel engagement, Tommy and his band hit the road. It was rugged. Jack Leonard says, "We paid our dues, playing innumerable one-nighters in every city and hamlet, in ballrooms, tobacco warehouses, any place that had a roof." Jack goes on to recall "the dominating force of Tommy himself . . . discipline, hard work, hours of rehearsal, and his beautiful playing. He was a true leader. Tough but true."

Gene Traxler, recalling the one-nighters, says, "Tommy always made the long bus trips bearable by stopping to play ball; or, if we were near his home in Lansford, we would go by his home and his mom and sister would cook Pennsylvania Dutch pot pie for the whole band, or we would stop at a famous restaurant in any part of the country and fill ourselves with the house specialty." Gene adds, "One of the most difficult things to get Tommy to do was to stop the bus for a rest stop. He either had a reserve tank built in or he had no bladder at all."

In the summer of 1936, Tommy and the band were the eight-week summer replacement for Fred Waring, sponsored by Ford, broadcasting from the Texas Centennial in Dallas. Hay McClinton, pro-

Jack Leonard, four years with Tommy, did the vocal on *Marie*

Glamorous Edythe Wright, Tommy's first girl vocalist in 1935, stayed aboard for four years

ducer of the Ford Sunday Hour, flew down from Detroit for a rehearsal. Hay says, "I remember that Tommy ordered a *case* of Dr.
Pepper and drank it." The fact that it was Dr. Pepper is believable;
Tommy was on the wagon. The fact that it was a case, not just a few
bottles, was characteristic; Tommy had to go the whole way.

During this period, the band played a two-week job at the St.
Anthony Hotel in San Antonio, travelling to Dallas each week to do
the broadcast. Paul Weston, Freddie Stulce, Joe Dixon, and a couple
of others were in a cab in San Antonio on the way to catch a train
for Dallas when they got hit broadside by someone driving too fast
at an intersection. Their car turned over three-and-a-half times. Paul
says, "Only the fact that we were packed in the little cab like sardines
kept us from having injuries more serious than cuts and concussions,
but a couple of the guys did miss one broadcast."

One of those who had to miss the broadcast was clarinetist Joe
Dixon. Bobby Burns, Tommy's manager, recalls "that was the day we
had scheduled our arrangement of *Finger Buster*, which featured Joe
on the clarinet. Anyway, when we got to Dallas, I found out that
Isham Jones was playing there and I quickly borrowed the services
of his clarinet player—Woody Herman."

"While in Texas," says Paul Weston, "all the guys used to go to a
musicians' hangout to jam, and they let me be the warm-up piano
player and Phil Harris the warm-up drummer until Howard Smith
and Dave Tough got ready to play. Musicians came from all over
Texas to play and be heard, and Phil Harris has always insisted that,
when one of the tenor players opened his case, a lot of fodder fell
out."

Bud Freeman recalls Tommy supervising the broadcast engineer,
who was setting up, testing, and positioning the microphones for a
broadcast from the St. Anthony Hotel in San Antonio. The engineer,
who felt that he knew how to do it, finally asked, "Why are you so
worried about it?" *"Because,"* replied Tommy, emphatically, "this is
going to the brother." Presumably, he thought Jimmy would be
listening from California, and he wanted him to be favorably impressed.

During the eight weeks, the band also played at the Baker Hotel
in Dallas. Carmen Mastren says, "We played for lunch, dinner, and
supper. In between, we would run back and forth to the Centennial
grounds and rehearse for the show. They paid us Dallas scale and it
was a joke. We told Burns we wanted to talk to Tommy, so we had

a meeting in his room. Out of a clear blue sky, Dave Tough said, 'Tommy, please don't get any more programs—I can't afford it.' It cost him more to tote the drums back and forth than he got for the show."

Paul Whiteman played at the Centennial. Opposite him was Joe Venuti with a small band. Paul Weston remembers, "That's where Venuti got annoyed at Whiteman's elongated baton with a light on the end of it, so he took the big long electric light out of his own music stand, and conducted his little band with it, much to the amusement of the musicians, if no one else."

In New York, advertisers and their agencies were making plans for the new season in radio. The Depression had lifted. Radio, which had matured during the Depression, was Big Time. The Brown and Williamson Tobacco Company was in the market for a radio show with a star comedian. Those high ratings of Jack Benny, Burns and Allen, Eddie Cantor, and Fred Allen looked mighty good. The advertising agency was looking, but there was no comedian who was available and who had a "guaranteed" rating. There was one possibility: Jack Pearl, who had built a huge following as the prevaricating Baron Munchausen, whose "Vas you dere, Sharlie?" had become a nationally popular saying. It was decided to take a chance on a Jack Pearl Show.

A band was needed. It would do only one number, but some of us took the position that it wouldn't hurt to have a *good* band. The reports of Tommy's drawing power on the road were impressive. His records were popular. And so Tommy was signed.

The Jack Pearl Show didn't make it. Jack was an able and experienced performer, a former Ziegfeld star, but the time had passed for Baron Munchausen. It was evident there would be a replacement.

Tommy's band was clearly headed for the top. The time was right. There was only one decision to be made. The Tommy Dorsey Show for Raleigh and Kool Cigarettes was launched.

8

Sentimental Gentlemen

RALEIGH and Kool introduced Tommy as "that Sentimental Gentleman of Swing—Tommy Dorsey, his trombone, and his orchestra —with Edythe Wright and Jack Leonard."

As anyone might guess, the opening number on the first show was *Song of India*, and the featured number was *Marie*. They were on the two sides of the hit record that was accelerating the pace of the band's rising popularity.

People still ask who made the arrangement of *Song of India*. It was a group effort, and we always knew that the introduction was Tommy's, but just how it all came about has not been generally clear. Carmen Mastren, Tommy's long-time guitarist and arranger, gave us the answer recently when he was talking about Tommy as a bandleader. Here is the story, as Carmen tells it:

"Tommy had a way of taking an arrangement apart, cutting and adding, and it always came out better than the original. Look what he did with *Song of India*. It was my assignment, but I forgot about it completely. Every time he would ask me about it, I'd say it's almost finished, but I had never written one note, until one night at the

Meadowbrook Tommy asked if it was ready, because he wanted to record it the next morning. I had to confess it wasn't ready, but I told him I would work on it between sets—and that we did. The intro was Tommy's idea, which I put down immediately. I had written the first part when Bud Freeman came back where we were working. That little sax bridge that comes in after the trombone solo is more or less Bud's idea. I just scored it for saxes. I sketched the rest, and Red Bone took it home and worked on it all night and brought it in the next morning. I had forgotten all about the second part, which I guess you could call the chorus. I told Red to make it a trumpet solo, because I knew Bunny Berigan had one more date to do before leaving the band. The rest is history. The only thing Bunny did on that date was play the choruses on *Marie* and *Song of India*."

The arrangement of *Marie* is a different kind of story. It happened at Nixon's Grand Theatre in Philadelphia. Bobby Burns, Tommy's manager, remembers, "We had been working at a restaurant in Boston, Levaggi's, and we were really dying from lack of business. Harry Squires, an agent, called and asked if we wanted to come to Philadelphia . . . I spoke to Mr. Levaggi and he was delighted to get rid of us." On the bill at Nixon's Grand were "a Negro chorus, Peg Leg Bates, and the Sunset Royal Serenaders." Tommy and the band closed the show. "The Sunset Royal's big number," says Bobby, "was *Marie*."

The arrangement was acquired for fifty dollars. They really didn't need the parts; one of Tommy's arrangers could have written them out from memory. Bobby gave Doc Wheeler, the Sunset Royal's leader, a check "to keep it legal." The dividend they got with the *Marie* arrangement was the patter, sung by the band in back of Jack Leonard's vocal chorus:

"Oh, Marie, 'tis true . . . Just breakin' for me . . . Girl of my dreams, I want you, I need you . . . Have a little faith in me . . . Tra, la, la, la, la . . . Here I go cryin' again . . . Take me, darlin', take me . . . On a night like thisssss . . . We'll go pettin' in the park . . . Oh, the way I like it, darlin', I'm yours . . . Spoken as it came from me . . . Oh, body and soul . . . I'm livin' . . . Livin' in a great big way . . . MAMA!"

Each line of the patter followed a line or word in the lyric, as if to comment on what was being said in the lyric:

Bunny Berigan graced many an early Dorsey Brothers record date, waxed two of his greatest solos on TD's immortal *Marie/Song of India* coupling

That Sentimental Gentleman of Swing

Jack: Ma - rie . . .
Band: (starting on fourth beat of "-rie")
         . . . Oh, Marie, 'tis true . . .
Jack: (starting over "'tis")
         . . . the dawn is breaking . . .
Band: (starting on fourth beat of "brea-king")
         . . . just breakin' for me . . .

Song of India and *Marie* each started a long line of descendants.
Song of India was the prototype of a series of "swing classics" includ-
ing *Liebestraum, Humoresque, Mendelssohn's Spring Song, Goin'
Home,* and *Hymn to the Sun. Marie* was followed by *Who, Yearning,
Sweet Sue, Blue Moon, How Am I to Know,* and *East of the Sun,* each
with a like treatment.

Song of India and *Marie* demonstrated Tommy's belief in having
a wide range of material. The book included standards such as Paul
Weston's swing treatment of *Night and Day* and Axel Stordahl's
Smoke Gets in Your Eyes; Howard Smith's easy swing arrangement
of *Nola;* Larry Clinton's swing original, *Satan Takes a Holiday;*
Deane Kincaide's *Beale Street Blues,* a highlight of the stage shows;
and Cahn and Chaplin's *Posin',* an entertaining swing specialty. In
the year following *Song of India* and *Marie,* there was a prodigious
production of material. From the beginning, Tommy was determined not to have a "style." There would be no trade-mark gim-
micks.

Rehearsals were not predictable. A visitor might venture in and
find Tommy in the role of raconteur, which he enjoyed and did very
well. Or he might find Tommy delivering a fight talk with a lucidity
and persuasiveness that would have been the envy of any coach. A
sluggish performance on the part of a musician had a traumatic effect
on Tommy. He wanted musicians who *liked* to play. He wanted none
who played, as he put it, like a "fat man on a full stomach." A phone
call from M.C.A., the talent agency booking the band, could always
be counted on to produce a crisis. Tommy and M.C.A. were natural
enemies.

During rehearsal breaks, band members wandered into the corri-
dor outside NBC studio 8G. Small talk touched on anything and
everything. Naturally, some of it concerned music and musicians. In
one discussion, the comparative merits of several leading musicians
were being overhauled. Tommy got mostly straight A's. Bud Free-

man, who was feuding with Tommy at the time, assumed a pained look and said, "Well, he makes the best sound." That much he had to allow, but no more.

Bob Weitman, Hollywood producer who was general manager of New York's Paramount Theatre in the thirties, got to know Tommy well. Weitman originated the band policy which was pursued by theatres across the country. Tommy played the Paramount many times, and Bob was a keen observer. Here is the way Bob tells what happened during a performance on stage:

"It goes without saying, Tommy was an extraordinary musician, and probably one of the outstanding soloists in the music business, not only as a jazz musician, but as a concert trombonist. He was a great stickler for musical accuracy and deportment amongst his musicians. He would fraternize with his men, was a great party guy, and fun-loving, but once he was on the stage with his musicians, all was business. . . . One New Year's Eve, during a midnight show, he did something before a packed audience of 4,000 people which proved to me that music and deportment and conduct were uppermost in his mind. One of his musicians, during a number, was not playing together with the rest of the group while Tommy was playing his trombone. Tommy detected it, and turned and saw the musician reading something from his stand other than the music. Tommy stopped the number right in the middle, in front of the 4,000 people, and said, 'Ladies and gentlemen, you came here to be entertained, and one of my boys is welshing on the job.' And he dismissed him from the stand right there. He got a tremendous ovation, and he continued on with the number. This was Dorsey—the musician, the leader, and the perfectionist."

The day-to-day business of the band included all sorts of knotty problems. A constant factor in this ever-changing scene was Bobby Burns, Tommy's band manager. He figured out the right way to do the job: he simply accepted crisis as the norm. His equanimity could counteract tension. When one of our radio shows—one which was running dangerously long—turned out well, Bobby complimented Tommy on the show, incidentally remarking that the show ended on time after all. Tommy denounced Bobby for not being aware of the irrelevancy of timing to entertainment value. Bobby smiled; he knew the difference. I knew that Bobby knew. And Tommy knew that Bobby knew. It was an exercise. They understood each other.

The Tommy Dorsey Scene had many settings: NBC Studio 8G, Victor recording studios, theatre dressing rooms, the Dorsey home in Bernardsville, ballrooms, hotels. A rallying point was the Pennsylvania Roof . . .

9

At the Pennsylvania Roof

THE Pennsylvania Roof, in what is now the Statler-Hilton in New York, is fondly remembered in any Tommy Dorsey reminiscence session. The first engagement there came at a time when the band's top position was assured. The radio show was a hit. The records were on the most-played list. The camaraderie in the band extended to friends of the band and to the fans who gathered there.

The band table, adjacent to the bandstand, was the dugout for us non-playing members. I say "us" because, although my only responsibility was the radio show, I was a sort of adopted member of the band. I figured I had to consult with Tommy on matters pertaining to the show, and there seemed to be nothing wrong in liking the music so much that nightly visits were deemed necessary.

This band table was a kind of Round Table. There were Edythe Wright and Jack Leonard, non-playing but working. Arrangers Axel Stordahl and Paul Weston were there, and p.r. man Jack Egan. People from other tables came by. Edythe held court. It was headquarters.

Those who came to dance, listen, and watch covered a lot of territory. There were movie stars Merle Oberon, Reginald Gardiner, and Hedy Lamarr. Tennis stars Gene Mako and Don Budge were regulars. Yankee pitcher Red Ruffing and catcher Bill Dickey were there; also the Red Sox's great right-handed slugger, Jimmy Foxx. There was always the college crowd, including Franklin D. Roosevelt, Jr., then a student at Harvard.

This was the year of the Big Apple, the swing square dance, contemporary of the jitterbug and the shag, forerunner of the twist. When the Big Apple came on, the listening-watching crowd around the bandstand made way for the dancers. It was worth watching. The dancers ad-libbed a performance that could have been conceived by a professional choreographer. It was as picturesque as the traditional square dance, and it was equalled in drive only by the dancers at the Savoy Ballroom in Harlem.

There was, naturally, a song, *The Big Apple*. It was recorded in August, 1937, by Tommy Dorsey and the Clambake Seven: Pee Wee Erwin, Johnny Mince, Bud Freeman, Howard Smith, Carmen Mastren, Gene Traxler, and Davey Tough, with Edythe Wright's vocal.

Song writers were well represented. The team of Cahn and Chaplin, who wrote *The Big Apple* and *Posin'*, a specialty number done specifically for the Clambake Seven, also wrote *If It's the Last Thing I Do*, given the full treatment by Tommy's trombone and Jack's sympathetic vocal.

Hoagy Carmichael dropped in often. *Stardust* was one of the early Tommy Dorsey recordings; it was released back-to-back with Benny Goodman's version of the same number. Hoagy loved the band, and he loved to go where there was good jazz to be heard. On one occasion, this led to an extended evening. When the Pennsylvania Roof closed at 2:00 A.M., Hoagy remarked that Albert Ammons and Meade Lux Lewis, the boogie-woogie pianists, were playing at Cafe Society Downtown in Greenwich Village. With only a slight whizzing sound, we were on our way, explaining to our wives Ruth and Bobbie that it was quite early.

We reached Cafe Society, and the carpet was rolled out for Hoagy. Ammons and Lewis were working on the two upright pianos. Before long, Hoagy and I joined them—eight hands on two pianos. At 4:00

A.M., the legal closing hour, the door was locked, drinks were on the house, and we played on. We finally left and climbed into a cab going uptown. At Thirty-fourth Street, we stopped for a traffic light, side by side with a milk delivery truck. We disembarked from the cab and joined the driver on his truck. The driver was congenial. As he drove us home, bottles of milk were opened. It was just the right morning's end to a lovely evening.

Another frequent visitor, when in town from California, was Johnny Mercer. Johnny still remembers one evening when he and his wife Ginger came in. Tommy, visiting at their table, learned it was Johnny's birthday. Later in the evening, the band played *Happy Birthday*, and Tommy sent a large birthday cake to the Mercers' table. "When I cut into it," says Johnny, "it turned out to be full of lead sheets of my flop songs, which amused Tommy greatly and also pleased Ginger and me."

Bobby Burns recalls the incident, but he doesn't say "flop songs." He says that Tommy "hollowed out the inside of the cake and filled it with old lead sheets of songs that never made it."

What makes it especially amusing is that Johnny seems to have had nothing but hits. It's easy to name them. The list is long; we can start with *Lazy Bones, Blues in the Night, That Old Black Magic, Skylark, One for My Baby, Laura, Moon River, Days of Wine and Roses.*

Jimmy McHugh was another who came to the Roof often. Every time he was there Tommy played a medley of his hits, which, Bobby Burns remembers, "would take the best part of an hour." The songs included *I Can't Give You Anything but Love, Sunny Side of the Street, I'm in the Mood for Love, You're a Sweetheart.*

A favorite visitor—everybody's favorite—was Mrs. Thomas Dorsey, Sr.—"Mom," as she was affectionately known to all of us. She always checked in at the band table; she was one of the group. When she had her own table, it was a popular checkpoint. Mom was fiercely loyal to her boys. Phyllis Condon remembers a guest mentioning the name of a trombone player whom she considered lacking in expertise. "Him?" she queried. "Why, he hasn't got enough wind to blow the dust off a fiddle."

Tommy loved to play trumpet for fun and relaxation. Just as, on the Paul Whiteman theatre tour, he entertained the band between shows, playing Louis Armstrong's record choruses on a C cornet, he customarily played trumpet in the last set at the Roof. Invariably, the tune was *Blue Lou*, a composition of Edgar Sampson, who wrote

Stompin' at the Savoy and *Don't Be That Way*. The chord structure of *Blue Lou* pleased him, and he didn't stop at one or two choruses. The band fell in, and it developed into a first-class jam session.

One night, we witnessed the birth of a song. There were periodic sessions to clear out the books. As new arrangements were added, the books became weightier, and it was necessary to eliminate those numbers no longer needed.

One of these sessions was fateful. It took place at the Pennsylvania Roof after the 2:00 A.M. closing. As always, it was attended by friends and associates, also by music publishers and song pluggers, who wanted to keep up with what was going on.

Tommy made decisions rapidly. Bobby Burns stood by, keeping the record and making notes. As each title came up, the word was "Keep it in" or "Send it to the file."

One of the titles was *Dancing with You*. This was a song with words and music by Michael Edwards, a family friend and musician who had played in the Lansford, Pennsylvania, band with Tommy's father. When it was submitted a year before, Tommy decided to put it in the books. Why not? It was a pretty tune. He gave it to Axel Stordahl to arrange, adding, "Don't waste time on it—just trombone on first chorus, vocal, eight bars and out."

Dancing with You had been played and sung for a year and got little attention.

"Send it to the file."

A voice was heard from somewhere among those in attendance. It was Jack Robbins, one of the greats among music publishers, maker of hits.

"Please, Tommy," Jack said, "don't throw it out. Let me take it, and you give me permission to assign a professional lyric writer to do a new lyric. We won't change a note of the tune. I know you'll have a hit."

"Sure—go ahead."

The lyric writer selected by Jack Robbins was Bud Green, writer of countless hit songs, including *Alabamy Bound, I'll Always Be in Love with You, Flat Foot Floogie, Sentimental Journey*.

The new song—that is, the same tune with the new lyric—was recorded with the same arrangement, the one Axel was told not to waste any time on. It was an immediate hit, a top seller, and was awarded the 1937 ASCAP Prize. It remains today a standard.

The original lyric began,

> "Dancing with you
> To the strains of a
> Beautiful mel-o-dy . . ."

With the new lyric, the song began,

> *"Once in a while,*
> *Will you try to give*
> *One little thought to me? . . ."*

It was the same beautiful melody—the original lyric was factually correct—but with a whole new feeling.

The happiest one of all should have been Michael Edwards. He had composed a fine melody. Writing lyrics is a special skill. Only a few composers have ever managed it.

One night between sets, several of the band members were engaged in a bull session. It had to do with the time-honored question: which is more important in a song, words or music? Jack Leonard, understandably, felt it was the words. The first trumpeter, Andy Ferretti, maintained it was the music.

The argument was getting nowhere. I ventured a question, "How about *Once in a While?*"

That ended the argument, but it didn't prove that the words are the more important. What it did prove was that a good song is the proper marriage of words and music.

There were nights when the scene shifted from the Pennsylvania Roof to Bernardsville, New Jersey. . . .

10

Expeditions to Bernardsville

THE closing hour at the Pennsylvania Roof was not always the end of the evening. Often it signalled a change of scene to Tommy's home in Bernardsville, New Jersey. The entr'acte was a fast ride in Tommy's Buick Roadmaster. Forty-eight miles in exactly one hour. On weekends, there were other cars in the cavalcade, loaded with the entourage Tommy had gathered up. Sometimes an invitation came without warning, a kind of friendly order. There was no time to ponder. Just get in and we're on the way.

There were no regrets. The expeditions were a welcome change, relaxing and congenial. On arrival, there were nightcaps for all except Tommy—the wagon still prevailed—then to bed.

Next morning, on at least one occasion, we found that Tommy had not been to bed at all. He had spent the rest of the night working his layout of Lionel trains on the top floor. This was relaxation, and it was characteristic. Tommy didn't sleep long at a time. He would wake up and start thinking of a project of some kind.

74

The train layout he put together was not a simple grouping of toy trains. Tommy went the whole way. It was fifty feet of tracks, representing the route from New York to Los Angeles, complete with signal devices and switching. Engines and cars in full detail. Accurate topography from plains to mountains to coast. The Santa Fe, from Chicago to Los Angeles, had all the important stops, including Dodge City and Albuquerque. And everything worked.

We started off the next day witnessing a transcontinental run on the Dorsey route from New York to Hollywood. It was a good performance and a receptive audience. After breakfast, we were on our own. A pleasant aspect of the Dorsey hospitality was that no fuss was made over anyone.

Our hostess was Tommy's wife, Mildred, known to all as "Toots," a much-loved member of the group. There was seldom any advance warning as to who would be there, or how many there would be, but Toots was never at a loss. Present also were Patsy, their attractive daughter, and Tommy, Jr., known as "Skipper." Skipper played a little drums, but he was more interested in football.

It was a twenty-eight-room house, with room for all. On the top floor, beside the train setup, was a dormitory. One morning, some of us were awakened by the radio. Dave Tough, in the opposite bunk, expressed his disapproval of the music. "Imagine waking up to music like that," he moaned. It was Schumann's *Traumeri*, and it did sound dreary.

The bar was a fun spot, a setting for stories told by Tommy and others. One who provided many laughs was Tommy's good friend, George Marlo, the music publisher. Others who were present from time to time included Lennie Hayton, Johnny Mercer, tennis star Don Budge, songwriter Clay Boland (*Gypsy in My Soul*), bandleader Bob Chester, jazz critic George Simon, the King Sisters, the Andrews Sisters . . .

Tommy sometimes acted as bartender, but guests could make their own. There was a phonograph and lots of records. But there was no live music on those weekends. All that was left behind. And there was no business talk, even if an agent had been among those scooped up. Outside, there were tennis courts and an Olympic-size swimming pool. The pool was heated, and stayed in use until Thanksgiving time.

The twenty-two-acre estate, as we saw it on those weekends, was developed over a period of several years. Jack Egan was there at the start. "I went out there," he says, "in late '34 or very early '35—the

Brothers band was playing at the Palais Royale at the time—on a Sunday morning with Tommy and Toots, either just before or right after he closed the deal. We went all through it and around the property, unoccupied at the time, of course, then had dinner, just the three of us, at the Bernardsville Inn."

When the Dorseys moved from Freeport, Long Island, to Bernardsville, they had furnishings for only five rooms in the twenty-eight-room house. "At one point," says Jack, "Tommy asked me to save him any furniture, especially bedroom, we might be replacing at home in Yonkers. I remember going out from the Onyx, leaving the city at 4:00 A.M., getting there at 5:00 A.M., and Tommy rooting Jimmy Plunkett out of bed so I'd have a place to sleep. It was done in shifts in those days. All this in the days before he knocked out five or six rooms on the second floor wing and made it into a playroom, then later had the place landscaped, and installed the pool and tennis court."

The Bernardsville place had recuperative powers. Friends who became ill lodged at the Dorsey home and regained health. It was likewise good therapy for those of us who came for a weekend.

11

❦ ❦

With Jimmy
in Hollywood

LANDING the band spot in the Kraft Music Hall with Bing Crosby
was a good break for Jimmy. With that Thursday night exposure on
the network, nobody had to wonder what had happened to him. Most
variety shows used a studio orchestra. Jimmy gave them a swing
band, but a versatile swing band, adaptable and musically tasteful. It
was right for Bing, and it worked well with the guests.

Jimmy and the band enjoyed the show, with its wide-ranging variety of guests. Yehudi Menuhin, then a child prodigy on the violin,
made his first radio appearance with Bing. Jim Crowley, the Ford-
ham coach, was in town on a scouting trip when he was invited to
drop in for a visit on the show. His conversation with Bing on the air
made an entertaining spot, with a script tailored for Bing's delivery.

Some who were in the band at that time still remember the night
John Barrymore was scheduled for the "Hamlet" Soliloquy. The
problem that night was that Barrymore had reached for the bottle
too many times. It didn't appear that he would deliver the Soliloquy

PALOMAR

VERMONT AT SECOND & THIRD . . . . PROGRAM WEEK OF JAN. 6th

Another "Dixieland Band"-and one of the Greatest!

JIMMY DORSEY'S ORCHESTRA

MASTER OF THE SAXA-
PHONE and CLARINET

THE TOAST OF THE
N. B. C. NETWORKS

WEST COAST PREMIERE, WEDNESDAY NITE, JANUARY 8th

JIMMY DORSEY WILL OPEN HERE FOR A LIMITED ENGAGEMENT
with all of his NATIONALLY POPULAR VOCAL & RHYTHM STARS of the **Bing Crosby** RADIO Program

PALOMAR'S FIRST MUSICAL SCOOP FOR 1936 . . . . DON'T MISS IT

in the usual Barrymore manner. But when the moment came, he straightened up and delivered it flawlessly. This was a feat for Barrymore and a credit to Bing for his expert handling of the preceding talk. When he finished the Soliloquy, Barrymore retreated to the comfort of his previous state.

Jimmy and his wife Jane rented a house in Burbank, just north of Hollywood in the San Fernando Valley. It was where Bob Eberly lived during that first stay in California. The house was Spanish style, with a balcony overlooking the entrance. It was equipped with a jukebox, which promptly buckled and crushed a rare Coleman Hawkins record which Bob had placed within.

At first, it was a two-day week. The radio show only required two days, and there were no local jobs to be had, because the musicians union imposed a period of restriction on outside bands. That meant time on their hands. Jimmy joined the Lakeside Golf Club. The golf and the company were good, and there was some overtime at the nineteenth hole. Jimmy wakened Bob, late one night, and told him there was someone in the yard, some sort of mysterious stranger. The stranger was not clearly visible through the trees, but Jimmy noticed he was wearing white flannels. Bob found a flashlight and began a stealthy approach. The stranger was cornered. He was not wearing white flannels. He was a white horse, whose legs had been visible through the trees.

Another time, Jimmy rolled in at about 4:00 A.M., his hair full of broken glass. He had driven into a filling station, toppling a steel pole which smashed through the top of the car, barely missing him. There was practically nothing left of the car; how he got it back to the house was not clear.

Jimmy found time for constructive work. He hired Tutti ("Toots") Camarata for second trumpet and as arranger. The addition of Camarata as arranger was an important step in building the band that was to achieve such a big success in the next few years. Jimmy's alto sax became increasingly important as an identifying sound in the band. Bob Eberly remembers that Jimmy originally played first alto, and he remembers the fine intonation. It was, incidentally, Tommy who advised Jimmy to feature his alto rather than clarinet. "Goodman got there first," said Tommy. "Nobody else is featuring alto."

There was work in films. One job was in the Fred Astaire-Ginger Rogers picture, "Shall We Dance?". Songs hits were *They Can't Take That Away from Me, Let's Call the Whole Thing Off,* and *They All*

Jimmy's band in Los Angeles, 1936. Back row: Len Whitney, Bob Eberly, Bruce Squires, Jack Ryan, Ray McKinley, Freddie Slack, Shorty Sherock. Front row: Don Matteson, Roc Hillman, Charlie Frazier, Toots Camarata, Dave Matthews, Bobby Byrne

Jimmy and the band at a New Year's Eve costume party in Hollywood, 1935. Front: Don Matteson, Roc Hillman, Bobby Byrne, Skeets Herfurt as Mickey Mouse, Bob Eberly, Bobby Van Eps. Back: Toots Camarata, Kay Weber as Topsy, Jack Stacey, George Thow, Jimmy, Jim Taft, Ray McKinley as Groucho, Joe Yukl

Laughed. The band was augmented to fifty pieces. Fud Livingston, who had joined the band as arranger and fourth sax, orchestrated and conducted the music. At one of the rehearsals a handsome, soft-spoken gentleman approached Fud and said, "If I may suggest, I believe the tempo should be a little slower."

Fud was deferential, even courtly, as he explained, "You see, I arranged it and that's the way I feel it."

"I understand, and I think the arrangements are wonderful, but I wrote the music." Fud had not recognized George Gershwin.

Bing's big interest was his racetrack at Delmar, near San Diego. It had been a farm, an ideal spot for a track. Bing and some partners acquired the property and developed the Delmar Racetrack. The opening in 1936 was a big day. Everybody was there. Jimmy and the band were appointed to launch the ceremonies with the playing of *The Star-Spangled Banner.*

It was decided to use the brass choir. Camarata arranged it for the two trumpets and three trombones. He elected to play first trumpet himself, with George Thow on second, and Bobby Byrne, Joe Yukl, and Don Matteson on trombones. Bobby remembers marching through the crowd to the appointed place. The moment for *The Star-Spangled Banner* arrived. There was silence. All eyes were on the brass choir. Then it happened: Camarata forgot the melody. The others improvised roving parts. The melody passed from one to another. When they all met toward the last eight bars (" . . .OH SAY DOES THAT . . ."), they played the melody in unison, maestoso.

During this period, Jimmy and Johnny Mercer organized a benefit for an old friend—Joe Sullivan, one of the jazz greats. Joe had been the pianist in the Bob Crosby band, launched only a year before, and he was suffering from tuberculosis. The benefit, staged at the Pan Pacific Auditorium in Los Angeles, had many stars taking part. Johnny Mercer took *Pinetop's Boogie-Woogie,* the piano composition of Pinetop Smith, the veteran jazz pianist, and wrote words for the occasion—"all about Pinetop and Joe," Johnny recalls. "We must have been doing something right," Johnny commented in November in 1971, "because that was in 1936, and Joe recovered to live until about three months ago, when he passed away in San Francisco. If we could find the poster, you would be surprised at the list of contributors to that benefit which Jimmy was personally responsible for."

Bobby Byrne found his own way to use spare time. He took flying lessons and became an expert flier. During the war, he became an instructor and bandleader in the Air Corps.

There were jam sessions on Central Avenue, the Harlem of Los Angeles, and at Sebastian's Cotton Club in nearby Culver City. When the hour was unusually late, it was Bob Eberly who had to explain to Jane, who evidently thought Bob was the instigator.

When the waiting period imposed by the union came to an end, so did the two-day week. A schedule of one-nighters made it day and night all week long. Up and down the coast, from Bellingham, Washington, to San Diego, all night in the bus, grabbing enough sleep to get through.

By this time, Kay Weber had returned east and joined the Bob Crosby band, whose leader was her co-worker in the Dorsey Brothers band. Kay married one of the Crosby trombonists, Ward Sillaway.

Bob Eberly was a big attraction on these one-nighters. He knew how to project a lyric. Bob is a baritone, with considerable range. One time, when he ended *Where or When* on the high F, the audience reaction was so enthusiastic that Jimmy had him do it over again —just the ending.

A favorite number with the crowd was *Parade of the Milk Bottle Caps,* which was a showcase for Ray McKinley at the drums. This was recorded that first summer and was a standard Jimmy Dorsey item. Another one that summer was the twelve-inch recording of the songs from "Pennies from Heaven," which Jimmy did with Bing and Louis Armstrong, Louis doing *Skeleton in the Closet.*

When there was a respite of a few days, some of the band would drive to Palm Springs. Their recollection of the Palm Springs of that day sounds delightfully primitive when compared to the Palm Springs of today. It was a sleepy hideaway. There were only a few hotels. The streets were dirt roads. Bob Eberly recalls getting good accommodations for a rate of $17.50 a week, with a swimming pool on the patio. With a few days off you could, as Bob says, "take forty dollars, go to Palm Springs, and live it up."

By the time the second summer in California arrived it was time for Jimmy and the band to journey to New York. They were due to open at the Hotel New Yorker in the fall. And there would be three months of one-nighters along the way. Motors were tuned up in preparation for the mileage. San Francisco, four hundred miles; then five hundred and twenty-five to Salt Lake City; seven hundred and twenty-five to Fargo . . .

Charlie Frazier, tenor sax player, who joined the band in California and stayed ten years, remembers "playing dances through Reno and small towns. Sometimes we could hardly find the place we were to play in. I remember in one town we were playing for about an hour and we heard the fire sirens. The whole crowd left the dance and went to the fire. We waited until they came back from the fire and finished the night. The roads were long, bumpy, and lonely. If you ran out of gas out there, it was too bad—miles and miles before a gas station."

There was a tense moment in Pottstown, Pennsylvania. It was between sets. Jimmy recognized the face of a huge man who stepped on the dance floor and was making for the bandstand with a determined step. Jimmy hastily drew Bob Eberly aside, pointed out the man, and told Bob, "Tell him I'm not here," then disappeared into a back room.

Years before, when Jimmy was about fifteen, an accident occurred when he was working in the coal mines. Jimmy's sledge hammer hit another worker on the head. Jimmy had not seen him from that day to this. Now he was approaching the bandstand and he looked as if he meant business.

The stranger spoke to Bob, said he wanted to see Jimmy. Bob said Jimmy had stepped out. Then Bob went to consult with Jimmy, who told him the story.

Bob returned to the bandstand. The man was insistent.

"Why do you want to see him?" Bob asked.

"He hit me with a sledge hammer a long time ago. I want to thank him."

"You mean you're not mad?"

"No. Back home, I've been famous for years as the guy who was hit on the head with a sledge hammer by Jimmy Dorsey. I want to shake his hand."

Bobby Byrne's snapshots of the Jimmy Dorsey band on a 1936 West Coast tour

The boss

Would you believe Ray McKinley?

Arranger-trumpeter Toots Camarata

Young Ray Eberly, younger Bobby Byrne

Jazz cornetist Shorty Sherock

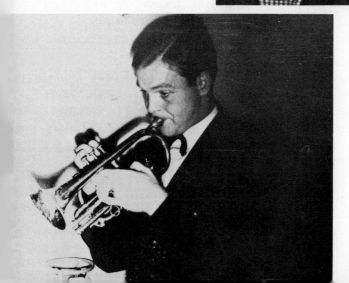

12

Meanwhile,
Back at the Onyx...

ONE place where Jimmy was sure to go, when he reached New York, was the Onyx Club on West Fifty-second Street. Jimmy was an old friend of the owner, Joe Helbock, and the Onyx was sure to have some good music.

As it turned out, when Jimmy returned from California in September, 1937, he received a special invitation from Joe Helbock. Tommy got one, too. It was a celebration, to let it be known that the Dorsey brothers' feud was ended. By this time, there really was no feud, but this was a sort of confirmation. Mrs. Helbock helped Joe preside. Those who helped make it official included Don Matteson, Bobby Byrne, Bob Eberly, and Mrs. Roc Hillman, from Jimmy's side; Skeets Herfurt, Jack Leonard, and Carmen Mastren, from Tommy's side; Cecil Stover, from Casa Loma; and bandleaders Artie Shaw, Joe Haymes, Lennie Hayton, and Wingy Manone; and a host of musicians like Jack Jenney.

Joe Helbock was a successful bootlegger during Prohibition. He loved jazz, and he liked being with jazz musicians. He and Jimmy were pals as far back as 1925, when Jimmy turned twenty-one and Joe got out of the under-thirty group. Joe was a customer at Plunkett's, where he often saw Jimmy and Tommy and the whole bunch.

It was a logical step—the most natural thing in the world—for Joe Helbock to open a place of his own, one which would be a haven for musicians. And so he started the Onyx Club, a speakeasy in the late twenties.

With Repeal and the advent of swing, Joe enlarged his duties from those of bartender and host to include those of entrepreneur. Some of the finest entertainment of the period was presented at the Onyx. Although it was a popular spot with the jazz-going public, the Onyx never ceased to be a meeting place for musicians. The musicians liked Joe and accepted him as one of them.

For a year or so, Joe had a partner—Carl Kress, one of the greatest of jazz guitarists. Carl's wife, Helen Carroll, was lead singer in the swinging Merry Macs, who appeared at the Onyx and on the Fred Allen Show.

Some of the performers made their first New York appearances at the Onyx and became stars there. One was Maxine Sullivan. The Onyx was an intimate place, with a small stage where Maxine sang under a pin spot, backed by the John Kirby Sextet. Claude Thornhill made the arrangements, which were evocative song-settings. Kirby's Sextet had Charlie Shavers on trumpet, Buster Bailey on clarinet, Russell Procope on alto sax, Billy Kyle on piano, O'Neill Spencer on drums, and Kirby on bass. The whole effect, with Maxine's appealing reticence, had the audience spellbound. The big number was the swing treatment of *Loch Lomond.* Other favorites were *Brown Bird Singing, The Folks Who Live on the Hill,* and *Nice Work If You Can Get It.*

The Spirits of Rhythm got their start at the Onyx. For some of those who remember, because they were there, the Spirits of Rhythm and the Onyx were inseparable. They remember Leo Watson's scat-singing, also the trombone sound Leo made with his voice. The trombone was amazingly close to the real thing, and Leo's choice of notes produced excellent jazz solos, attested to by both Tommy Dorsey and Jack Teagarden. Leo's "trombone" was, in fact, the group's "melody instrument." The others were guitars and rhythm. Virgil Scroggins played a newspaper-wrapped suitcase for drums. Teddy Bunn played a fine jazz guitar; he also sang numbers like *Riptide.*

Ernest Myers was the bass player. They called him "Serious" because, when Ernest took a chorus, he concentrated, and his look
became very serious. The Spirits of Rhythm were a big entertainment attraction for the general public, and they also played good
notes for those who knew.

Stuff Smith was another who was brought to New York by Joe
Helbock and introduced at the Onyx Club. Stuff played swing fiddle
and put on a lively floor show with his quintet, which included Jonah
Jones on trumpet and Cozy Cole on drums. Some of their specialty
numbers, like *I'se a' Muggin'* sung and acted by Stuff and Jonah, were
shows in themselves. And when Stuff did the vocal on *I've Got You
Under My Skin,* Cozy responded with "Won't you please let me in?"

It happened for Mike Riley and Eddie Farley at the Onyx, for that
was where *The Music Goes 'Round and Around* happened. The song
originated with Red Hodgson, a Chicago musician, but it was thrust
into national prominence when Riley and Farley put on an act with
it. As Riley delivered the words ("You press the middle valve down,
the music goes round and around . . . and it comes out here"), he took
his trombone apart and demonstrated. It was, as the television movie
trailers say, "action-packed."

The Onyx was a coming-out spot for jazz pianists. Joe Sullivan was
the original. There was Willie ("The Lion") Smith, who stood out on
the sidewalk, surveying the scene and greeting arrivals, and display-
ing a weighty gold watch chain across his vest. His piano compositions, *Morning Air* and *Passionette,* are gems. And there was the
great Art Tatum. People came to listen; Tatum held them spellbound.

It seemed that everybody, at one time or another, stopped in at the
Onyx. It was a haven for Johnny Mercer, during the period when he
was singing with Whiteman. It was where Johnny first met Tommy
and Jimmy Dorsey. Paul Douglas, popular radio announcer and,
later, co-star with Judy Holliday in "Born Yesterday," was a regular.
Paul, who liked jazz as much as Joe Helbock, emceed the mammoth
swing concert which Joe staged at Town Hall in May, 1936.

A familiar presence at the Onyx was the prominent radio actor,
Jack Smart. Jack played hundreds of parts on the air, including the
lead in the thriller, "The Fat Man." Jack weighed three hundred
pounds, but was light on his feet. He loved the Onyx. He showed up
almost every night and proceeded to have the time of his life—
singing, tap dancing, and playing suitcase drums with Riley and

Farley. If he forgot to duck when Mike Riley swung his trombone 360 degrees, he came up smiling.

The Onyx was a regular stop for some of us every Wednesday, following Tommy Dorsey's radio show. One night Edythe Wright, Jack Leonard, and I persuaded Johnny Mince, Tommy's star clarinetist, to join us. It was Johnny's first trip to the Onyx. Maxine Sullivan and the Kirby band were on. They were doing a dulcet number. He listened for a moment, then said, slowly, "What beau-ti-ful music." Not "Swing it, man." Just simply, "What beautiful music."

Occasionally, we strayed to the Hickory House to hear Joe Marsala play clarinet and Adele Girard (Mrs. Joe Marsala) play jazz harp, or to the Famous Door to listen to Teddy Wilson or Joe Bushkin, or to Kelly's Stables when Coleman Hawkins was there. But we always came back to the Onyx. It was like going home.

13

Travelogue

IT was good to hit the road. It was good to get away from New York. Playing a top spot in New York was important. But it was equally important to get out and Meet the People. It was important to have fans meet the band, to find out at the source what goes over best, what new trends are worth pursuing.

The road was also important financially. In a string of one-nighters, a single date could gross more than a week in New York. The appearance of a top band was an event. The spot, in most cases, had high capacity and the crowd turned out in big numbers. Tommy's grosses were high, but I recall one instance in which, for some reason, the receipts were not enough to justify the guarantee. Tommy gave the promoter a refund.

There was only one real advance man, in the professional public-relations sense. That was Jack Egan. But there were three other "advance men" who moved ahead of the band, roosting at the next origination point for the radio show. The others were Paul Weston, Axel Stordahl, and I.

We all had plenty to do. Paul and Axel were constantly working on new arrangements, including special material for the radio show. Jack, in daily touch with Tommy, made contact with the local media. Distance can lend autonomy. The script for the radio show was written in pencil in the hotel room. There was no one to approve or disapprove. It was typed at the local station, never submitted to NBC's "Continuity Acceptance" department.

A one-nighter schedule usually skipped broadcast dates, which were scheduled where there was a network station. With the station as origination point, technical facilities were no problem. The problem was apt to be in finding enough space to accommodate the crowds who wanted to get in and see the show.

But when a broadcast date and a one-nighter coincided, the reverse was true. There was room for the crowd, but no technical facilities. The band would likely play in a huge ballroom or auditorium—any place, as Jack Leonard said, "that had a roof." We actually did—in Raleigh, North Carolina, I think—originate one show in a tobacco warehouse.

Such an origination was a "remote." Engineers from New York or Chicago brought in technical equipment. We brought along a blueprint for a portable temporary control room to be made of beaverboard with room for engineer and equipment, plus three of us. Reaction would be mixed. The engineers were delighted. But the promoters, who were prevailed upon to produce carpenters, thought we were crazy. They'd had bands on the air before. Why not just turn on the mikes? When there was a week at a theatre, the manager was happy to build the control room. It was an audience gimmick. But those beaverboard control rooms worked, especially in warehouses, armories, and the like. We put out a good sound.

The band travelled by special bus, Carmen Mastren remembers. He said, just recently, "Of course you remember that first bus we had. Joe Bauer used to aim for every hole in the road, hoping it would fall apart. It took a long time and about three motors before we finally got a Greyhound." Sleep did not come quickly or easily in a bus. Deane Kincaide customarily used the time making an arrangement. It is not surprising that Deane heard the whole thing in his mind and could do it without a piano, but in a bus? His arrangement of *Boogie Woogie* is still in jukeboxes in 1972.

Before leaving New York, we stumbled on a watchword. The band had played at the Commodore Hotel. Across the street, on Lexington Avenue, there was a Kelly's Tavern, which became a rendezvous

TD flack Jack Egan

Bud Freeman: "Fired twice, quit three times"

between sets. When we moved to the Pennsylvania Hotel, there was a Kelly's directly across on Thirty-fourth Street. When we left town, first stop was Cincinnati. Sure enough, there was a Kelly's across from the hotel. The conclusion was obvious: there's always a Kelly's. It sounds apocryphal, but it held up. Of course, in Chicago it was easy. Just point in any direction.

Wherever we went, Tommy enjoyed seeking out unusual restaurants, Italian preferred, where there was no stint on portions. He found some good ones, but they were no match for the dinners Mom served up when the band—his or Jimmy's—got close enough to Lansford to come to the house for dinner. Yank Lawson recalls a dinner with pork roast, steak, chicken, and five or six vegetables.

There were minor mishaps. At the Stanley Theatre in Pittsburgh, Edythe missed her cue and did not appear on stage for her first vocal. While the band played through the accompaniment, Tommy dashed to the wings and screamed a summons aimed at Edythe's upstairs dressing room. Edythe screamed her reply all the way downstairs and onstage. The band repeated the accompaniment and Edythe sang. On stage, it was all smiles, but the dialogue in the wings would be rated "X."

A suspenseful moment occurred at the Metropolitan Theatre in Boston. Bobby Burns recalls, "In those days, the first show was around 10:00 A.M. I was rooming with Jack Leonard at the Statler Hotel. We both slept over, and Jack and I didn't get there for the opening. It wasn't a big thing for Jack, because he didn't appear until later in the show. With me, it was different, because I had Tommy's trombone, and Tommy was pretty upset when the show opened and he had no trombone."

A high point in the stage shows was Bud Freeman's solo performance on the tenor sax. It was infectious. With waves of approval from the audience, momentum would grow. This delighted Tommy, who would stand aside with a happy grin as Bud continued downstage. Tommy would continue to signal "One more." This sometimes lasted fifteen minutes or longer.

This was the scene when Bud was performing on *Beale Street Blues* at the Fox Theatre in Detroit. Before the show, he and Tommy had had a difference of opinion over something or other. This time, instead of signalling for more, Tommy gave the band the coda signal after Bud had played exactly one twenty-second chorus. Bud returned to his chair with an expression of philosophic contempt.

Tommy grinned broadly. Next show, Bud was on for his customary tour de force. Everybody was happy.

Louisville was home ground for the radio sponsor. There was a trip through the Brown and Williamson factory and a pause at the Pendennis Club for mint juleps. We were shocked to learn that the Brown and Williamson people began work at 8:00 A.M. But then we learned that they finished at 4:00. That made sense. It allowed a longer pause at day's end for those good mint juleps.

The first place we visited in Chicago was the Blackhawk on North Wabash. This was the stand for the Bob Crosby band. We were drawn to the Blackhawk because we liked the band, and because it was one of the places where paths crossed. We heard Billy Butterfield's lyrical trumpet on *I'm Free*, Bob Haggart's beautiful melody—later, with lyric, re-titled *What's New?*. Bob Zurke played *Little Rock Getaway*, originally performed with the band by the composer, Joe Sullivan. And the band played Sullivan's *Gin Mill Blues*. The place was electrified by Bob Haggart and Ray Bauduc with their unique bass-and-drums performance on *Big Noise from Winnetka*. The band played Yank Lawson's tune, *Five Point Blues*. so named because, in Yank's home town of Trenton, Missouri, five streets converged at a point in the center of town. It included solos by Yank on trumpet, Irving Fazola on clarinet, and Eddie Miller on tenor sax.

Squirrel Ashcraft recalls a time he and his wife Jane took Libby Holman to the Blackhawk when the Crosby band was playing there. "As I remember, it was rainy, and the place was almost deserted. It was long and narrow, as you will remember, with the long, narrow bandstand along one of the walls. We were seated right opposite the band, across the little dance floor, just the three of us, and the band played a couple of numbers. Then, with the lights quite low, Eddie Miller came across the dance floor and played *Can't We Be Friends?* to Libby. She cried, and so did just about everybody else."

Johnny Mercer was among those we met up with at the Blackhawk. One evening, Johnny was in a singing mood. The hour was late. The crowd had thinned out, leaving an intimate group, many of whom knew each other. Johnny was invited up to the stand. We were expecting to hear some of his currently popular hits—*Too Marvelous for Words* or *You Must Have Been a Beautiful Baby*. Instead, Johnny asked the band for the blues—just the standard twelve-bar blues. He proceeded to improvise verses about people in the room, shifting from one to another without a perceptible pause. Recently,

I asked Johnny to write just one verse in blues form, to illustrate what
he continued to do for nearly an hour on that evening at the Blackhawk.

> (Traditional blues form)
> *"When Jimmy plays the alto*
> *   he makes the people scream and shout,*
> *The others run for cover—*
> *   it is a saxophonists' rout . . .*
> *And when he plays Oodles of Noodles*
> *   he even straightens Tommy's trombone out!"*

When we saw Squirrel Ashcraft at the Blackhawk, it usually meant
moving the action to his house in Evanston, about a half hour's drive
from Chicago. Squirrel had been a leading jazz musician at Princeton, Class of '29. His love of jazz and his activity in the field have
never ceased.

The house in Evanston, all through the thirties and up until the
war, was a General Headquarters for jazz music and musicians.
Squirrel's wife Jane loved every minute of it. Joe Rushton was a kind
of executive officer for the sessions. It was not an assignment; he fell
into it naturally. Joe played all the reeds, but he is most remembered
for his bass sax. He is also remembered for the decibels tallied by his
motorcycle at each arrival and departure. Bill Priestley, who, with
Squirrel, was co-leader of the jazz band at Princeton, checked in
whenever he came to Chicago, bringing his guitar and the cornet
which Bix taught him to play. Another moving spirit was Crickie
Wheeler, who was to become Mrs. Bill Priestley.

Squirrel's place was a regular stop for both Jimmy and Tommy
Dorsey. They brought into the group an old friend from the Goldkette days, Howard Kennedy. Howard, who was a student at University of Michigan when Tommy and Jimmy were with Goldkette in
Detroit, played guitar on jobs with various Goldkette groups. Occasionally, he sat in with the "first team," sometimes with the "second
team." Squirrel recalls, "Howard was in Chicago, working for Penn-
Central (later Capitol) Airlines, knew nobody, and was very lonely for
music. Tommy came into the Blackhawk hurriedly one night with
the purpose, it later turned out, of stealing Yank Lawson and Charlie
Spivak from the Crosby band. He stopped and said hello and left at
high speed; then, as an afterthought, came running back and brought

Howard over from another table and introduced him. We asked him
to come out to the house a few days later, and he was with us on every
session from then on."

Monday was the night. It was the off night for all the spots in
Chicago. According to Bill Priestley, "Almost anyone was apt to show
up and, over the years, almost everybody we knew took part in
'Sessions at Squirrel's.' " One of these players was cornetist Jimmy
McPartland, who often came back to his home town to play at the
College Inn or the Three Deuces.

Another was legendary clarinetist Pee Wee Russell. There was the
night Squirrel excused himself early, retiring at 3:00 A.M. because he
had an important appointment at 9:00 A.M. The music carried on
until daylight. Pee Wee started for home, stopping at a milk wagon,
as was his custom, to buy a bottle of milk. The driver was out of sight,
making deliveries. As Bill Priestley tells it, "Pee Wee, who had no
change and was not going to leave a bill, got tired of waiting and took
a bottle. Of course, the driver returned at this moment, yelled blue
murder, and Pee Wee ended up in the pokey. When Squirrel came
out of his meeting, he got the S.O.S. and found that the judge before
whom Pee Wee would come to trial was a good friend and a jazz buff
who particularly admired Pee Wee's playing. So it was in the bag, but
rigged as follows: the judge was very stern with Pee Wee, who was
shivering in a dishevelled tuxedo and in need of a shave, and finally
dismissed Pee Wee with a suspended sentence and the grim admoni-
tion: 'Mr. Russell, never let me hear of you touching milk again as
long as you live!' "

Tommy and Edythe Wright and Jack Leonard drove with Squirrel
to Evanston, one night after the radio show. On the way, Tommy said
that Jimmy had often spoken of the completeness of Squirrel's record
collection. Squirrel asked Tommy what he would most like to hear.
Squirrel recalls that Tommy seemed to think this over carefully.
Then he asked for three: first, the Gennett recording of *Davenport
Blues*, the one he made with Bix; then Louis Armstrong's *Oriental
Strut;* and "anything of Miff's." This checks with Bill Challis' story
of Tommy entertaining the Whiteman band backstage with Louis'
record choruses, played on a C cornet, and Miff's record choruses on
trombone. In the case of *Davenport Blues*, it is not surprising that he
liked to remember that historic record date.

The "Sessions at Squirrel's" ended with the coming of the war. But
the custom, as we shall see, was revived later on in the Bix Festivals

Tommy cuts the cake celebrating the band's second birthday in the fall of 1937. Looking on are arranger Paul Weston, attorney-business manager Johnny Gluskin, arranger Axel Stordahl

Tommy Dorsey and band on stage of NBC Studio 8G for Raleigh-Kool radio show, autumn, 1937. Left: Edythe Wright, Jack Leonard, Axel Stordahl. Trumpets: Lee Castle, Andy Ferretti, Pee Wee Erwin. Trombones: Les Jenkins, Earle Hagen. Rhythm: Moe Purtill (drums), Carmen Mastren (guitar), Gene Traxler (bass), Howard Smith (piano). Saxes: Johnny Mince, Skeets Herfurt, Freddie Stulce, Bud Freeman. Right: Paul Stewart, co-m.c. with Tommy, and announcers Dwight Weist and John Holbrook

that grew out of Sunday afternoon gatherings at the Priestleys'.

During our stay in Chicago, we made frequent stops at the Three Deuces. It was only a block from the Chicago Theatre; we couldn't skip it. Jimmy McPartland was the m.c. and band leader. He was playing the cornet given him by Bix Beiderbecke. Jimmy still has that cornet and he makes beautiful music with it.

Returning from a string of one-nighters in June of 1937, Tommy and the band played a date that did not appear on the itinerary. Tommy had learned the date of my tenth reunion at Princeton, and he knew I was responsible for the entertainment. Tommy decided that the band would play at the Class of 1927's tenth reunion. To me it was an impossible dream. I tried weakly to explain that we didn't have that kind of budget. Tommy wouldn't listen. The date was set.

Came Friday night of the reunion. Tommy Dorsey and the band played at our reunion! There had been no advance announcement, but the word spread all over town. We had visitors, invited or not, from everywhere. We were the talk of the town.

The band had not been entirely happy when Tommy first told them that this date was to be tacked on the schedule. But the reception they got was overwhelming. All was forgiven.

The whole thing was characteristic of Tommy. He was generous. He loved doing it. And he couldn't do anything half way.

Among the visitors to our reunion headquarters were two Princeton seniors who were especially interested in the band. One was Kirk Alexander, who joined the production staff of Tommy's Raleigh-Kool radio show, later on becoming television director of the Jack Paar Show and the Merv Griffin Show. The other was Bill Borden, who went on to become arranger for Claude Thornhill's band and is now president of Monmouth-Evergreen Records.

The string of one-nighters ended at 7:00 A.M. one morning at the Paramount Theatre in New York. It had been an all-night bus ride. The band was opening at the Paramount that day, first show at 10:00 A.M. There had to be a rehearsal, if only to set the routine and review the music for the other acts. An opening number was needed. Tommy looked through the book and picked out *Weary Blues.* They hadn't played it in a long time, and the run-through was incredibly bad. Everybody, including Tommy, was just tired. This time, nobody was bawled out. Tommy quietly talked it through, bar for bar. They tried it again; it sounded marvelous. *Weary Blues* was, incidentally, recorded on Tommy's first session at Victor with his new band in September, 1935.

Travelling was over for a while. There would be five shows a day at the Paramount, but that would be comparatively easy. Then would come a stretch at the Pennsylvania Roof and the weekly radio show.

14

"Evolution of Swing"

"EVOLUTION of Swing" . . . a formidable title, suggesting a prodigious tracing of musical history and development. Actually, it was the title of a mini-documentary special in Tommy Dorsey's series of Raleigh-Kool radio shows.

As the show became established and its following grew, it was important to make use of ideas that would attract the interest of the general public as well as the aficionados. We included in each show a production number, usually an amplification of a published number, with extra verses telling a story and with spoken interpolations in rhythm-and-rhyme, bringing in various band members by name for solos. Sometimes we brought in guests, such as Hoagy Carmichael, Connee Boswell, Jerry Colonna, and Shirley Ross, whose material and performance fit in our kind of show. Periodically, we introduced the music from a new show or picture, or a song we hoped would be a hit.

Occasionally, we did a special program. "Evolution of Swing" was one. It was a change of pace. It delivered extra publicity and critical comment. The idea was to pick milestones and recreate them as they originally sounded, using exact notes annotated from recordings. This meant not merely reading the notes; it meant *acting the parts*.

It was, after all, only a half hour. We couldn't start at the beginning. We started with *Memphis Blues* as it was played by a street band in a parade for a 1909 mayoralty election in Memphis. The original title was *Mayor Crump*. The band stopped playing in the seventh and eighth bars (presumably stopping the parade), while the clarinetist, according to the composer, W. C. Handy, improvised a figure which was subsequently adopted by others and became standard.

Then we jumped to *Tiger Rag*, as played by the Original Dixieland Jazz Band in 1916. We included excerpts from the 1920 Paul Whiteman arrangements of *Japanese Sandman* and *Song of India*—not that these were jazz, but they helped illustrate the growing importance of the organized background.

Especially interesting were *Sweet Georgia Brown*, as played by the California Ramblers, and *Clementine*, as played by the Jean Goldkette band. We, naturally, pointed out that Tommy and Jimmy were alumni of both bands. Pee Wee Erwin played Bix Beiderbecke's solo on *Clementine* precisely and affectionately. Adrian Rollini's solo on *Sweet Georgia Brown* was played by Adrian himself. We couldn't impersonate Rollini and his bass sax. Tommy got Adrian to join us for that one number.

In the final part of the program we did the Tommy Dorsey arrangements of *Song of India* and *Night and Day*, and we brought in a bit of *Posin'* with Edythe Wright and *Marie* with Jack Leonard.

We knew that the usual rehearsal on the afternoon of the broadcast was not enough time. The Commodore Hotel, where Tommy and the band were playing at the time, was the scene of an all-night rehearsal. Only the bare night lights and the lights on the music stands broke the darkness.

There was no problem with the notes; they had been carefully written out by Paul Weston and Axel Stordahl. Nor was there any difficulty impersonating the California Ramblers or the Goldkette band. But playing *Japanese Sandman* straight, without any syncopation, took some doing. It was written with four eighth notes and a quarter note leading to two half notes:

Involuntarily, the musicians came in after an eighth-note rest, dotting the eighth notes on the second and third beats:

When they tried to play it straight, they unconsciously played it corny. Tommy screamed, "No! Just play it as written—straight— *legit.*"

They got the point. The show came off well, on January 14, 1938. Paul Stewart, then one of the Mercury Theatre actors with Orson Welles and a leading radio performer, delivered the script in dialogue with Tommy. The program was elementary and minuscule, but it proved entertaining, both to the general audience and to those who already knew the markers that led to swing, which was what they called the jazz of that day.

And there was nostalgia: when Adrian Rollini heard Pee Wee Erwin play Bix's chorus of *Clementine,* he burst into tears. So much seemed to come back in that moment.

The musical content of this show was incorporated in some of Tommy's concerts, starting with the one at the University of Michigan at Ann Arbor a month later. The program for that concert shows the variety of material in the Tommy Dorsey book. Arrangers represented in the program included Fletcher Henderson, Larry Clinton, Carmen Mastren, Benny Carter, Paul Weston, Axel Stordahl, Howard Smith, Glenn Miller, and Deane Kincaide. It was too early for Sy Oliver or Bill Finegan.

The program follows:

TOMMY DORSEY

Swing Concert—Ann Arbor, February 22, 1938

I

1.   *Swing That Music*
        . . . anything can happen.

2.   *Dipsy Doodle*
        —a swing hit of the day introduced by Tommy Dorsey

Tommy's trumpets in late 1937-early 1938 were Lee Castle, Andy Ferretti and Pee Wee Erwin. Trombonist is Earle Hagen, later a top Hollywood composer-arranger

1938: Jack Leonard, front and center

3.   Three Moods in Swing:
     (a)   *Dark Eyes* (Swing Classic)
     (b)   *Satan Takes a Holiday* (Swing Novelette)
     (c)   *Symphony in Riffs* (Swing a la Harlem)

4.   *Trombone Man*
     —a musical biography

5.   Three songs popularized by Tommy Dorsey:
     (a)   *In the Still of the Night*
     (b)   *You're a Sweetheart*
     (c)   *Once in a While*

6.   *Marie*
     . . . a gal who needs no introduction

7.   Evolution of Swing
     (1)   From Then Until Now:
           (a)   *Memphis Blues*, as played in Memphis in
                 1909
           (b)   *Tiger Rag*, as played by the Original Dixie-
                 land Jazz Band
           (c)   Excerpts from Paul Whiteman's arrange-
                 ments of *Japanese Sandman* and *Song of
                 India*
           (d)   *Hot Lips*, an early hot trumpet solo
           (e)   *Gypsy Blues*, a synthesis in early swing
           (f)   *Sweet Georgia Brown*, as played by the
                 California Ramblers
           (g)   *Clementine*, as played by Jean Goldkette's
                 Orchestra, reproducing a Bix Beiderbecke
                 cornet solo
           (h)   *Christopher Columbus*, Fletcher Hender-
                 son's contribution
     (2)   Today: Two Tommy Dorsey Hits in the Swing
           Cavalcade
           (a)   *Song of India*, No. 1 Swing Classic
           (b)   *Night and Day*, swing with light and shade

8.   *Devil's Holiday*
     . . . the lid is off.

(Intermission)

II

1.   *Who*
       . . . sequel to *Marie*

2.   *Stardust*
       . . . a pastel in swing

3.   Two Impressions by the late Bix Beiderbecke
      (Piano solos arranged for orchestra)
      (a)   *In a Mist*
      (b)   *Candlelight*

4.   *The Big Apple's Family Tree*
      "A square dance in swing time, as you can see,
      That is the Big Apple's Family Tree."

5.   *Stop, Look, and Listen*
       . . . let swing be unconfined.

6.   Three Scotch Songs in Swingtime
      (a)   *Comin' Thru the Rye*
      (b)   *Loch Lomond*
      (c)   *Annie Laurie*

7.   Three Moods in Swing
      (a)   *Goin' Home* (Swing Classic)
      (b)   *Just a Simple Melody* (Swing Novelette)
      (c)   *Down South Camp Meeting* (Swing a la Harlem)

8.   *If It's the Last Thing I Do*
       . . . introduced by Tommy Dorsey
       . . . sung by Jack Leonard

9.   The Clambake Seven
      (a)   *Posin'* (Edythe, Tommy and the gang)
      (b)   *Nice Work If You Can Get It* (Edythe Wright
            sings)
      (c)   *Pagan Love Song* (That lid is off again)

10. Three Popular Tunes
      (a)   *Down with Love* (a rock and a bounce)

  (b) *Bewildered* (a recent Tommy Dorsey introduction)

  (c) *Little White Lies* (power a-plenty)

11. *Peckin'*

  . . . wherein the band goes dizzy and daffy.

12. *Beale Street Blues*

  . . . which more or less sums things up.

(Encore: *Bugle Call Rag*)

15

Amateur Swing Contest

THERE are times when things happen fortuitously.

The Tommy Dorsey Show was sailing on a high level. Ratings were good. The press raved. Studio audiences screamed. Stacks of fan mail. Sales were up. All was well . . .

And then a voice was heard in the advertising agency. The cry was: "We need a gimmick!"

It wasn't surprising. It seemed to me we'd heard that song before. But how to answer?

Of course, there were all kinds of suggestions. One was that we interpolate a quiz of some sort. That, some of us thought, was the exactly wrong thing to do. "Information, Please" was a good show and it didn't need music. In like manner, a show built around a top swing band would not be improved by interrupting it for a quiz.

We finally hit on an idea for a feature that was related to our show: an Amateur Swing Contest. In a ten-minute segment, we introduced four young instrumentalists, selected from auditions held during the preceding week. Each player, after a few get-acquainted words, played a tune of his choice. Studio audience reaction, registered on an applause meter, determined the winner, who received a $75 prize and the chance to swing with Tommy and the band.

The word went out and the contestants rushed in. We had to add several people to the production staff to handle the auditions. The aspirants were mostly high school kids and college students. A few were somewhat older—they probably played when they were in school and were still hooked on jazz. Some knew exactly what notes they were playing. Some chose their notes intuitively, feeling what they were playing. Others explored their way through chords, guided by an ear not, as yet anyway, entirely reliable. But in all of them, interest in jazz was real.

All the instruments were represented—drums, clarinet, sax, trumpet, piano, guitar, trombone. There were a few girls, but, despite the success of Phil Spitalny and his All-Girl Orchestra, we found no girl trombone players. Our girls stuck with piano and guitar.

Auditions were held at the agency, BBD & O. A conference room had been converted to a radio studio but continued to function as a part-time conference room. There were times when a meeting lasted right up to our scheduled time for auditions. Advertising executives would emerge from the soundproof room and run square into a legion of tyro musicians coming on strong with riffs and tune-ups. For the more traditional-minded executives, schooled in print media, this was a far cry from the old days.

On the air, it was good fun. The capsule interviews were breezy and amusing. When those kids played, they went for broke. When they played with the band, the studio rocked. There was no doubt that we were reaching the youth market, which was just fine with the sponsor.

The Amateur Swing Contest was enormously successful. It was in tune with the times. It was a ratings-builder. It produced new publicity. Best of all, it heralded our arrival in cities throughout the country. The kids flocked to the auditions at the local stations, the papers took note, and everyone knew we were in town.

In Cincinnati several of us, who arrived in advance to audition the young musicians, were guests of my friend, Groverman Blake, then drama critic on the *Cincinnati Times-Star*. Grove asked me a question: "How did you happen to decide on a *seventy-five*-dollar prize? Why wasn't it fifty or a hundred?" I thought it was a good question, but I didn't have an answer. Somebody must have figured it out, possibly the keeper of the budget.

Some of our winners went on to become professional musicians. Our sixteen-year-old winner in Chicago became a jazz star—George Barnes, whose fine guitar work is widely known. Not long after his appearance in our show, he got a job with Jimmy McPartland at the Three Deuces in Chicago. George has since appeared with many leading bands, including the Lawson-Haggart band, co-led by the same Yank Lawson and Bob Haggart who now lead the World's Greatest Jazz Band. Many will recall George teaming with the late Carl Kress, one of the all-time great guitarists. The recording they made with tenor sax star Bud Freeman, "Something Tender," is unique. George later teamed with another fine guitarist, Bucky Pizzarelli, for records and personal appearances.

Immediately at the conclusion of the broadcast in which George was winner, he joined Paul Weston and me for a snack. George ordered ginger ale, Paul ordered a coke. George didn't approve of the coke. He said to Paul, "Don't forget—there's just as much caffeine in coke as there is in coffee." He made no comment on my scotch-and-soda. I was beyond the pale. Some years later, when George and I met at a tavern near Carnegie Hall, it was evident he had changed his thinking.

16

Swinging with the Stars

WE left Chicago behind us. Next stop, Denver. Then on to Hollywood. Tommy and I rode to Denver on the fast and elegant Burlington Zephyr. After a long stretch on the road, and with summer coming on, we were anticipating a pleasant two-month plateau in California.

We talked about what we would do with the show in Hollywood. Naturally, we wanted to take advantage of the locale.

We felt that the Amateur Swing Contest had run its course. It had done a good job, functioning best when we hit a different city each week. We would be in Hollywood for most of the summer, and there would be better ways of renewing and maintaining audience interest. "But," I said, "let's have one final fling. Let's get four picture stars who play instruments and have them be the amateur contestants. We'll treat them exactly the way we treat the kids—pretend we don't know they are stars."

"I like the idea," Tommy said, "but how can we do it? We don't have the budget."

He was right. We didn't. But there might be a way. "You're a pal of Bing Crosby," I reminded Tommy. "I'll bet that, if you ask him to play drums, he'll do it. And if he says yes, I know we can get the others."

Tommy's eyes lit up and glowed. "Okay," he said, with just the right inflection.

Tommy had planned to call Bing anyway, naturally. We got together at Bing's house, Tommy greeting Bing as "the Groaner," a bit of nomenclature from the Whiteman days. Tommy asked Bing if he would join us and play drums in this special edition of the Amateur Swing Contest. Without hesitation, Bing said, "Sure, it sounds like a fun idea." A Crosby film was in production at Paramount, and the lot was right next to the NBC studios, then located on Melrose Avenue.

We recalled that Dick Powell, whose current picture was "Cowboy from Brooklyn," had played trumpet when he was a singing master-of-ceremonies. A Warner Brothers talent scout discovered him in a neighborhood theatre near Pittsburgh. And we had heard that he still had an affectionate spot in his heart for the horn.

We arranged to meet Dick at his home in Beverly Hills. Neither Tommy nor I had met him before. We had nothing to go on except the idea itself and the fact that Bing was playing drums. Dick seemed amused at the idea. He thought for a moment, then said, "You say Crosby is going to do this? Count me in."

We were getting on fine. We had drums and trumpet. Next we remembered that Ken Murray did a vaudeville routine in which he played clarinet. Next day we called on him at his Sunset Towers apartment. He was not hard to convince. By all means yes, he would be there.

We needed a fourth. How about a girl? True, there was no television, but it would be a nice touch. Shirley Ross had recently completed "The Big Broadcast" with Bob Hope and Jack Benny, and "Thanks for the Memory," in which she and Bob Hope had introduced *Two Sleepy People*. We learned that Shirley had played piano when she was at UCLA, and we were told she was better than ever. Shirley was invited, and she said she would love it.

That gave us our complement of four. There were no business arrangements. We were in no position to ask for advance meetings or rehearsals. But they all agreed to show up for dress rehearsal on broadcast day. Tunes were selected. There would be no script to worry about. We would plot the questions; answers would be up to them. The date was set for two weeks ahead.

One day, during a rehearsal break, Tommy and I were having a hamburger at the Melrose Grotto, next to the NBC studios, when Jack Benny strolled in and sat down with us. "I hear you're having some kind of swing contest. You're not going to leave me out, are you?"

We were transfixed. This was incredible. *He* was asking *us?*

If Tommy and I were not entirely coherent in our reply, there could be no doubt that we extended a welcome.

Now we were five. And a violin, too. It happened because Bing had met up with Jack Benny bicycling on the Paramount lot. He stopped Jack and told him what was going on the next Wednesday. Jack's next stop was our cubicle at the Melrose Grotto.

As it must to all shows, broadcast day arrived. July 20, 1938. Rehearsal was in progress—*Honeysuckle Rose* for Bing, *Ida* for Dick, *Three O'Clock in the Morning* for Ken, *Thanks for the Memory* for Shirley, *My Honey's Lovin' Arms* for Jack. Dick was taking it seriously. He asked for a separate studio, where he could work on his embouchure alone. If one stepped into the hall, the sound from the adjoining studio gave proof he was working at it.

Jack Benny did not arrive for dress rehearsal. We slipped in an extra number for the band, to be used only if he didn't make the show. About two minutes before air time, Jack sauntered in, smiling under his snap-brim hat, smoking a cigar, holding violin and bow at the ready. There was only time to make sure of the key for his number, and we were on the air.

At the top of the show, Tommy introduced a representative of *Metronome* Magazine who presented him with the magazine's award for best all-around band. Then came the "amateurs."

As each of our "amateurs" came to the mike, he was asked the usual questions—name, occupation, and so on. Dealing with the stars exactly as we had dealt with the actual amateurs gave us a natural, built-in comedy situation.

Jack Benny was asked what his name was. After a pause of just the right length, he answered, "My name's Jack Benny."

"What is your line of work?"

"I work in pictures."

"You mean you're a movie actor?"

(Deadpan.) "Yeah." (Pause—deadpan.) "I'm a lover." (Big laugh.)

There is nothing inherently funny in that line. But Benny's timing and delivery, aided by the situation, made it very funny indeed.

At Tommy's Amateur Swing Contest, amateurs Benny, Powell, Murray, Crosby, Ross and one ringer, the trombone man

Why is that leader smiling?

The drummer meditates mayhem. He must be a music lover

Tommy with his favorite 39-year-old fiddle player

Edgar Bergen, Shirley Ross, Jack Benny, TD

After each one had performed, it was time to ascertain the winner and award the seventy-five-dollar prize. We pretended that the applause meter was so overwhelmed by the swinging performances that it ceased to function. We declared a five-way tie. Then the five of them launched into an animated discussion of just how they would handle the seventy-five dollars, including such matters as Social Security and agents' commissions.

We closed with a jam session, all five playing *When You and I Were Young, Maggie* with Tommy and the band. It was terrible. The audience howled with delight. Over the applause, Bing was heard to holler, "Hey, Tommy, you better tell that man from *Metronome* to take back the award."

One thing was sure. Tommy and I never forgot what Bing did for us.

17

House in Beverly Hills

WHILE we were travelling across the country, on our way to Hollywood, there was the question of where to stay when we got there. We would be there eight or ten weeks, so it wasn't just a matter of checking in at a hotel. Maybe there was something better.

Four of us—Jack Leonard, Paul Weston, Axel Stordahl, and I—decided we would combine our resources and see what could be found. Since it might take too long if we waited until we were there, I got in touch with Randy Hall—the same Randy Hall who had been on the expedition to hear the California Ramblers when we were college musicians. He and his wife Jean had moved to Hollywood two years before, and I thought they might have a suggestion.

The reply was that we should not worry, they would find something suitable for the four of us. We were to call the minute we arrived. We got there with no idea of where we would be staying. We telephoned the Halls and they took us to our new address: a house in Beverly Hills. It wasn't a mansion, but it was a commodious house, and it *was* in Beverly Hills, on Colgate Avenue, not far from the Beverly Wilshire Hotel.

The original Pied Pipers were eight, not four

There was a grand piano in the living room. There were four bedrooms and a large kitchen, completely stocked by Jean and Randy. We figured we would come out all right, financially, because there were four of us. We did all right; the cost was ninety-five dollars a month, and we split it four ways.

That wasn't all. There was Buck, who had been engaged to take care of us. He was friend, counselor, valet, and cook.

We saw a lot of Jean and Randy. Jean had been a leading show girl in the "Earl Carroll Vanities." Randy was program director at Standard Radio, a transcription firm; he produced programs featuring the music of Duke Ellington, Nat Cole, Spike Jones, Alvino Rey, David Rose, Buddy Cole, and, later on, George Barnes, the guitarist who had won our Amateur Swing Contest in Chicago.

Our house in Beverly Hills was an easy stop on the way from Hollywood to the beach at Santa Monica, and so became a rendezvous. It was a work room for Paul and Axel. It was also the place where the Pied Pipers were discovered, when the King Sisters brought them around for us to hear. Later in the year, Tommy hired the Pied Pipers and brought them to New York. I'm sure Paul remembers the day we auditioned them. The girl in the group was Jo Stafford, who is now Mrs. Paul Weston.

The band was working at the Palomar Ballroom in Los Angeles every night from 7:00 P.M. to 2:00 A.M. It was an especially rough schedule on Wednesdays, when there was also the radio show to do. In those pre-tape days, we had to do the show twice—first at 5:30 P.M. for broadcast in the east at 8:30 P.M., eastern time, then again at 8:30 P.M. for broadcast to the western and mountain states.

Wednesday was a shuttle. Rehearsal for the radio show began at 9:00 A.M., which meant little sleep the night before. Rehearsal led into the 5:30 broadcast. Then to the Palomar, where it was necessary also to play for a set of variety acts. Back to NBC for the re-broadcast at 8:30. Then back to the Palomar for the rest of the night, including another show. Every two weeks, the situation was aggravated by the band having to rehearse for a new set of variety acts at the Palomar. Everybody was exhausted. Tommy appeared grim, resentment building up inside. This had to lead to something.

Deane Kincaide tells what happened one time. "A new show came in one week. We rehearsed long and arduously for the new acts, then came the Headliner. Out came a tall, imposing-looking gentleman, neatly dressed in a business suit. He wore glasses, had a heavy German accent, and brought a violin and bow with him. His music was passed out to the band, but there was no conductor part. Tommy let him have it.

" 'How the hell am I supposed to conduct your act without a conductor part?' he hollered.

"Fixing a withering gaze on TD, the violinist replied, 'I ton't neet your gottam music. If dot's de vay you feel, no music at all. Who do you t'ink you are, anyvay?' His tone was ominous. All the while he spoke, he was edging nearer and nearer to Dorsey.

"Tommy went livid. 'Well, I know who *I* am, but I sure as hell don't know who *you* are!' he raged, and kept backing away little by little as the other guy kept edging toward him. 'Do your act *without* music. Band, get lost 'til time for the job.'

"About an hour before the job, Tommy reconsidered and called everybody back to rehearse this man's music. Everything went smoothly. Now comes the show that evening. We play the first few acts, and in comes Mr. Fiddler, the Headliner. He wore nothing but tights and gymnast's shoes, and he made Charles Atlas look like a runt. He had two short but very stocky assistants, and these guys had muscles and did acrobatics like you wouldn't believe!

"For the climax of this act, the two assistants brought out a sawed-off but thick telephone pole, about twelve or fifteen feet in length. Meanwhile, the fiddler man, the giant, lay down on the floor and put a big chock under his rear, sticking his legs and feet up in the air. The assistants put the telephone pole on his feet, draped themselves over each end, and the fiddler started whirling them around his feet, all the while playing *My Hero* on his violin, and very commendably, too.

"Our accompaniment to all this was pretty hysterical, believe me, and Dorsey did all the takes in the book! He must have had a bunch of ESP going for him that afternoon at rehearsal, the way he backed away from the fiddler."

There was a new Irving Berlin song that summer, *Now It Can Be Told.* Tommy was asked if he would introduce it on the air. We surrounded it with some Berlin favorites and made the whole show an Irving Berlin Cavalcade. We opened with *Alexander's Ragtime Band* and moved through succeeding Berlin cycles, including *A Pretty Girl Is Like a Melody* ("Ziegfeld Follies"), *Oh, How I Hate to Get Up in the Morning* (World War I), *Pack Up Your Sins* ("Music Box Revue"), *Blue Skies* (the twenties), *Heat Wave* (Ethel Waters in "As Thousands Cheer"), and *Cheek to Cheek* (Fred Astaire-Ginger

Rogers). *Say It with Music* led into the new song and we closed with *Marie*. Yes, Tommy Dorsey's *Marie* is an Irving Berlin song.

Before the 8:30 show, Tommy received this wire:

MY COMPLIMENTS ON ONE OF THE FINEST PROGRAMS I'VE EVER
HEARD OF THE REALLY CORRECT RENDITIONS OF MY SONGS.

IRVING BERLIN

Mr. Berlin had apparently heard the 5:30 show at 8:30 New York time, sent the wire, and the wire reached us before we did the repeat show at 8:30 California time.

It was a good summer for Tommy Dorsey recordings. And the band was in fine form. Intonation and phrasing in the brass section were assured with Andy Ferretti on first trumpet. The other trumpets were Pee Wee Erwin and Lee Castle, which guaranteed both solos and section work. Les Jenkins, Earle Hagen, and Tommy were the trombones. The sax section achieved a beautiful blend with Hymie Schertzer on first, Deane Kincaide and Skeets Herfurt on tenors, Freddie Stulce and Johnny Mince on altos, Johnny also doing the clarinet solo work. The rhythm section was unbeatable, with Howard Smith on piano, Carmen Mastren on guitar, Gene Traxler on bass, and Moe Purtill on drums.

Deane Kincaide's influence showed up strongly in the numbers recorded that summer. His *Washboard Blues* arrangement was completely in character with Hoagy Carmichael's composition. Deane's voicing—particularly in the clarinet figures in back of Tommy's trombone—gave it a peculiar sensitivity. Deane also contributed new swing treatments of two jazz traditionals, *Panama* and *Copenhagen*. The ending of *Washboard Blues* was arranged so that, on the stand, without the time limitations of radio and recording, Tommy could extend his blues improvisations indefinitely, and the listener would be lost in another world.

Lou Bring's *Lightly and Politely* and Benny Carter's *Symphony in Riffs* demonstrated two different approaches. *Lightly and Politely* was gentle, perceptive, and reticent—and it did swing. *Symphony in Riffs* was all-out, just what the title promised. It rolled and sailed to a triumphant finish. It was Benny Carter all the way.

Other recordings were *I'll See You in My Dreams*, sung by Jack Leonard; *A-Tisket A-Tasket*, done by Edythe Wright and the Clambake Seven; and *Stop Beatin' Around the Mulberry Bush*. Edythe and Skeets Herfurt together gave *Mulberry Bush* a real vocal work-out.

Just to even everything up, they recorded *Sweetheart of Sigma Chi*, with vocal chorus by the Three Esquires, and *The Sheik of Araby* by the Clambake Seven.

We were getting to like it in California. We enjoyed the good times at Bing Crosby's and the occasional trips to Hollywood Park Race-track. It was good seeing old friends—Johnny Mercer, Victor Young, Hoagy Carmichael, Lennie Hayton. The Palomar was a tough job, but the crowd loved the band. And the stay in Hollywood revitalized the radio show.

In August, we were on the move—back to New York, with, of course, a pause in Chicago.

18

"I Love My Band"

WITH the coming of summer, 1937, after a year and a half in California and the happy experience of working with Bing Crosby on his radio show, Jimmy and the band ventured out. They had been settled in one area for a long time. Although millions of radio listeners were aware that Jimmy Dorsey and his band appeared on the radio show with Bing Crosby, the band did not have much to do on its own. It was time now to stretch and get moving, to let more people hear and see the band perform. Action would create news; news would give the publicity people something to write about.

It would take three months to get to New York, three months filled with one-night performances along the way. The going would be rough, but it was an opportunity to make sure that the band would be in top form for the upcoming season. The workout would have a solidifying effect on performance. There would be publicity resulting from the trip. And one-nighters are money-makers.

The band was ready. The make-up was almost the same: two trumpets instead of one, three trombones, four saxes instead of three, four rhythm. For solos there were Jimmy's alto sax and clarinet, Bobby

Byrne's trombone, and Shorty Sherock's trumpet. Ray McKinley was at his post on drums, Tutti Camarata was chief arranger, and Bob Eberly was featured singer. Jimmy was ready, too. He was no longer the scared young leader who had suddenly had to take charge at Glen Island two years before.

When the summer ended and the band arrived in New York, Cork O'Keefe and the Rockwell-O'Keefe office were ready. The awareness on the part of the public, which the band's presence on the radio program had created, had built a following. The band was a salable item, and the association with Bing was a help. Bookings were solid, starting in New York with the New Yorker Hotel and the Paramount Theatre. With hotel engagements, there was time on the air, which resulted in bigger crowds at subsequent one-nighters. Demand increased, and so did the price. Before long, the band was drawing $12,500 for a week at a theatre.

In the next year, during one of the Chicago engagements, Jimmy, as he always did, got together with two of his closest friends—Squirrel Ashcraft and Jimmy O'Keefe (no relation to Cork). They were both prominent attorneys. In addition, Squirrel continued active in jazz as patron and participant. Both Squirrel and Jimmy O'Keefe followed Jimmy Dorsey's progress with great interest. They discovered that the band was grossing over one million dollars per year. "Great big, real dollars," says Squirrel. And it appeared to them that Jimmy's financial affairs were in an appalling state of disarray.

"We told him," Squirrel remembers, "that a well-run foundry would gross about that much and that maybe he had better put things on a more businesslike basis." Squirrel and Jimmy O'Keefe argued that, if he got rid of some of the supporting group of handlers, stopped enlarging the band, and would use a smaller, compact group, "he could make really wonderful *net* dough. It made Jimmy furious. When we saw him off this time, he was almost in tears, and said:

" 'I love my band. You leave it alone.' "

In retrospect, it was a predictable reaction on the part of Jimmy Dorsey. It was an emotional reaction. He was willing at least to listen to a suggestion if it dealt purely with finances, but don't touch the band. He did love the band, and Squirrel and Jimmy O'Keefe left it alone.

The next time Squirrel saw Jimmy Dorsey was a year or so later, when the band played the Chicago Theatre. Squirrel's young daughter Avis had a part in the story this time. As Squirrel tells it, "Young

Jimmy's 1939 trombone section: Don Matteson, Sonny Lee and Bobby Byrne (then a four-year veteran at the ripe old age of twenty)

Avis had always been a great pet of Jimmy's. One reason was that Jimmy and Jane Dorsey and their daughter had been separated for so long, and Avis was close to his child's age. Avis, aged six or seven, managed to talk our maid and semi-nurse, Madeline, into taking her in to hear her friend Jimmy—'in' meant twelve miles from Evanston to Chicago via elevated, which was a first for both of them. When they located the theatre and had finished a big movie and Jimmy's show, they managed to get down the alley and through the autograph swarm Jimmy had picked up by that time. Neither, of course, had ever been backstage anywhere, but apparently both were full of confidence and sent up word that 'Miss Ashcraft' wanted to see Mr. Dorsey. Jimmy apparently came down the iron staircase in a bathrobe, sighted Avis and said, 'I'll be right with you. I had hoped so much you would come to the show.' He then hurriedly called up Jane Ashcraft in Evanston and said that he was terribly ashamed, but that he couldn't recall her daughter's first name. Jane said 'Avis,' and Jimmy said he would call back later, that this was an emergency. According to Madeline, he showed up in no time at all, showed them all over the Chicago Theatre backstage, and assured Avis that he would have been very disappointed if he had not heard from her."

Squirrel considers the incident "a wonderful key to Jimmy's character and way of going. It was important to me, because I felt that very, very few guys in Jimmy's position would have gone to such trouble to make sure of a little girl's name, when he could have gotten along perfectly well simply by not using it."

While the band was still at the Chicago Theatre, Jimmy got together with Squirrel and Jimmy O'Keefe. They naturally remembered the discussion, a year or so before, which Jimmy Dorsey had brought to a finish when he said, "I love my band. You leave it alone." Squirrel recalls, "All was forgiven. The band was an undisputed success, and Jimmy acted as if had won a big one over both of us."

Another of Jimmy's good friends in Chicago was Paul Mares, the trumpeter who had been leader of the legendary New Orleans Rhythm Kings and co-writer of *Tin Roof Blues, Farewell Blues*, and *Milenberg Joys*, Four of the New Orleans Rhythm Kings were from New Orleans, and four from downstate Illinois and Indiana. They included such jazz pioneers as George Brunis, Leon Rapollo, and Elmer Schoebel, the pianist who wrote *Nobody's Sweetheart*.

Paul Mares operated a barbecue place on Chicago's near-North Side. "I remember arguing all night there once," says Squirrel, "with

Jimmy Dorsey and Paul on the rather vague subject of whether music was going on indefinitely on its then current path toward more and more 'modern' and complicated stuff. Jimmy was sure that it was and that it should; Paul agreed that it was but was not happy about it. I can't imagine why I was so sure that a big resurgence of the Rhythm Kings' way of going was just around the corner; however, Fud Livingston, who was the only other guy in the place, agreed with me." Fud had done arrangements for the Ben Pollack band and for Jimmy Dorsey. He and Squirrel "took the attitude that the Bix melodic line and a beat like Davey Tough's would always succeed, where the complicated things, so much easier for lesser musicians than originality, could exist only if they changed often and never took permanent form. Needless to state, it grew later and later and there was no conclusion."

Squirrel adds, "Bear in mind that Paul really quit because he couldn't stand reading music, which was to him something that 'somebody else' had written."

19

How to Hire
a Trumpet Player

PERSONNEL changes were not unusual in the big bands. Some top musicians moved from one to another. Bud Freeman was in and out of the Tommy Dorsey band. "Fired twice, quit three times," according to Bud.

When Yank Lawson joined Tommy Dorsey in 1938, it was news, because Yank had been with the Bob Crosby band from its beginning in 1935. There had been almost no turnover. What made the move particularly interesting in retrospect was the way Tommy maneuvered it—after the manner of secret diplomacy.

It began, we later learned, in June, when we were in Chicago on our way to California. Tommy stopped in at the Blackhawk, which in itself was not noteworthy. What drew attention was the fact that he came in hurriedly, disappeared from view for a few minutes, reappeared and left without lingering. Squirrel Ashcraft remembers this because Tommy, passing Squirrel's table on the way out, stopped just long enough to say hello, then "left at high speed." Yank told me

Tommy raided the Crosby Bobcats to land searing trumpeter Yank Lawson in 1938

recently that, during Tommy's brief stop, they had discussed matters informally. "Let me know," Tommy said.

The next month, when we were in Hollywood, Yank received a wire addressed to him at the Blackhawk:

MUST KNOW IMMEDIATELY YOUR PLANS. HOW SOON CAN YOU ACT. PLEASE ADVISE BY WESTERN UNION.

                                                    TOMMY DORSEY

To cover any contingency, the following instruction appeared on the envelope:

PERSONAL DELIVERY ONLY. IDENTIFICATION OF ADDRESSEE MUST BE ASSURED FOR DELIVERY. MUST SHOW UNION CARD OR DRIVERS LICENSE.

While we were still in California, Tommy confided to me that he would soon have some exciting news having to do with a personnel acquisition. Presumably this was before it was confirmed, because he didn't say who it was. I have never understood the classified nature of the imminent announcement. Throughout my long association with Tommy, I was always in possession of confidential information. But in this case, secrecy was the pattern.

However, he did tell me before we took off for Chicago on our way to New York. Yank Lawson was joining the band in Chicago. Tommy was really happy. There was great enthusiasm and anticipation.

Yank joined without learning how much he would be paid. Tommy didn't say and Yank didn't ask. It turned out to be a top salary. Along with Yank there was another from the Crosby band joining Tommy —Charlie Spivak, first trumpet. A third new member was the young trombone player, Buddy Morrow. Lee Castle remained on trumpet, as did Les Jenkins on trombone. The sax and rhythm sections remained as they were throughout the summer.

We were in Chicago just long enough for a recording date and the August 17th radio show, in which *Panama* was included to feature Yank. We arrived in New York with the Hurricane of '38. The hurricane struck, causing the Empire State Building to sway, while we were rehearsing in Studio 8G at NBC in Rockefeller Center.

Yank's presence in the band was unmistakable. Deane Kincaide completed a new arrangement of Jelly Roll Morton's jazz standard,

Milenberg Joys, in which Yank gave out with an extended solo that said it all. It was introduced on the radio show and recorded the following January on two sides. It is a collector's item, notable for the Kincaide arrangement, the drive and energy of the ensemble, and the solo work of Yank, Tommy, tenor saxophonist Babe Russin and Johnny Mince.

It was the beginning of a long and happy association for Yank and for his wife Harriet. Harriet thinks of it as a "family band," the wives knowing and liking each other. She remembers that Tommy made sure they had comfortable places to stay when the band was on the road.

There were some memorable Tommy Dorsey recordings that fall, including *Boogie Woogie,* Deane Kincaide's arrangement with Howard Smith at the piano. This became one of the all-time big sellers and is still heard on radio and in jukeboxes. There was *Davenport Blues* with an extended ending, which, on the stand, where there was time, repeated and built to a pinnacle. And *Hawaiian War Chant,* another which set off fine solo work by Yank. There was also *Sweet Sue,* a new one in the *Marie* cycle.

At the Pennsylvania Roof again, Tommy reverted to his custom of playing trumpet during the last set. This time, Yank got in the act by playing sax. I was unaware that he played anything other than trumpet; it turned out he had also played sax in college. The tune, naturally, was Tommy's favorite, *Blue Lou.*

About this time Eli Oberstein, recording director at RCA-Victor, and George Simon, editor of *Metronome,* arranged for a recording by the winners of the magazine's popularity poll. The first tune they recorded was—*Blue Lou.*

The other side was *The Blues.* Tommy Dorsey and Jack Teagarden were the winners in the trombone category. All who were present at the date remember how Tommy would not do a solo when there was Jackson T. to do it, so great was his regard for Jack. He finally agreed to do it straight, with Jack playing the blues around him. It was beautiful.

Earlier in the year, we asked Tommy to play an excerpt from Tschaikovsky in the radio show—the introductory theme of the second movement from the *Fifth Symphony.* This is the timeless melody written for French horn in the symphony. Tommy played it on trombone. The studio audience was spellbound, and we learned from comment and letters that listeners were equally affected.

Bergen could make McCarthy talk—but Tommy?

For Herb:
"Thanks for the
Memory of a swell
jam session, + of
making such a
fine friend —
Sincerely
Shirley Ross

Shirley Ross is thankful for the memory of her appearance as an "amateur" swing pianist on Tommy's radio show, 1938

We decided to venture again outside our customary programming area. Paul Weston and I spent an hour in the NBC music library looking through Bach. We selected a fugue and Paul voiced it for the band. No change was made in melody, harmony, or note valuation. Paul simply voiced it for the instrumentation of Tommy's band. Visitors who stopped in at rehearsal thought it was a new swing arrangement. The relationship was no surprise; if Mr. Bach had been alive, he would have been a swing composer.

Shirley Ross, on a trip to New York, paid us a visit. She sang *Two Sleepy People*, which she had introduced with Bob Hope. And, recalling the fun we all had when she was with us for our "Amateur" Swing Contest in Hollywood the previous summer, we did *Thanks for the Memory*, with special lyrics written for Shirley, Edythe, Jack, Tommy, and the band.

Before the year was out, Jo Stafford and the original Pied Pipers —all eight of them—came east for a five-week engagement on the show. They made their first appearance on the show of December 28, 1938, singing *All of Me* and *Joshua Fit the Battle of Jericho*.

It had been a good year. A Very Good Year.

20

Downstage: Two Bands

IN three and a half years the Tommy Dorsey and Jimmy Dorsey bands had both reached top-level positions. During this time, the brothers saw each other occasionally, and it was always an agreeable meeting. When they were not working side by side, there was nothing to fight about. Each was a booster for the other's band.

In January of 1939, there were two occasions which gave proof that Tommy and Jimmy were friends beyond doubt. One of those occasions took place at the Terrace Room of the Hotel New Yorker, the other on Tommy's Raleigh-Kool Show.

Tommy finished an engagement at the New Yorker on January 10. Jimmy was scheduled to open on January 11. Instead of playing until 2:00 A.M. on closing night, Tommy and his band played *Auld Lang Syne* at 12:00 midnight and segued to *Sandman*, the Dorsey Brothers theme, which Jimmy had continued to use. Jimmy made his entrance and introduced his own band with his new theme, *Contrasts*. Both Dorseys were beaming.

The room was filled with friends, in and out of the music business, and with devotees who were surprised and delighted to find they were getting a double bill. Robert Taylor, Dick Foran, Dan Healy, Max Baer, Larry Clinton, Glen Gray, and most of the Casa Loma band were among those present. Jack White, the wild master-of-ceremonies at the Club 18 on Fifty-second Street, showed up with his highly visible and audible entourage, led by Pat Harrington and Frankie Hyres.

Mr. and Mrs. Thomas Dorsey, Sr., were seated at a front table and were cheered when they were called upon to take bows. Mrs. Dorsey cried tears of pride when her boys embraced and traded sentimental stories and ribbings. Mr. Dorsey was handed a trumpet, and he played a number with his sons. This was the first time the members of this ad hoc trio had played together since the Lansford days, when Tommy and Jimmy were pupils and their father was the teacher.

Jimmy's new theme, *Contrasts*, was impressive. It was Jimmy's composition, incorporating an earlier one, *Oodles of Noodles*, which had been a Dorsey Brothers specialty featuring Jimmy. In slow tempo and with pronounced beat, *Contrasts* projected an imposing chord sequence by the full band, with Jimmy's alto sax over. The release picked up the tempo for a jazz interlude, followed by a return to the expansive slow tempo.

The event at the Hotel New Yorker gave Tommy and me an idea. We frequently introduced a guest performer on Tommy's radio show. So let's have fifteen guest performers—that is, three trumpet players, three trombone players, five saxophonists, and four rhythm players. We promptly engaged Jimmy and his band to appear in our show the very next week, on Wednesday, January 18.

Rehearsal was a clambake, the good kind. Most of NBC's eighth floor was occupied by Studio 8H, the big one where Toscanini and the NBC Symphony broadcast. The stage in our more intimate studio, 8G, was barely large enough to accommodate both bands. It was "Mac" and "Lad" again. Occasionally, Tommy tossed in "Harve," addressing it to anyone at hand. The name had always amused him, and it came to mind at this time. Everyone was in a jovial mood.

In the first half of the program, Tommy and his band did *Marie*, and the Pied Pipers did *Dixieland Band*. About halfway through the program, we introduced Jimmy and his band. They opened with *Contrasts*, and followed it with a swing arrangement of *Pagan Love Song*. Then we turned the calendar back to the Dorsey brothers— not the Dorsey Brothers band, but Jimmy and Tommy, the Dorsey brothers aged ten and eight. In a three-minute sketch, two child

Radio recreation of Dorseys' younger days. Tommy plays peck horn,
Jimmy plays cornet, and young actors Ronald Liss and Kingsley Colter
take the speaking roles

Combined bands of Tommy and Jimmy rehearsing for joint appearance on Tommy's Raleigh-Kool Show over NBC in 1939

actors portrayed Jimmy and Tommy having a music lesson at their father's music school in Lansford. The instruments were cornet and "peck horn" (baritone), respectively, played off mike by Jimmy and Tommy. The composition they were practicing was *Semeramide Overture*, a staple in the libraries of traditional concert bands, like those of John Philip Sousa and Arthur Pryor. The young actors were Ronald Liss (Jimmy) and Kingsley Colter (Tommy).

Then came the finale. There was only one number to have chosen: *Honeysuckle Rose*, as originally played by the Dorsey Brothers, the Glenn Miller arrangement recorded on two sides. For the first and only time, it was rendered with six trumpets, seven trombones, ten saxophones, two pianos, two guitars, two bass viols, and two sets of drums. The execution was amazingly light, considering the doubling and sheer weight. In any case, it sounded just the right note.

When we rehearsed *Honeysuckle Rose*, Tommy spoke into the microphone, addressing those of us in the control room. "For this," he said, "we won't need microphones. Just open the windows."

21

Editor & Publisher

THE editor was Jack Egan. The publisher was Tommy Dorsey. The publication was *The Bandstand,* issued monthly and described on the masthead as "A Newspaper for Musical Students and Fans."

The paper was sent, free of charge, to all who requested it. *The Bandstand* reported, and commented on, the entire music scene. Each issue gave notice of the Tommy Dorsey band's movements from one location to another during the month ahead. Copies were available on the tours, and the "subscription" list grew.

The Bandstand was astute promotion; it was not a stuffer or a "mailing piece." It was an honest-to-goodness newspaper, tabloid size. It included straight news reporting of people and events in the world of swing music, by-line articles from names prominent in the field, news of other bands, letters to the editor, feature articles, and a center spread of pictures. There were articles by members of the band, announcers, disc jockeys, and by those in the areas of radio production, band management, and recording. These articles were intended to be helpful to students, especially those who might want to go to work in the field.

One might conclude that it was a big job to put it all together and get it off the press. It was, and Jack Egan, Tommy's public relations man, did it. Jack was city editor, managing editor, and editor-in-chief.

Not many copies of *The Bandstand* have been preserved, but I found that Yank Lawson has a copy of Volume One, Number Two, the issue of February, 1939. The headline on page one at top left reads, "Tommy Dorsey and Band Head for Midwest After Breaking Records." Subhead: "Orchestra Does Vaudeville Stands in Pittsburgh and Indianapolis to Start Second Leg of Tour." The story listed the itinerary throughout the middle of March, and concluded with the announcement of engagements at the New York Paramount in April and the Hotel Pennsylvania Roof for the summer.

The headline at top right on page one carries Artie Shaw's by-line and reads: "Artie Shaw Expresses His Opinions on Swing and Its Various Forms—'Smooth Swing' and 'Sophisticated Swing' Mislead—Public Kept in Dark About Real Swing Music." This seemed to merit reading on.

Shaw gave a hint, regarding a future activity of his, in his opening comment on Tommy's publication. "Having had certain journalistic, not to say literary, ambitions of my own, it always gives me a little self-assurance and a great deal of pleasure to see a fellow-musician starting out in that field."

". . . I think it's time to debunk swing," Artie states in his article. "Let's take all the nonsense, ballyhoo and jive jargon out of it. The two outstanding types of swing that are now being played often merit the ridicule and somewhat harsh criticism directed from more erudite circles. The first type of swing is that which attempts to blast off the roof . . . Offensive to most ears and definitely of the musically punch-drunk variety, it is an out-and-out menace. The second classification bears the alliterative titles of 'smooth' or 'sophisticated' swing. For sheer monotony I don't believe this type of music can be surpassed . . . Instrumentalists can almost doze off on the bandstand and it would have no effect on their playing. Swing—and I mean real swing—is an idiom designed to make songs more listenable and more danceable than they are in their original form. It is, in sum, the creation and sustenance of a mood. In it, there is blasting, purring, sublety, obviousness—all in their proper places naturally."

Shaw made good on his words. His recording of *Carioca* had just been released, six months after *Begin the Beguine*.

A boxed item on page two, entitled "Meet the Orchestra," listed

birthplaces of the band members. None was born in Manhattan. Jack
Leonard was born in Brooklyn, but his home town was Freeport,
Long Island. There were two born in Chicago—Johnny Mince and,
of course, Dave Tough, of the Austin High School Gang. There were
six small towns in the east represented: Bayonne, New Jersey
(Edythe Wright); Revere, Massachusetts (Andy Ferretti); Indiana,
Pennsylvania (Elmer Smithers); Stoughton, Massachusetts (Dave
Jacobs); Cohoes, New York (Carmen Mastren); and Chambersburg,
Pennsylvania (Gene Traxler). Texas was twice in the list—for Dallas
(Freddie Stulce) and Houston (Deane Kincaide). There was Ardmore,
Oklahoma (Howard Smith); also Pittsburgh (Babe Russin); Cincinnati
(Skeets Herfurt); Milwaukee (Ward Sillaway), Boston (Bobby Burns),
and Yonkers, New York (Jack Egan). Birth dates were listed; average
age was twenty-seven. Tommy was thirty-three at the time; he was
not yet thirty when he organized his band.

Writing assignments were handed out to all band members. There
was no shirking these assignments. Edythe, in her column, stated
that Jack Egan was standing over her with a whip. Among the by-line
articles were Edythe's "The Feminine Viewpoint"; "Sing, It's Good
for You," by Jack Leonard; "Advice to Clarinetists on Jam-Legit
Playing," by Johnny Mince; "Just Take Your Pick, String Along on
Guitar," by Carmen Mastren; "Theories on Blues—Origin, Arrangement, and Execution," by Deane Kincaide; and "Sleep and Musicians," in which Ward Sillaway dealt with the problem of getting
sleep on one-nighter tours.

Bobby Burns, in his article, "Get Lift with Bus Best Bet," explained
that air transportation on tours was eliminated from consideration,
because the band carried two tons of baggage and equipment. "Many
people ask us," Bobby wrote, "why, when we travel by bus, we leave
a city as soon as we finish an engagement. It seems offhand that it
might be more sensible to get a good night's sleep and then start out
on the trip. Experience has taught us, however, that our way is much
easier, since we travel over less-congested highways at night, avoid-
ing traffic jams when passing through large cities, and, with a large
bus, travelling at night, the driver can be sure he will have the road
to himself, thus making it safer."

Eli Oberstein, manager of Artists & Repertoire at RCA-Victor,
contributed an interesting piece in which he commented on the fact
that outsiders thought his job must be "interesting." They thought
that all he had to do was find the fellow "who does something just

At the Pennsylvania Roof, 1938–39. Front row: Tommy, Deane Kincaide, Johnny Mince, Freddie Stulce, Babe Russin. Middle: Carmen Mastren, Gene Traxler. Back: Pee Wee Erwin, Andy Ferretti, Yank Lawson

At the Pennsylvania Roof, 1938–39. From left: Tommy, Carmen Mastren, Dave Jacobs, Ward Sillaway, Elmer Smithers (trombone beyond Sillaway), Howard Smith, Bunny Shawker, Andy Ferretti, Pee Wee Erwin (top of head showing), Yank Lawson

a bit better or just a bit different." Eli answers this: "For every orchestra that records for us on our Victor or Bluebird label, there are approximately 2,000 who do not. A simple formula covers this situation. You have one friend and 2,000 enemies." Discussing the importance of style in a recording band, Eli observes that "we meet the bugaboo of style—monotony. Unless an orchestra has sufficient versatility, either in repertoire or interpretation, it may find itself stagnant. In my experience, the most versatile organization is that of Tommy Dorsey, and its life is extended by this versatility indefinitely through the coming years."

One story, without a by-line but written, I am sure, by Jack Egan, reported a visit to the Philadelphia Zoo by the Clambake Seven. They held a jam session for the apes. Scientists, psychologists, and reporters were on hand to observe the reactions of the animals. "When the boys played *Getting Sentimental Over You,* [the animals] got dreamy-eyed and rocked back and forth slowly. Then the boys swung out . . . there was bedlam in the monkey house as the primitive jitterbugs went into a jungle version of a cross between the Big Apple, Shag, Lindy, and Truckin'."

The Bandstand's circulation reached 180,000, and was growing. Tommy's enthusiasm grew to crusading proportions. There were twenty young people at work in the office of his lawyer, John Gluskin, taking care of mailings and other chores. But it became too expensive to maintain. When Tommy proposed going into rotogravure, "that," according to Jack Egan, "was when Johnny Gluskin said 'No!'" *The Bandstand* was discontinued after six months and a cost of $65,000. Copies are rare. Yank Lawson must have kept his under glass.

22

༄ ༄

Stardust in
Indianapolis

TOMMY and I looked at the itinerary for the spring tour. Charlottes-
ville, Wilkes-Barre, Rochester, Pittsburgh for a week at the Stanley
Theatre, Indianapolis for a week at the Lyric Theatre . . .

Indianapolis . . . for a week . . . doing the radio show from the stage
of the Lyric Theatre. We would be near Richmond, Indiana, where
Tommy had recorded *Davenport Blues* with Bix Beiderbecke and a
pick-up band at the Gennett studio fourteen years before. Hoagy
Carmichael was there. We would be near Bloomington, where
Hoagy was born, home of the University of Indiana. When Hoagy was
a student at the university, Bloomington was headquarters for Bix
and other musicians, who gravitated there for jam sessions at the
Book Nook, a favorite haunt. Hoagy's *Riverboat Shuffle* was born
there and became a jazz standard. Bloomington was also the birthplace of Hoagy's then avant-garde tune which, with Mitchell Parish's
lyric, became *Stardust*.

With only a look and a nod, Tommy and I understood each other:

144

we would get Hoagy to join us for the radio show in Indianapolis and we would do an all-Carmichael program. The Hollywood magnet had drawn Hoagy west, but we knew he would come back home to Indiana and be our guest star.

There was plenty of material for the program—*Rockin' Chair, Lazy Bones, Lazy River, Georgia on My Mind, Heart and Soul* . . . Tommy's recording of *Stardust* was a best-seller. There was plenty to talk about. Hoagy and Tommy were Paul Whiteman alumni. Tommy and Jimmy were both with Whiteman when he made the famous recording of *Washboard Blues* with Hoagy singing.

The Lyric was a large theatre, comparable to the New York Paramount. Like many theatres across the country, it followed the policy, originated by the Paramount's general manager, Bob Weitman, of presenting the big bands of the day on stage. It was the height of the Swing Era. The Paramount made page one in the papers when the kids lined up around the block as early as 7:00 A.M. to get in for that first show at 10:30 A.M. to hear Tommy Dorsey, Benny Goodman, or Glenn Miller. That's the way it was when Tommy played the Lyric in Indianapolis.

Hoagy arrived in town, and we were introduced to his father and mother, Mr. and Mrs. Howard Carmichael. Their charm and hospitality made us feel that we had all been friends for years. We were entranced by Mrs. Carmichael. She was a lovely cameo, with a twinkle that telegraphed a sense of humor; gentle, kindly, and spunky. She was the heart of America. She had taught piano to Hoagy years before, when she was playing in a silent movie theatre. We knew immediately that we must have her with us for the show. We put *Maple Leaf Rag* in the program for Mrs. Carmichael. She would be accompanied by Tommy and the band.

Tommy's five shows a day for the theatre gave us a bit of a problem: one way or another, we had to rehearse the radio show. We did it on the run, in bits and pieces—in a distant loft in the theatre, after midnight and between shows.

March 1, 1939, was a bright spring day. The headline in the *Indianapolis Star* was "Governor Gets Beer Reform Bill." The marquee of the Lyric proclaimed: STAGE—TOMMY DORSEY, HIS TROMBONE AND HIS ORCHESTRA—EDYTHE WRIGHT— JACK LEONARD—HOAGY CARMICHAEL . . . SCREEN—NANCY DREW, REPORTER—WITH BONITA GRANVILLE, FRANK THOMAS, JR. Turning to the entertainment section, we saw a

Guitarist-arranger Carmen Mastren and producer-author Herb Sanford flank Hoagy Carmichael as they prepare for TD's 1939 salute to Hoagy on his radio show

HOAGY CARMICHAEL RETURNS· FOR MOTHER'S RADIO DEBUT

HOAGY CARMICHAEL LISTENS . . . HIS MOTHER PLAYS.

By CORBIN PATRICK.

Hoagy Carmichael, the Indiana boy who writes songs the nation sings, came home yesterday afternoon for the most exciting event of his mother's life.

Mrs. Howard Carmichael, housewife, 3120 Graceland avenue, will make her radio debut with her famous son and Tommy Dorsey's band in a broadcast on the NBC-Red network from the stage of the Lyric Theater at 7:30 and 10:30 o'clock tonight.

His mother will play a special arrangement of the "Maple Leaf Rag," Hoagy declared. He'll play a "little piano" himself, he said, featuring a number of his own compositions, as he did in a similar broadcast with Dorsey in New York several weeks ago.

Hoagy Is Excited, Too.

Hoagy was excited himself at the chance of presenting his mother to a nation-wide audience. "She played for the same Indiana University sorority and fraternity dances in 1903 and 1904 for which I played 20 years later," he declared. In the meantime, Mrs. Carmichael raised a family of four children but "she can play the piano today better than I can," Hoagy admitted.

The author of "Star Dust," "Lazy Bones," "Little Old Lady," "Small Fry" and numerous other universal favorites will join Dorsey in tonight's program in paying tribute to the memory of an old friend and associate of his Indiana University days, the late Bix Biederbecke, whose genius on the cornet still is a marvel to bandmen. They will recall their early recording dates with Bix in Richmond, Ind.

Family Stays on Coast.

Hoagy didn't bring his family with him this trip. The infant Hoagy Bix Carmichael was not considered big enough to travel and remained at home on the coast with his mother. Hoagy is anxious to get back to them, but has business in New York which will keep him in the East for a couple of weeks. He may get to Bloomington this trip only for a couple of hours to visit with his grandmother Thursday. Later that day he will leave for New York.

There he has several irons in the fire which bear watching. He has to see about a contract to write the music for a new show and has a picture deal under consideration. He recently completed a short for Paramount, in which he introduces a new song, "That Right I'm Wrong," it will be released in about two months.

Hit Will Be Featured.

His latest hit, "I Get Along Without You Very Well," will be featured Saturday night on the Hit Parade radio broadcast. The song was based on a poem given Hoagy by a friend 10 years ago. When the song was written, he conducted a search for the author of the poem with the aid of Walter Winchell. They finally found her, Mrs. Jane Brown Thompson of Philadelphia, Pa., but she died Jan. 19 without having heard the song.

Hoagy and his mother were having a little rehearsal at home last night when this reporter called. They were to rehearse with Dorsey and the band at the Lyric at midnight, after the last show. Mrs. Carmichael, who taught Hoagy the first things he knew about the piano, was rising to the occasion beautifully.

"This is the price of fame," she sighed as she held her pose "just another minute, please, for the photographer."

theatre ad with this announcement at the top: TONITE 7:30 AND
10:30 TOMMY DORSEY WILL BROADCAST FROM OUR STAGE
HIS NBC RALEIGH AND KOOL CIGARETTE PROGRAM,
HOAGY CARMICHAEL GUEST STAR.

People queued up all day long. A moment before 7:30 P.M., the
screen rose, revealing Tommy and the band on stage. The signal was
given from the temporary control room in the wings. The sound of
Tommy's trombone on *Getting Sentimental Over You* was heard on
the coast-to-coast NBC Network.

Next day, the *Indianapolis Star* reported:

> A capacity audience that had gathered hours in advance
> whooped and hollered, whistled and clapped for Hoagy Carmi-
> chael and his mother, Tommy Dorsey and his band as they
> broadcast an NBC radio program from the stage of the Lyric
> Theatre at 7:30 o'clock last night . . . An estimated 1,500 persons
> who packed the sidewalk in front of the house while the show
> was on then moved in to witness a repetition of the program for
> Pacific Coast stations at 10:30.

The program opened with *Song of India,* to let the swing fans in
the audience know we hadn't forgotten them. The response of those
in the theatre proved that they got the point. We did *Riverboat
Shuffle* with Hoagy at the piano. For this we used the Clambake
Seven, because Hoagy had originally composed and played it with a
small jazz band. Hoagy introduced some words he had recently written to fit the tune. It had never had words; it was strictly a jazz
instrumental. It was astonishing how these words coincided with the
syncopation in the tune, including the riffs.

> *Good people, you're invited tonight*
> *To the Riverboat Shuffle.*
> *Good people, we got rhythm tonight*
> *At the Riverboat Shuffle.*
> *They tell me that slide-pipe tooter is grand,*
> *Best in Louisiana.*
> *So bring your freighter,*
> *Come on alligator,*
> *That band! Mr. Hawkins on the tenor.*
> *Good people, you'll hear Milenberg Joys*
> *In a special orchestration.*

Even Mama Dinah will be there
To strut for the boys
In a room full of noise.
She'll teach you to shuffle it right,
So bring your baby.
I'll be seein' you
At the Riverboat Shuffle tonight!

Judy was sung by Jack Leonard. *Small Fry* was half sung, half recited by Hoagy and Tommy, somewhat after the manner of Bing Crosby and Johnny Mercer. *Davenport Blues* was included for the band. The composer was Beiderbecke, not Carmichael, but it belonged. It evoked the memory of that recording session in Richmond, Indiana. This was followed by *Stardust,* the record arrangement, with Edythe Wright singing the vocal chorus.

Then came the closing number, *Maple Leaf Rag.* The tune had been heard many times, in many places, played by many performers. But I am sure that this was a rendition the like of which had never been heard before. Mrs. Carmichael attacked with an enthusiasm and a confidence that would have been the envy of Fats Waller. Her head moved with the beat and the notes leaped out. The band's accompaniment was affectionate even in the crescendos. The guys wanted her to look good, but they needn't have worried.

The audience was electrified. They hadn't expected anything like this. They thought we just wanted them to meet Hoagy's mother. The response was overwhelming. They didn't just applaud. They cheered. They screamed. Some were even moved to tears. Mrs. Carmichael had stolen the show right out from under Tommy and Hoagy. It is a miracle that we somehow managed to squeeze in a closing sponsor credit as we went off the air under the continuing ovation.

I don't believe we could possibly have been foolish enough to have placed *Maple Leaf Rag* anywhere other than in the closing spot. We could never have followed it.

23

Clear Road Ahead

ON the night of January 10, 1939, at the Hotel New Yorker, there were two big bands side by side. This was the night Tommy Dorsey closed an engagement and turned over the bandstand to Jimmy Dorsey, who was opening at the same spot that same night.

Reflecting on the two bands, as they appeared that night, we see that their relative situation, during the three preceding years, had been changing and developing in clearly recognizable stages.

The Dorsey Brothers in 1935 were going places. Their band was sending out waves, signalling things to come. We can only speculate, but it seems reasonable to believe that the split, resulting in two bands, would have occurred even if Tommy's dramatic walkout had not brought it about fortuitously. Jimmy might have been slower to take the step, but undoubtedly they both would have reached the conclusion that their modus operandi was not workable. Harry Goodman played in Benny's band, but as a sideman. The Guy Lombardo band is a family affair, but there has never been any question about who is leader. If there could ever have been two brothers successfully co-starring as leaders of one band, it would not have been the Dorseys. Tommy was, functionally, leader of the Dorsey Brothers, but authority was divided. The two-leader policy could not have produced a band equal to either of the two bands which developed in the wake of the split.

After the split, Jimmy carried on alone, but he did it with a functioning organization. Tommy was on his own, alone, and had to start all over again.

The job with Bing in 1936 was a break for Jimmy. It gave him good visibility in a top spot. Throughout much of this time, Tommy was struggling along in outlying places.

The following year found Jimmy travelling on a comfortable plateau. Tommy's popularity was rising and spreading.

In the following year, 1938, Tommy reached the top. Jimmy, no longer situated on Bing's show, mustered new energy and started moving.

Tommy's drive, energy, and resourcefulness had caused him to outdistance Jimmy. But never, during this time, did Tommy view their relative progress as a race between them. Never was it his aim to "win." He wanted to have the best possible band, but not for the purpose of outdoing Jimmy. Tommy was a great supporter of Jimmy; he took every opportunity to boost him. Jimmy knew this.

By 1939, it was evident that Jimmy was no straggler. He had achieved a band of first rank, and he had done it on his own. Following the split in 1935, Tommy and Jimmy were both in tough spots, but for different reasons. In 1939, each had made it independently. The juxtaposition of the two bands at the New Yorker symbolized a clear road ahead.

Eight of the musicians who were in Jimmy's band in 1937 were still there in 1939: Shorty Sherock, trumpet; Bobby Byrne and Don Matteson, trombones; Charlie Frazier, sax and clarinet; and the rhythm section intact: Freddie Slack, piano; Roc Hillman, guitar; Jack Ryan, bass; Ray McKinley, drums. Tutti Camarata was another veteran. He had joined in 1936, as second trumpet and arranger; in 1939, he was devoting full time to arranging. Bob Eberly was there, of course, and Helen O'Connell made her entrance early in 1939.

The band was enlarged to include a third trumpet and a fifth sax (baritone). What made the band different was more than size and instrumentation. It was the impression it created. There was more assurance. The band seemed to step out. Much of this was the work of Camarata. It was evident that a great deal of thought had gone into

Helen and Bob

the writing he had been doing over the past year. The library of arrangements was not only larger, it was more *interesting*. The performance helped, too; it was precise, in both the section work and the ensemble. Solo work—by Shorty Sherock, Herbie Haymer, Bobby Byrne—was excellent. There was a kind of elegance in the ensemble. Above all, there was taste.

Helen O'Connell turned out to be the right one at the right time. Singers were becoming more and more important in the bands. In this department, Jimmy was well off with Bob Eberly. But, since Kay Weber's departure, he had not found a girl singer who was just the right one for the band. Helen was the one.

The band liked Helen from the start, and she enjoyed being a part of the band. When she appeared on the Merv Griffin Show in October, 1971, Griffin fondly recalled the big bands. Helen remembered "flipping" over Jimmy and Bob Eberly. "Did you have a crush on Bob Eberly?" Griffin asked. "Didn't everybody?" was Helen's reply. In that same conversation, Helen remembered that the first arrangement made for her to sing with the band was *All of Me*. Before long, Helen acquired a large following, and, in 1940, she won the *Metronome* Magazine poll.

Bob Eberly, at this time, had become one of the most popular singers in the nation. Bob had many opportunities to set out on his own, as Frank Sinatra did. There is no doubt that he could have made it, and made it big, but he wanted to stay on with Jimmy. Besides feeling a personal loyalty, Bob liked the spot he had with the band.

Bobby Byrne was thinking about organizing his own band. Although he had, as yet, no definite plans, he decided on the move early in 1939. In orderly and business-like fashion, he gave Jimmy a year's notice. Jimmy didn't like the idea of Bobby's leaving, not one bit. He was mad. He gave him the distant look. Jimmy continued to feature Bobby, but he looked right past him.

Later on, when Bobby had his own band, he met up with Jimmy one time, and Jimmy asked him if he wanted to come back. When Bobby declined, Jimmy was mad again. The same thing happened a few months later, in exactly the same way. This was very Dorsey-like. It could as well have been Tommy. Jimmy and Bobby, through all of this, were actually good friends, and they both knew it. This also was very Dorsey-like.

When Jimmy and his band came east in the fall of 1937, there was some catching up to do. Tutti Camarata remembers one-nighters where fans requested *Song of India* and *Marie.* "You've got the wrong Dorsey," they had to be told. In 1939, there was no such confusion. The requests were for *My Prayer* and *John Silver.* The catching up had been done. The road ahead was clear.

24

Bix Lix

WHILE Hoagy Carmichael was in New York, during the month preceding the Indianapolis visit, he came on Tommy's radio show to introduce his new song, *I Get Along Without You Very Well.* About a week before show date, he suddenly appeared in my office. It was late in the afternoon, time to leave, he said, and maybe we could stop in across the street and discuss the show. Hoagy was excited about a new tune he had just figured out, and I wanted to hear about it.

"Across the street" meant a little bar at the Ritz-Carlton Hotel on Madison Avenue at Forty-sixth Street. Not the men's bar or the main bar, but the little one with the red-lacquered tables and chairs, tucked away, downstairs in the corner. It would be a good place to talk. In no time at all we were settled, and drinks were ordered.

I asked Hoagy about the new tune. He told me about the plans for a Broadway production of "Young Man with a Horn," a play based on the Dorothy Baker novel inspired by the career of Bix Beiderbecke. Hoagy had been retained as music consultant. The production was not to be a musical, but it would require incidental music and a trumpet player who could play the Bix kind of notes offstage, synchronizing with the actor onstage.

While he was looking around for the right trumpet player, Hoagy was working on the notes to be played. He didn't want to use a familiar tune—it might draw attention away from the character. What he wanted was music that would sound like Bix, something characteristic.

Hoagy remembered that Bix frequently made use of a single note accented three times in succession, lingering the third time.

For example:

Hoagy called it the "one-two-three." For use in "Young Man with a Horn," he wrote a new tune with a flowing melody line, making use of the "one-two-three." DA . . . DA . . . da-de-da-da-da-da-ONE-TWO-THREE. The working title was *Bix Lix*.

Since there was no piano within reach, Hoagy compensated with an explanation so eloquent and graphic that it amounted to a performance. I was fascinated with the whole idea—especially so because it was a good tune, quite aside from its pragmatic qualities.

A sidelong glance confirmed my suspicion that the other people in the small bar were watching and listening. The full significance of the one-two-three may not have reached them, but they seemed to go along with it.

I had some doubts about a production of "Young Man with a Horn," for reasons having nothing to do with Hoagy, but I did want to hear more of that tune. The play was never produced, and the tune found a resting place in Hoagy's trunk. Three years later, the tune was lifted out and given to Johnny Mercer, who gave it a lyric. *Bix Lix* became *Skylark*.* The tempo was slower. It was legato. But it still had the one-two-three.

A week or so after *Bix Lix* emerged at the Ritz, Hoagy was on hand
in 8G at NBC to help introduce his new song, *I Get Along Without
You Very Well*, in Tommy's radio show. Long before this, a lyric had
been submitted to Hoagy. It had arrived in the mail from a Mrs. Jane
Brown. It might have been just another unusable amateur effort. But
this one seemed different to Hoagy. There was a thought—"I get
along without you very well, except sometimes, when evening shad-
ows fall . . ." The thought was directed to the author's deceased
husband.

It was not really a song lyric. It was a poem, rewarding to read, but
without the kind of construction that would have made it suitable for
a song. It was worth working on, and so Hoagy put it in proper shape
and wrote a melody to go with it.

When the song was completed, Hoagy tried to get in touch with
the author. He wanted her to have credit for the lyric. But there was
no Mrs. Jane Brown to be found at the address on her letter. The
effort to reach Mrs. Brown continued, with help from Walter Winchell in his column. The song was published, credit for the lyric going
to "Mrs. J. B. (?)."

Eventually, an address was located in Philadelphia for Mrs. Jane
Brown Thompson. It was the address of Mrs. Jane Brown, who had
remarried. She had died on January 19, 1939, without hearing her
song. How she would have loved to hear Tommy play it and Jack
Leonard sing it when it was introduced a few weeks later on February 15.

On the same show, Hoagy played and sang his *Hong Kong Blues*.
The song is not easy to explain to someone who has never heard it.
It is a character song, a sort of Chinese-jazz blues in minor with a sort
of rock beat. It tells the story of a musician stranded in Hong Kong,
who is "bobbin' the piano just to raise the price of a ticket to the land
of the free."

Later in that same season, Tommy and Jack Leonard introduced
another Carmichael song, *Blue Orchids*, surely one of the most
beautiful of all songs. Hoagy wrote his own lyric for this one—"Two
orchids only bloom in your eyes." The record is one of Jack Leonard's
favorites of all the many ballads he recorded with Tommy.

It was always a pleasure having Hoagy come on the show. The long
friendship and early association with Tommy gave us a foundation.
Around 1930, Hoagy assembled a group for some recordings at Victor. The group was Bix Beiderbecke, Jack Teagarden, both Dorseys,
Pee Wee Russell, Bud Freeman, Benny Goodman, Gene Krupa, and

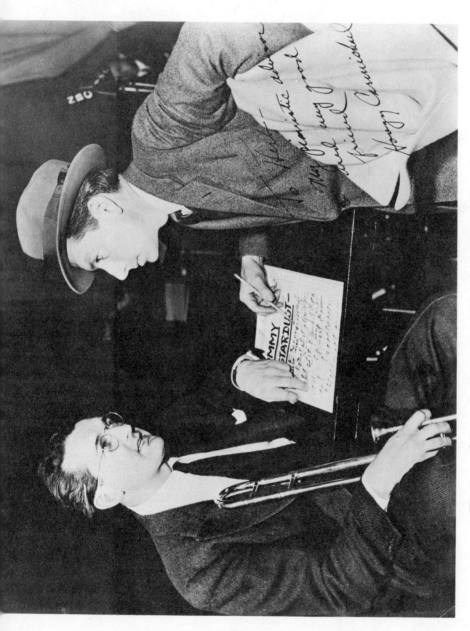

Tommy and Hoagy in 1939. They made their first record together in the mid-20s

Joe Venuti. The recordings were *Barnacle Bill, Rockin' Chair, Bessie Couldn't Help It,* and *Georgia on My Mind.* The assembling was done at Hoagy's New York apartment, which was a rendezvous and checkpoint for jazz musicians.

Hoagy has always been a special kind of writer. He doesn't go for a hit, although hits do come his way. He writes what he feels, honestly. He has given us music with character, songs that are a segment of Americana, and also some big hits, including the Oscar-winning *In the Cool, Cool, Cool of the Evening.*

Years ago, an all-knowing recording executive rejected a Carmichael tune, marking the test pressing "Not commercial." Hoagy keeps a loose-leaf book at home, containing a copy of every song he has written. On the leather cover, embossed in gold lettering, is the inscription, "It's Not Commercial."

25

"Sing, Sing, Sing,"
Mr. Krupa

FOLLOWING the show with Hoagy Carmichael, Tommy and the band played a week at the Stanley Theatre in Pittsburgh, a week at the Lyric in Indianapolis, which included the Carmichael show with Hoagy's mother, then on to Chicago. This time, we crossed paths with Jimmy McPartland and Gene Krupa.

Chicago was home territory for both Jimmy and Gene back in the days of the Austin High School Gang. Much had happened since then. Jimmy had been with the Ben Pollack band, along with a friend of the Austin High Gang, Benny Goodman. After the Pollack band broke up, Jimmy returned to Chicago to play in and emcee the show at the Three Deuces, where the singer was Anita O'Day. Gene was the drummer with Benny Goodman soon after Benny organized his band in 1934. Gene became one of the top stars of the day, remaining with Goodman until he started his own band in 1938.

When we were in Chicago this time, Jimmy was emceeing the show in the new Panther Room at the Sherman Hotel, where the star

160

attraction was Gene Krupa and his band—which Anita O'Day would join a couple of years later. During several weeks of midwestern dates, Tommy did the weekly radio show from Chicago. In one show, Jimmy McPartland was guest, playing the cornet Bix Beiderbecke had given him. In another show, we introduced Gene and his band.

This was Gene's second appearance in Tommy's show. The first one, the year before, was a send-off for the new band, which had since become a top attraction. Gene had also become an actor—in the picture, "Some Like It Hot," with Bob Hope and Shirley Ross; and he composed the music for the title song.

Tommy wanted to present Gene the right way. Thinking about it a couple of weeks ahead of show date, he said, "Last year, Gene only did one or two numbers. That's not enough. Let's have him do the whole show. That way, people will really hear the band. We'll give my band the night off."

That was Dorsey, and that was it. Our band had a night off and the Tommy Dorsey Show was Gene Krupa's that night. The sponsor approved. The change of pace was a good idea, and the two-week interval gave us time to get it in the papers.

We had a preconditioned crowd in the Panther Room. They gave Gene a welcome that must have been heard all around the Loop. They remembered *One O'Clock Jump* and *Sing, Sing, Sing*. Gene gave them *Nagasaki* and *Big Crash from China*. Irene Daye did *The Madam Swings It* and *My Heart Belongs to Daddy*. The program included the timely *Some Like It Hot* and closed with *Bugle Blues*.

There had been only a few drum-playing leaders—Ben Pollack, Chick Webb. Soon there would be Ray McKinley with his own outfit, and, in a few more years, Buddy Rich. Gene was a showman. But he was more: he was, and is, an artist. In a performance that was visually entertaining, he gave the crowd a great show. This may have obscured his musicianship for the less perceptive. But most people recognized his musicianship and found his showmanship entertaining.

It was about this time that Gene made an album demonstrating every kind of drumbeat, from primitive African to swing. No tonal instruments were used, only drums. The album was 78 r.p.m., which meant a lot of record changing, but it was worth it. The sequence had light and shade, variety and contrast, pacing, surprise effects—all the elements that might be expected in a well planned and routined musical program.

This talent, knowledge, and performance produced an interesting result some years later. In the fifties, Gene and another great drummer, Cozy Cole, operated a school for drummers, located in midtown Manhattan. We introduced Gene and Cozy on Garry Moore's daily television show for a demonstration. It was an entertaining spot, and our band joined Gene and Cozy for some real good jazz.

Gene Krupa seems to be indestructible. *The New York Times*, in June of 1970, carried a story by John S. Wilson with the heading, "Krupa, Back on Drums at 61, Leads Quartet at Plaza." The story begins, "Gene Krupa, who went quietly into retirement in October of 1967, is back at his drums again, slim, trim and tanned, leading a quartet at Plaza-9 in the Plaza Hotel." In the story Mr. Wilson observes, "Mr. Krupa's once jet-black hair has turned a misty gray but a lock still dangles down his forehead just as it did when he was establishing himself as the first virtuoso jazz drum soloist with Benny Goodman's band 35 years ago."

After the Gene Krupa entry in the Tommy Dorsey Show on March 29, Tommy and the band had to get back to New York for an April opening at the Paramount Theatre. The engagements at the Paramount and other theatres, as we have observed, were never without incident. Just recently, Johnny Mince recalled one. It occurred as a stage show was about to begin.

The stage show was always preceded by the cartoon on the screen, during which the band was seated on the stand in its lowered position in the pit. All lights were out. The exit signs in the back of the theatre were usually visible, but, on one occasion, Johnny was aware that not even the exit signs could be seen. Something was not right, but Johnny did not know what. The cartoon ended, lights came on as the band platform rose to stage level, facing the audience. Standing squarely in front of Johnny was a giant bum who had somehow found his way in from the street and onto the bandstand. Johnny says, "You could see Tommy go pale, even under all that makeup." The ushers hustled the bum out, but not before he strode to the mike and began to recite, "Fourscore and seven years ago, our forefathers brought forth on this continent a new nation, conceived . . ."

26

"Next Week—"

"NEXT week" in the Tommy Dorsey organization was not "East Lynne," although there is no denying that there were occasional incidents that verged on the melodramatic. However, each week would likely bring with it some kind of new development. There was always something brewing in Tommy's mind, whether it was a new business project or a new direction for the band.

Tommy looked ahead. He wanted to widen the scope of the band's performance. In the arranging department, Tommy was in magnificent shape with Paul Weston, Axel Stordahl, Deane Kincaide, and others. But there might be something new to add.

This was comparable to a comedian recognizing the desirability of expanding his writing staff. If Jack Benny hired a new writer, it probably meant he had found one who could deliver something additional, something that would enhance the overall result.

The radio show was a sounding board. Newly recorded arrangements were always introduced there. In the spring and summer of 1939, two new arrangements were heard—Bill Finegan's *Lonesome Road* and Sy Oliver's *Stomp It Off*. These arrangements constituted a forecast of new sounds that would characterize the Tommy Dorsey band in the next few years. *Lonesome Road*, recorded on two sides, was massive, deliberate, powerful, with chord sequences that demanded attention. *Stomp It Off* was smooth, easy, joyful, with an irresistible beat and swing.

Neither Bill Finegan nor Sy Oliver was on the Tommy Dorsey staff at this time. Sy Oliver was the first to join. Tommy had always liked Jimmie Lunceford's band, and he especially admired the writing Sy Oliver did for that band—*Swanee River*, *Cheatin' on Me*, and Sy's own tune, *Dream of You*, among many others. I can remember a rehearsal, long before Sy's time with the band, when a new swing arrangement was being run through. The notes came out right, but it wasn't getting through with the right effect. Tommy was exasperated. "Look," he said, "make it sound like Lunceford." This was direct and clear. He was thinking about those Sy Oliver arrangements.

Another Sy Oliver arrangement, *Easy Does It*, came along that fall, and, before the year was out, Sy went to work for Tommy. He contributed much in the period, beginning in 1940, characterized by the rise of Frank Sinatra and Buddy Rich.

Looking through some of the programs we did in the radio series, there was usually something "next week" that had some special interest. There was always a ballad, such as *You Taught Me to Love Again*, *If It's the Last Thing I Do*, or *All the Things You Are*, given emotional impact by Tommy's trombone and Jack Leonard's voice. And there was sure to be good jazz—*Wolverine Blues*, *Copenhagen*, *Tin Roof Blues*, *Clarinet Marmalade*.

Shirley Ross came back to visit the show in April with *Blow, Gabriel, Blow*, *The Lady's in Love with You*, and a first performance of *The Lamp Is Low*. Special lyrics were written for Shirley and Tommy to do *Thanks for the Memory* as a dialogue in song.

Hoagy Carmichael, in his book, *Sometimes I Wonder*, quotes Ernest Hemingway: "We all had a girl—and her name is Nostalgia." We frequently called upon nostalgia. Howard Smith did an arrangement of Bix Beiderbecke's *Candlelights*. Bix would have loved both Howard's piano and the faithful interpretation given in the arrangement. Howard was especially good at arranging piano compositions for the band. Two of Willie ("The Lion") Smith's compositions, *Morning Air* and *Passionette*, were among them.

In the same program, we repeated Tommy's legit rendition of the

Jerry Colonna, Tommy, Bud Collyer

Sy Oliver

second movement of Tschaikovsky's *Fifth Symphony*, using it to introduce *Moon Love*, a new popular song based on the Tschaikovsky melody. The music that night had nothing if not variety. We included a medley of favorite ballads—*How Deep Is the Ocean?*, *These Foolish Things*, and *Out of Nowhere*. We opened with *The Jumpin' Jive*, closed with a swing arrangement of *Beach at Waikiki*, and—just to make sure—we threw in *Honeysuckle Rose*.

Among our first on-the-air performances were songs from the "George White's Scandals of 1939" in our show of August 9. The "Scandals" had opened on Broadway only a few days before. Here was a current event which brought forth a rich vein of nostalgia. In the twenties, George White and the "George White's Scandals" were very much a part of the scene. In 1939, there was no more "Ziegfeld Follies" or "Earl Carroll's Vanities," but there was George White producing a new edition of his "Scandals."

In 1925, Helen Morgan was in the "Scandals," and Tommy and Jimmy Dorsey, a few miles to the north on Pelham Parkway, were playing in the California Ramblers. Miguel Covarrubias came out with a book that year entitled *The Prince of Wales and Other Famous Americans*, which included sketches of Calvin Coolidge, Babe Ruth, Jack Dempsey, Paul Whiteman, and the "Scandals" star, Ann Pennington. "No, No, Nanette" was a hit in 1925, as it is in 1972. Charlie Chaplin's "Gold Rush" was playing then, as it is in 1972. In 1925, people were doing the Charleston.

We included the popular tune, *Charleston*, on the radio show because it was in "Runnin' Wild," an all-Negro revue produced by George White in 1923, and because the music was composed by James P. Johnson, the stride piano player who was one of the greats of jazz. Another tune on the same show, also from "Runnin' Wild," was *Old-Fashioned Love*, which is a jazz standard.

Also in our radio show were *Somebody Loves Me*, by George and Ira Gershwin, from the 1924 "Scandals," introduced by Tom Patricola and Winnie Lightner; *Birth of the Blues* and *Black Bottom*, by Buddy DeSylva, Lew Brown, and Ray Henderson, from the great 1926 edition with Ann Pennington, Frances Williams, Harry Richman, and Willie and Eugene Howard; *Life Is Just a Bowl of Cherries* and *The Thrill Is Gone*, also by DeSylva, Brown and Henderson, from the 1931 "Scandals," with a cast that included Ethel Merman, Rudy Vallee, and Ray Bolger.

Sammy Fain and Jack Yellen wrote the songs for the 1939 "Scandals." The cast included Ella Logan, Ann Miller, Ben Blue, and Willie and Eugene Howard. On Tommy's radio show, Edythe Wright sang the rhythm song, *Are You Having Any Fun?*, Jack Leonard sang the ballad, *Good Night, My Beautiful*, and the band played *Mexiconga*.

Jack Yellen wrote us a letter: "George White isn't a very demonstrative fellow, but I think, had you and Tommy Dorsey been around here after last night's program, he'd have kissed you both. Little did the audience waiting impatiently in the theatre realize what was holding the curtain. White wouldn't start the show until he had heard the last word and note of the broadcast. As for myself, I haven't had such a kick since I've been writing songs."

Variety wrote: "White couldn't have asked for a better sendoff. The makeup of the program in both music and narrative treatment brought credit to Dorsey and all others concerned." The review began, "Tommy Dorsey gave over practically his entire half hour of the Raleigh cigarette show (NBC) last Wednesday (9) to a buildup for George White's new 'Scandals.' "

Variety was right. We gave over *practically* the entire half hour, but not quite *all*. Just to make sure that the listeners knew who was doing all this, we saved out time for *Marie*.

27

The Graduates, Summer of '39

AMONG the bandleaders of the late thirties were some Dorsey graduates: Bunny Berigan, Glenn Miller, Larry Clinton, Bob Crosby, and Bobby Byrne. Soon there would be Ray McKinley, Freddie Slack, Charlie Spivak, Sy Oliver, Ray Anthony, Shorty Sherock, and Buddy Rich.

In June of 1939, a handpicked group of musicians, including several Dorsey graduates, were selected by some Princeton graduates to play at the Class of '29 Tenth Reunion. The Dorsey graduates were Bud Freeman, Dave Tough, and Max Kaminsky. The Princeton graduates were Bill Priestley, architect and musician, and Frank Norris, a *Time* editor.

The musicians were all graduates from somewhere. Eddie Condon and two of the Dorsey graduates, Bud and Dave, were graduates from the Austin High School Gang. Bud and Dave were also graduates from another Austin High sidekick, Benny Goodman. The third Dorsey graduate, Maxie Kaminsky, had also matriculated with Shaw.

Condon was not a band graduate; he had always been his own institution. The other four graduates in the outfit were Pee Wee Russell, from Red Nichols and Louis Prima; Brad Gowans, from the Memphis Five; Dave Bowman, from Jack Hylton, the English bandleader; and Clyde Newcombe, from Lennie Hayton and Bobby Hackett.

This ad hoc band made a big hit at Princeton—both as beer drinkers and as music makers. Bud Freeman was out in front as leader. Dave Tough was on drums. There was Max Kaminsky, trumpet; Pee Wee Russell, clarinet; Brad Gowans, valve trombone. Pianist was Dave Bowman; bassist, Clyde Newcombe. Through it all was Eddie Condon and his guitar.

The venture worked out so well that the graduates decided to stay in business as a cooperative band, sharing profits equally. John Chapman, in his *Daily News* column, "Mainly About Manhattan," reported, "Bud Freeman's name was put on the band because he's good-looking and well known and you got to have a name to get anywhere in the band business."

They needed a name for the new band. Considering that they played their first engagement at a graduate affair, and considering that they were all graduates of one kind or another, and, moreover, in good standing, they decided on "Summa Cum Laude."

The Summa Cum Laude opened in June at Nick's, then the foremost jazz spot in New York's Greenwich Village. At the same time, they embarked on a recording contract with Bluebird Records; their first sides were *I've Found a New Baby, Easy to Get, China Boy*, and Bud's old sax specialty, *The Eel.*

Nick's was a jazz center rivaling the Onyx as a rendezvous. It was not far from the spot where Eddie Condon was to open his place a few years later. It attracted lovers of swing, including those who danced in the aisles at the Paramount a few years earlier and were now graduated into the young married set. It was also a favorite spot for professional athletes and sports writers.

The only entertainment at Nick's was the band. That was because the owner and proprietor, Nick Rongetti, was a band buff. He also played acceptable piano; he moved in a second piano to facilitate his sitting in with the band without the necessity of removing the pianist. A collateral attraction at Nick's was Duchess, a blue-ribbon-winning boxer dog, who loved to join the party and meet people. Duchess stayed in her own quarters most of the time, coming out occasionally to see friends. Duchess sat at our table one night, in

Eddie Condon

dignified fashion on the chair at an unoccupied place. Her behavior was faultless; she followed the conversation around the table, looking directly at the person who was speaking. After a while, her expression communicated "Thank you," and she then descended and returned quietly to her quarters.

The one thing that bothered Nick was the practice, pursued by some of the band members, of going across the street to Julius' for a drink between sets. It was explained to Nick that this was done because business was so good at his place that there was no room at the bar. And besides, Julius' was not competition; it didn't swing. Nick still didn't approve.

Tommy Dorsey made Nick's a late stop on nights when he did not drive out to Bernardsville. Sometimes he was accompanied by Yank Lawson and others in his band, or by old pals like Lennie Hayton and Frank Signorelli. Jimmy Dorsey stopped in when he was in town, sometimes with cornet. They always sat in and played. If only we could have taped some of those sessions.

Twenty-three blocks up the street, at the Pennsylvania Roof, Tommy and the band were playing to joyful crowds. There would be personnel changes and new developments by the end of the year, but for the summer things were rolling along in pretty much the same way. Yank was captivating the people with his eloquent trumpet choruses. Johnny Mince was better than ever on the clarinet. Babe Russin was great on tenor, in the spot formerly occupied by graduate Bud Freeman. Graduate Dave Tough's spot was being filled in fine fashion by Cliff Leeman.

Cliff remembers that Tommy sometimes sat out in front during the dinner session, talking with friends and listening to the band, listening especially to his solo parts being played by one of the other trombone players. Tommy's parts were always written in higher-than-usual keys. Occasionally, there were "bloops." When a bloop occurred, it was followed by the appearance of the dignified head waiter, approaching the bandstand, bearing a silver tray on which was a coffee urn and a heap of crullers.

It was a good laugh. No one minded, the trombonists least of all. Tommy's expertise on the instrument was a phenomenon and was so accepted.

The Summa Cum Laude produced a spinoff. Bud Freeman, who always leaned toward becoming an actor, provided he could fit it in with jazz, teamed with Minerva Pious and recorded "Private Jives," a sketch by John DeVries taking off Noel Coward and Gertrude Lawrence in "Private Lives." It was hilarious and is now a collector's item.

Toward the end of the summer, there was an event which concluded a period of suspenseful waiting. Tommy began signing off his sustaining broadcasts with "Good night, Ma." This undoubtedly was not clear to listeners, but it was clear to Harriet Lawson, for Harriet and Yank were expecting an addition to the family. When the coming event became long overdue, Tommy closed with "Hurry up, Ma." Flowers arrived daily at the hospital in Jackson Heights on Long Island, marked, "To Mom."

Six weeks late but healthy and happy, on August 24, 1939, the Lawson twins arrived—Margaret and John, Jr. Eight weeks later, Harriet and the twins flew to Chicago, where the band was then playing, for a week's visit. Harriet recalls, "Tommy enjoyed taking everyone to Italian restaurants after work. I must have gained ten pounds, which I badly needed. Tommy delighted in ordering for everyone and, of course, enjoyed the attention he received from waiters and captains. We really had fun during that period."

As the summer of 1939 ended, there was serendipity in Toronto. On September 8 the *American Flagship* was chartered to fly the Tommy Dorsey band to Toronto to appear at the Canadian National Exhibition. I am told by Yank Lawson, Cliff Leeman, and others that this was the first time an entire band had travelled by air. At the airport they unpacked their instruments and played a few numbers to mark the occasion.

At the Exhibition, there was a girl at the stage door after every show. She had with her a demonstration recording of a song she had written, and she wanted Tommy to hear it. This happened often. People would show up with songs, hoping Tommy would look at them, play them, maybe record them. This was understandable, but not workable. Not one in a thousand would be worthwhile, and there just wasn't time to deal with them all.

But in this case the girl would not give up. Bobby Burns remembers she was there after every show. Carmen Mastren, guitarist and arranger, listened to the demo. The song had been done on a Toronto radio station by a singer and a studio orchestra, and recorded off the air. Carmen says, "I flipped when I heard it, and it took months to get Tommy to listen to it."

Carmen took the demo record back to New York. Cliff Leeman,

Yank Lawson's solos drove TD's band on *Losers Weepers, Milenberg Joys, Stomp It Off, Hawaiian War Chant,* many others

Backstage at the Paramount, Tommy chats with old sidekicks Lennie Hayton and Glenn Miller

Tommy Dorsey and band after flight from New York to Toronto for Canadian National Exhibition, September 8, 1939. They were first band to fly. Left to right: airline official, Dave Jacobs, Elmer Smithers, Richie Liscella, Johnny Mince, Andy Ferretti, Gene Traxler, Hymie Schertzer, Jack Leonard, Cliff Leeman, Yank Lawson, Ward Sillaway, Deane Kincaide, Edythe Wright, Tommy Dorsey, Carmen Mastren, Jimmy Blake, Howard Smith, Freddie Stulce, Babe Russin, Bobby Burns, two airline officials

who had heard the record and liked it, says, "We were back at the Statler for three weeks, and neither Carmen nor I could get Tommy to listen to it in the back room."

One afternoon, during this period, several of us were sitting in the office Tommy kept in the RCA Building in Rockefeller Center. Carmen Mastren, Paul Weston, Axel Stordahl, and I were hoping Tommy would come in, because Carmen had brought the record and we wanted to play it for him.

Ray Henderson, who had an office on the same floor, dropped in. We told him about the song and how it had come our way in Toronto, and asked him if he would listen to it. Ray liked it the first time through. Ray Henderson's opinion was worth having. He had written so many hits, including *Five Foot Two, Eyes of Blue, Birth of the Blues*, and *The Best Things in Life Are Free*. Listening to the record, Ray remarked on the sentimental quality of the song and said, *"Those are the songs, boys."*

Tommy was finally persuaded to listen to the demo record. The song was called *I'll Never Smile Again*. The girl at the stage door was Ruth Lowe. The orchestra conductor on the demo was Percy Faith. He had made the arrangement and conducted it as a favor to Ruth Lowe.

Tommy had the song, but he didn't seem to be in a hurry to do anything with it. He gave it to Glenn Miller to record, but nothing ever happened with Glenn's record. Tommy finally recorded *I'll Never Smile Again* with Frank Sinatra and the Pied Pipers in May, 1940, eight months after it had been stumbled on in Toronto.

28

It Wasn't Always Music

The Die Is Cast

When we were in Indianapolis for a week, earlier that year, what happened wasn't always music. One night, after Tommy's last show at the Lyric Theatre, several of us were ready to relax. The logical place, suggesting itself silently and telepathically, was the nearest oasis. There was no delay. We were there, as if we had been catapulted.

For some reason, the oasis did not seem to be the right thing. Still, it was too early to turn in without first unwinding. The moon and the tides must have taken command. Resembling a fast cut in a motion picture from one scene to another, we found ourselves in somebody's room at the Indiana Hotel clearing off a large round table. Chairs were moved back against the wall, allowing plenty of room for action all around.

The dice were tossed on the table. The sound was brittle and tempting. Grouped around the table were Yank Lawson, Carmen Mastren, Andy Ferretti, Johnny Mince, and I—plus Mr. Lowe, who was on the bill at the theatre in a comedy act known as "Lowe, Hite,

and Stanley." Hite was more than seven feet tall, Stanley was average, and Lowe was a midget.

Lowe could reach up and throw the dice on the table, but he could
not see them land. If he was entitled to roll again, there was a slight
operational problem in that he could not reach the dice. This was
solved by Yank, who is six feet four, twice Lowe's height. Yank simply
reached and picked up the dice and laid them down on the other side
of the large table, right over Lowe's head. Lowe would then reach
up and roll again.

The game moved along like many another. Winnings moved
around the table from one spot to another. For a while I was winning,
and I was embarrassed. It didn't seem right for the producer to be
taking money from the guys in the band. But the need for such
embarrassment did not last.

Hours passed. It was beginning to resemble a scoreless tie. But the
game went on. The entertaining part of the action was Yank span-
ning the table with his long arms, returning the dice neatly to Lowe's
position.

Then, at one point, Yank was forced to repeat those motions con-
secutively for what seemed an interminable length of time. He
looked like an assembly-line worker. It was comparable to a one-joke
routine that lasts too long, but it wasn't exactly a joke. The money
piled up in the spot over Lowe's head. He was quite evidently incapa-
ble of throwing a combination that would surrender the dice. He was
giving everybody a chance to recoup, but it was no dice.

When all the money in the room was in a large mound over Lowe,
along with several checks that had been written, the game ended.
And all this time, Lowe had not once seen the dice. He thanked one
and all for a pleasant evening, gathered up his winnings, and departed with a smile.

Maybe we should have stayed in that nice, relaxing oasis.

Dig a Little Deeper

During one of the runs at the Chicago Theatre Bobby Burns appeared in Tommy's dressing room and announced a caller downstairs
at the stage door. Tommy looked at the name and remembered it
was the man Morton Downey had told him about. "Tell him to come
up." There were several of us present, the usual complement between shows.

The caller entered, shook hands around, and proceeded to the point of his call without delay—or, rather, to what was the preliminary to the main point. He drew from his pocket an enormous handkerchief, tied around to hold in the contents, after the manner of a sack of Christmas candy. He set the handkerchief on a table, untwisted its folds, and revealed what appeared to be nuggets of gold.

"Do you see those?" he asked, as the nuggets rolled a few inches and settled down, shining. No one answered; it was obvious we saw them. "I mined those myself."

It was quite an opener. Clearly, he had planned his routine and believed in having an opening number that would grab the attention of the audience. The nuggets established him as one who didn't fool around. He then got right to the main business, and it was not a gold mine. It was an oil well—that is, a potential oil well—in Texas.

A short time before this, while the band was in California, Morton Downey had given Tommy a tip on an investment plan for an oil well. Downey and others were planning to go in on it. Tommy was sold. The oil well became Tommy's newest project.

While Tommy's lawyer, Johnny Gluskin, was looking into the legal and financial aspects, Tommy looked for confirmation of another sort. Dallas was the home town of Freddie Stulce, Tommy's saxist and arranger. Tommy remembered Freddie mentioning that his mother knew a gypsy fortune teller. He asked Freddie to write to his mother. "Ask her to speak to the gypsy. How does it look?"

We may assume that the gypsy did not render an unfavorable opinion. The project was activated. Tommy called a meeting of the band and announced that each one could invest whatever amount he chose. Some were hesitant, but Tommy told them he would pay them back in case the well didn't come in—"an unheard-of deal for us," says Johnny Mince. Most of the band came in for an investment of around $150. Gene Traxler says, "I remember some heavy investors, like single Johnny Mince, and I myself only put in $150." (Johnny was still a bachelor at the time, while Gene had embarked on rearing a family.)

Drilling moved ahead. Keeping abreast of the drilling became an extra duty for Johnny Gluskin. Johnny was fully occupied with the numerous problems facing a lawyer-business manager; those frequent trips to Texas were not easy to fit in. The band watched these trips with keen interest. Each time Johnny returned, he was surrounded. "How's it going? What's the word?" Invariably, the word was that it would be necessary to dig a little deeper. And that meant that Tommy would have to dig a little deeper to keep the drilling going.

If the caller at the Chicago Theatre recited the prologue, then Tommy was the protagonist and the band was the Greek chorus. It wasn't really Greek tragedy; there was no inevitability. But, as months passed, the oil well did take on an air of doom. The end came before a year had passed.

"Well, he sure kept his word," says Carmen, "and paid us back every cent, and it was a verbal agreement, nothing on paper. He really went for a bundle."

Johnny Mince remarks, "The oil well pooped out and everyone forgot what Tommy had promised, so one day in late 1940 we got our checks as usual, but with a much larger amount. Tommy had paid us back that day."

It was a calculated risk. If they had struck oil, Tommy and all concerned would have been heroes. But it didn't happen.

This was not the end of such projects and business ventures. There were more to come—successful ones, too—but no more oil wells. It was back to music.

Cream Puffs and Champagne

Several of us, including Lennie Hayton and Paul Weston and Bobby Burns, were sitting in Tommy's dressing room one afternoon at the New York Paramount Theatre. The show on stage was coming to an end. We could hear the last chorus of the closing number.

We heard the sound of intermission voices and footsteps on the stairway leading to the various dressing rooms. Tommy burst into the room, addressing Bobby Burns.

"Order up a case of champagne."

No one made any comment. We were not prepared for anything like that at this time. A case of champagne? Why? It was no special occasion . . . or was it?

In recent weeks, we had noticed that Tommy was keeping handy a bottle of Fernet Branca, the Italian bitters reputed to be good for settling the stomach. The alcoholic content was high but not intolerable, even for one who was on the wagon.

Could it be that Tommy was going off the wagon, putting an end to the seven-year stretch begun way back at Plunkett's speakeasy? Maybe he figured a little wine occasionally would be all right, like the Fernet Branca. But a *case?*

The case of champagne arrived almost immediately. I could never have negotiated so fast a delivery, but Bobby knew how to do it.

As it turned out, the event was a trial run. Tommy was venturing off the wagon—just a few steps. We had been chosen to participate. Fernet was medicinal and could be administered, when needed, in solitary. But for his first real drink in so many years, Tommy needed company. Paul was a non-drinker, but there was no sidestepping a sip of champagne on this occasion.

"Bobby, we need something to go with the champagne. Telephone Sardi's." Sardi's was around the corner on West Forty-fourth Street.

I thought of something I had read in *The New Yorker* about a party given by Isadora Duncan on a Sunday evening in her Paris apartment, at which guests were served champagne and strawberry tarts. The party, with the same people, gathered momentum two weeks later in Naples, and finished two months later in a houseboat on the Nile . . . no, that was going too far, both in the case of the strawberry tarts and the Nile.

What we got were cream puffs. Another fast delivery. A few cream puffs in a bakery box might not have been too great a surprise. But we were confronted with a caterer's tray—four dozen bulging cream puffs. I don't remember Tommy specifying the quantity. Bobby probably made the decision; he knew the idea would be to do it right, go the whole way.

The caterer's tray was more than enough to go around for the five of us. I am certain that no one wanted even one cream puff. Paul was more hesitant at a cream puff than he was at a glass of champagne. But the tray was passed again. And don't refuse.

A couple of times, someone looked in, did a fast take, and fled. My thoughts again went to *The New Yorker* story . . . Isadora Duncan's party was on a Sunday evening in Paris . . . this was a weekday afternoon on Broadway . . . the refreshments were comparable, only we had cream puffs instead of strawberry tarts . . .

Soon it was time for the next show. The champagne was put away. I don't know what happened to the cream puffs. The trial run was over. Back on the wagon. I believe it was a first of some sort.

29

Fate Takes a Hand

ON a night in the fall of 1939, Jack Leonard was with Tommy, driving to Bernardsville after work at the Pennsylvania Roof. Jack asked Tommy if he had heard the Harry James record, *All or Nothing at All.*

"No," replied Tommy. "Why do you ask?"

"There's a guy who does the vocal and he scares the hell out of me. He's that good."

In that moment, Jack may have been the first to tell Tommy Dorsey about Frank Sinatra.

Jack, at this time, had reached top place among band singers. The popularity polls were evidence of this. So were the comments about his singing on two best-selling Tommy Dorsey records, *You Taught Me to Love Again* and *All the Things You Are.* When Jack sang those songs at the Pennsylvania Roof, the dancers drew close to the bandstand.

Jack and Tommy were not communicating well at this time. There were rumors that Jack was making plans to start out on his own. It is true that Jack was thinking of doing a single. But he was not making any plans. He had not discussed such a move with anyone. If he had been seriously considering taking the step, he would have talked it over with Tommy. The rumors, of course, reached Tommy. The communications gap widened.

In November, Jack got into a dispute with Tommy over the treatment some of the musicians were receiving. The band was playing the Palmer House in Chicago, and it was there that Jack left the band. Everyone, including Jack, and possibly Tommy, thought he would be back. But that is not what happened. Harry James was at the Sherman Hotel, and his vocalist was the one whose singing on *All or Nothing at All* had been the subject of Jack's comment to Tommy, driving to Bernardsville that night. Tommy asked brother Jimmy and Jimmy's close friend, Jimmy O'Keefe, to stop in at the Sherman and ask the vocalist if he was interested. A few weeks later, Frank Sinatra went to work for Tommy Dorsey.

Sinatra's debut with Dorsey took place on February 2, 1940, in Indianapolis at the Lyric Theatre. Indianapolis was the scene of other noteworthy musical events. It was where Bix and Frank Trumbauer had joined Whiteman thirteen years before. The Lyric Theatre was where the people turned out to see their townsman, Hoagy Carmichael, and his mother when they appeared there with Tommy Dorsey the year before. The Lyric seated about two thousand. Tommy and the band were the draw, but the response of the overflowing crowd, when Sinatra sang, was a forecast of the next two years.

Before the month was out, Tommy recorded *I'll Be Seeing You*, with Sinatra doing the vocal. The song is still associated with the World War II period, and there are many who fondly remember Frank singing, "I'll be seeing you in all the old familiar places . . ."

Sinatra's emergence in the Tommy Dorsey band coincided with, and accented, a period of development that was taking place in the band. There were the Sy Oliver arrangements—*My, My* came along in March. There was the sound of Jo Stafford and the Pied Pipers, which, with Sinatra, was to become so characteristic. Connie Haines was there. And Buddy Rich was at the drums. The band was getting bigger.

The Raleigh-Kool sponsorship had come to an end. It was explained as some sort of change in advertising policy. The company had had the benefit of the acclaim accorded Tommy during the band's rise to the top, but it lost out on the cumulative benefit it would have enjoyed with the band's continuing rise in popularity.

The enviable standing of the band did not eliminate the one-nighters. The comparative ease and regularity of theatres and hotel work had to be reckoned against the irregularities of those one-night stands. Johnny Mince tells of the time in Baltimore when Frank Sinatra was in the line of fire and volunteered his services above and beyond the call. A drunk wandered on stage while Johnny was capturing the attention of the crowd with his clarinet solo. The drunk wandered off, then immediately rushed back on. He wasn't threatening; what was almost worse, he was exhibiting the antics of a stage drunk. It was Sinatra who finally grabbed the drunk and, with help from Richie Liscella, forced a swift exit. All this time, Johnny, hopelessly outnumbered, was trying valiantly to rise above the upstaging.

Carmen Mastren had left the band by this time. He wanted to stay around New York for a while. "I went right back to the Hickory House with Joe Marsala. Tommy used to come in," recalls Carmen, "and one night he asked me when I was coming back. I told him we were having too much fun. Not making any money, but I didn't have to worry about the bus leaving. He came back often when he was in town. I asked him if he would ever tire of the road, and he said he was the happiest when out of town. He really enjoyed being on the road. Most of us had tired of it long ago, and I don't think it was all a question of money with Tommy."

Beginning with the 1940 season, there came a succession of Tommy Dorsey records with Frank Sinatra vocals—*Fools Rush In, East of the Sun*, and, with the Pied Pipers, *I'll Never Smile Again* and *Stardust.*

I'll Never Smile Again is almost unique; the general excellence of the recording is due to a combination of several factors. No song is intrinsically a sure hit. It takes doing. The recording of *I'll Never Smile Again* is a classic example of *performance.* First of all, tempo. With some musicians and singers, the tempo might well have been too slow to be effective. In this case, it was the right hunch. In the attitude of both band and singers, there was an intimate personal quality that was communicated to the audience—more surely in the chosen tempo than could have been done in a faster tempo. The reflective quality of the lyric registered, beautifully punctuated by Joe Bushkin on the celeste. The blend of voices is about as good as a blend can be. Sinatra and the Pied Pipers stayed with the phrasing of Tommy's trombone, and the result was a masterpiece.

Coming when it did, Sinatra's joining Tommy Dorsey seemed al-

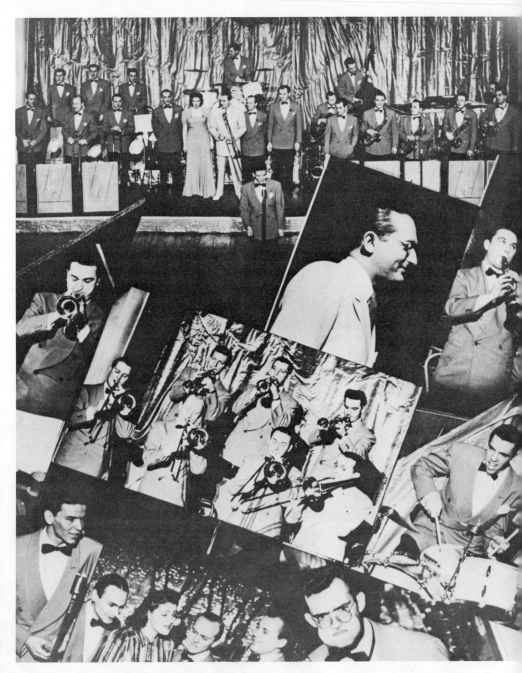

The band in early 1940. Clockwise: band, Johnny Mince, Buddy Rich, Freddie Stulce, Frank and the Pied Pipers, Lee Castle. Inside: Tommy and the brass

most as if it happened according to plan. Sinatra was ready. Tommy's band was the right spot.

With the entry of the United States in the war getting closer, Jack Leonard joined the Army. He did not return to singing after the war. But he did stay with music; he became associated with the management of Nat Cole. Today, Jack is west coast professional manager for Screen Gems-Columbia Music. In later years, Tommy and Jack resolved their differences and were once again the friends they always were.

There are many of us, friends and fans alike, who can never forget the sensitive, sympathetic quality of Jack Leonard's singing, a quality which reflects Jack as a person. We cannot help speculating on what might have happened with his singing career if he had returned to it after getting out of the service. Jack has thought about it, too. He says, "I, along with fans and music critics, have often wondered what my role as a pop singer would have been had I not been called to serve Uncle Sam at the height of my career."

Tommy gets around better on the trumpet than young Andy Hardy does on the trombone *(from the collection of Rev. Kenneth C. Spence)*

30

Ninth Birthday

IT was February of 1940, and Jimmy Dorsey and his band were coming to town—to Chicago, that is. On the band's east-west travels, Chicago was always a good place to stop, whether the stand was to be the Panther Room at the Sherman Hotel, the Joseph Urban Room at the Congress Hotel, or the big Chicago Theatre. There were kindred souls in Chicago. The band's arrival was always happily anticipated there by friends and followers—in particular by two of Jimmy's close personal friends, Squirrel Ashcraft and Jimmy O'Keefe.

On one occasion, travelling by train, Jimmy and the band arrived at Chicago's Union Station. As they filed past the gate and into the station, they were forced to step over or around a mob of people lying on the floor, apparently sound asleep, clutching placards proclaiming, in large letters, "It's the dreamer in me!" or some variation of the statement.

Jimmy and the band broke up. It was the title of Jimmy's song, *It's the Dreamer in Me*. Jimmy O'Keefe had enlisted the help of some of his law-student friends. There were a dozen or so of them, enough

At Jimmy's "ninth" birthday party: Jimmy, Charlie Frazier, Jerry Rosa, Jack Ryan, Bob and Florine Eberly. Roc Hillman is up front

At the same party, Joe Rushton, Dode O'Keefe, Jimmy Dorsey, Jane Ashcraft, Gloria Fay. Jimmy O'Keefe is seated on the floor

Scene of Jimmy's fabled "ninth" birthday party (February 29, 1940—
he was a leap-year baby) at Chicago's Hotel Sherman

to look like a crowd, lying there asleep, holding the signs upright.

Jimmy Dorsey composed the melody of *It's the Dreamer in Me*. The song is remarkable, in that the lyric was written by Jimmy Van Heusen, known as the composer of the music for so many hit songs. A year later we were hearing a lot of *I Thought About You*, which had Jimmy Van Heusen's music and Johnny Mercer's lyric. The recording of *It's the Dreamer in Me*, with Bob Eberly's vocal, was enjoying hit status at the time Jimmy O'Keefe and his legion met Jimmy Dorsey and his band at the gates of the Union Station.

Jimmy O'Keefe is a prominent Chicago lawyer, important in state political affairs. I asked him how he and Jimmy Dorsey happened to become such good friends. "For starters," he replied, "let me say that I met Jimmy Dorsey in 1937 when he opened at the Joseph Urban Room in the Congress Hotel. I simply walked up to him, profferred my hand and told him that I was a hoofer studying law, that I had worked in the Whiteman band for a couple of years and that we ought to be friends. And what a friendship that turned out to be!"

Bob Eberly confirms the fact that the friendship was a lively one. "Whenever we were due in Chicago, to Jimmy Dorsey Chicago *was* Jimmy O'Keefe. He was there, regardless of the year, month, or hour. It was hoo-ray time." Jimmy Dorsey enjoyed Jimmy O'Keefe's sense of humor and the practical jokes he engineered. Bob remembers that Jimmy O'Keefe once telephoned Ted Lewis ("Is ev-'rybody happy?") at 4:00 A.M. Awakening Lewis from a sound sleep, and pretending to be a radio personality, Jimmy informed him that he was the winner of a case of wine and that it must be picked up early that day. Bob says, "I can just imagine Ted Lewis saying, 'Oh . . . thank you . . . that's fine . . . uh . . . why so early?' "

There was a side laugh to this. Jimmy Dorsey had once played in Ted Lewis' band, on a European tour back in the barnstorming days of 1928. He used to do an imitation of Lewis playing the clarinet, complete with all of the jazzy gestures and attitudes. It was an entertaining party stunt. As the story goes, Lewis thought it was an excellent imitation, but was furious when he found out it was done for laughs.

Jimmy marked off a birthday during this particular sojourn in Chicago. He didn't have a birthday every year; it occurred only once in four years. This one was his ninth, on February 29, 1940, a leap year. He was thirty-six.

This was cause for celebration. Jimmy O'Keefe and his wife Dode, with the help of Jane and Squirrel Ashcraft, organized the party, held at a private dining room in the Sherman Hotel. There was additional cause for celebration. Bob Eberly and his bride, the former Florine Callahan, had been married only four weeks before. A photograph, taken at the party, reveals a happy bridegroom, whose thoughts were only slightly occupied with the birthday party.

Florine was a dancer in the Rodgers and Hart musical, "Too Many Girls," which had songs like *I Didn't Know What Time It Was* and *Give It Back to the Indians*, and a cast which included Hal LeRoy, Eddie Bracken, Mary Jane Walsh, Dick Kolmar, Van Johnson, and Desi Arnez.

Several members of the band were present, including guitarist Roc Hillman, bassist Jack Ryan, Charlie Frazier, who played all the reeds, trombonist Jerry Rosa, and Buddy Schutz, who had replaced Ray McKinley on drums. Joan Enzinger and Gloria Fay were there; Gloria sang with Jimmy McPartland's band at the Sherman. Present also were Joe Rushton, who played bass sax with Jimmy McPartland; Joe and Jimmy were both regulars at the sessions at Squirrel's.

No one seems to remember what the presents were. Charlie Frazier offers a clue. He says, "Jimmy always liked silk pajamas and underwear for birthdays and Christmas presents. He liked silk."

According to the dictionary, leap year is an "astronomical year," containing one day more than the ordinary year. In 1940, Jimmy's birthday was the one day more which made it an astronomical year. The band was riding high, fulfilling the promise of 1939. Squirrel Ashcraft and Jimmy O'Keefe must have been thinking of this when they picked out the room for the party. Maybe it was Jimmy O'Keefe's influence with a future governor, Adlai Stevenson, which was responsible for obtaining the room. It had a sign on the door: GOVERNOR'S SUITE.

31

Toscanini Pays a Call

WITH the approach of summer, in 1940, Tommy and his band settled in for a run at the Astor Roof in New York. A few blocks away, Jimmy and his band moved into the Pennsylvania Roof. Tommy's recording of *I'll Never Smile Again* was Number One. Jimmy's recording of *The Breeze and I,* with Bob Eberly's vocal, was runner-up. Helen O'Connell was entertaining the customers with *Six Lessons from Madame La Zonga.*

Both bands were appearing in radio series. The program in which Jimmy's band appeared, sponsored by Twenty Grand Cigarettes, called for a weekly three-minute number featuring Bob Eberly and Helen O'Connell along with Jimmy Dorsey. For this, Tutti Camarata devised what he calls "three-in-one-tempoed arrangements"—a device which was to have a dramatic effect on the band's future. Tommy and his band were the summer replacement for Bob Hope in the Tuesday night spot sponsored by Pepsodent.

Tommy's band, with Frank Sinatra, Buddy Rich, Connie Haines, Jo Stafford and the Pied Pipers, was doing fine. And Bunny Berigan was back. It was great to have Bunny back again, if only for a short time, but it was also a problem for manager Bobby Burns. One night, Bunny told Bobby his wife was coming in for dinner, and he asked if it would be all right to sign the check. Bobby said that it was okay. Bunny sat at the table with Mrs. Berigan between sets.

At the end of the dinner session, Bobby okayed Bunny's dinner check, which came to about $21.00. The band taxied to NBC to do the 9:30 radio show. *Marie* was in the program. When Bunny stood up for his solo, he fell off the stand.

"When we got back to the Astor Roof," says Bobby, "Tommy asked me to dig out Bunny's dinner check and see what he had for dinner. On close scrutiny it showed a tab for twelve scotch and sodas and one ham sandwich." This was a rough period for Bunny.

"That same summer," Bobby recalls, "the Lombardos were playing at the Roosevelt, and Lebert used to come over several nights each week and listen to Bunny. Naturally, Bunny would always sit at Lebert's table and talk to Lebe about trumpet technique. In the meantime, Lebert would buy drinks for Bunny all through the evening, and pick up the tab."

Bunny didn't stay long with the band this time. He was followed by Ziggy Elman, who had won fame as a soloist with Benny Goodman.

There was one night when the maitre d's list showed one reservation that stood out from the rest. Toscanini was bringing a party to the Astor Roof to hear Tommy Dorsey and the band. It is well known that Toscanini thought highly of Tommy's musicianship; he is quoted as saying that Tommy was the world's finest trombonist. This promised to be a good night.

Toscanini was a familiar figure around the eighth floor at NBC. He was conductor of the NBC Symphony, which was broadcast from 8H, the big studio adjoining the more intimate 8G, where Tommy and his band originated. Fred Allen, in one of his famous letters, this one to NBC executive John Royal, referred to Toscanini as "your house man."

Toscanini did not fraternize. Most of the time, he was in his ivory tower, lost in his own world. But the musicians in both symphony orchestra and swing band knew each other and often traded stories. Toscanini and Dorsey had much in common. Both were demanding. Each was satisfied with nothing less than perfection. This made for rigorous rehearsal, even if those involved knew the result would be enviable.

Bunny left Tommy to form his own band in 1937, rejoined briefly in 1940

The musicians told of one Toscanini rehearsal with more than the usual number of hurdles. It seemed they could not get beyond a certain passage in the music without the maestro flying into a rage at a mistake he detected in the brass section. The mistake was laid at the feet of one of the trumpet players. The passage was tried repeatedly. Each time, the result was a tantrum, with invective aimed at the trumpeter.

Finally, the trumpet player decided that, even though it was Toscanini, he had had enough. He rose and walked, slowly and deliberately, down from one level to the next below, until he was on stage level, approaching the maestro. He stopped, looked Toscanini squarely in the eye, and gave out with some invective which rivalled that of Toscanini.

Completely oblivious to what the musician was saying, Toscanini waved him away and shouted, "Don't apologize!"

At the Astor Roof, the word got around. Toscanini was coming. There was some speculation. Would he like the band? The party arrived and was seated at a table advantageously placed for listening to the band. The next set began and Toscanini was attentive, apparently taking in every nuance. He looked pleased.

During the intermission which followed, Tommy was invited to Toscanini's table. The maestro smiled and commented:

"Tommy, the band sounds fine, the boys play with a great deal of feeling, but they play too goddamn loud!"

It seems presumptuous to attempt to qualify Toscanini's statement, but, from a safe distance in time and space, it may be said that Toscanini played loud, too—and good! In Respighi's *Pines of Rome*, he conducted the orchestra in a powerful succession of crescendos. Hearing the next to last, the listener might have thought that there was room for no more. But there was yet another. It was an emotional experience, made possible because Toscanini knew where to start and how to build. It was loud. It was great!

The maestro smiled when he volunteered his opinion. It could be that he understood more than he said. I think Tommy did, too.

After the summer at the Astor, the destination was Los Angeles. Tommy had been chosen to open the Palladium, the shining new colossus which replaced the old Palomar Ballroom, which had burned to the ground.

The opening date was set for October 16, 1940. Making it on the final stretch was something of an obstacle race. The band was booked

in Ogden, Utah, on the night before the opening. The truck—with
two tons of equipment, including instruments and music—broke
down in Wyoming, en route to Ogden. Bobby Burns managed to get
the instruments and music to Ogden, in a rented car and in the cars
of some band members, in time to play the date. The truck was
repaired; Bobby rode with the driver through Salt Lake City and Las
Vegas. In Barstow, California, approaching Los Angeles and racing
against time, Bobby remembered it was the last day to register for
the draft. This was accomplished at a garage in Barstow, five minutes
before closing time.

They made it to Los Angeles on time. But if only they had known,
they needn't have hurried. Bobby remembers, "The Palladium was
nowhere near ready to open. The carpeting wasn't even laid down.
The next day, we called MCA and they quickly invented a week for
us for Fanchon and Marco at the Paramount Theatre in Los Angeles.
This filled in the time until the Palladium was ready to open."

The Palladium finally opened on the night of Halloween. Bob
Hope and Gracie Fields were there, and they helped make it a big
night. Mickey Rooney was also among those present. Johnny Mince
remembers that "Mickey Rooney played drums with the band, and
did a big solo. He was pretty good and the crowd loved it, as you can
imagine."

While they were playing nights at the Palladium, Tommy and the
band were getting up at 5:00 A.M. to go to work in the filming of "Las
Vegas Nights" at the Paramount studios. "We got paid as extras,"
recalls Johnny, "Frank Sinatra, the Pied Pipers, Buddy Rich . . . I
think it was about fifteen dollars a day. Shortly after we got to the
studios, the band would be asleep all around the set. There just wasn't
that much to do. A lot of time is wasted making pictures."

Bing Crosby called Tommy for a guest appearance on the Kraft
Music Hall. Tommy appeared in a bit with Minerva Pious, who
played Mrs. Nussbaum on the Fred Allen Show. In the bit, Tommy
used Mrs. Nussbaum's New Yorkese dialect. At one point, Tommy
expressed disdain for Min, who was playing the part of a swing fan.
She snapped at him, "Don't gimme dat; if it wasn't for jitterbugs like
me, you'd still be playing a horn in some jug band."

When Bing brought Tommy on as guest star, he showed he had not
forgotten an earlier time on the Kraft Music Hall. He introduced
Tommy as "brother of Jimmy."

32

The Bands
Are Getting Bigger

FOR the last twenty years, bands had been getting bigger. In the early twenties, that meant increasing from six to ten men. This created the need for arrangers. Equipped with arrangers, bands grew to from twelve to fifteen in the mid-thirties. In the early forties, Jimmy Dorsey's band reached a total of eighteen, including nine brass. Tommy Dorsey's band numbered twenty-six, including ten strings.

Increased size meant increased capability. Grand effects could be created which could not be achieved with a smaller band. This was not a matter just of size. Having four- and five-part harmony in a section gave arrangers more possibilities for voicing. Increased size also meant a bigger and more varied repertoire. The strings made this especially true of Tommy's band. It was possible to pick almost any sort of material and achieve the desired effect.

None of this—not even Tommy's strings—succeeded in edging out

Jimmy at his September 1942 Palladium opening. Parts of Helen, pianist Johnny Guarnieri, bassist Jack Ryan and drummer Buddy Schutz are dimly visible

Summer, 1941: Ziggy mutes his wail. Pied Piper Clark Yocum doubles on guitar *(Down Beat)*

Petite Connie Haines sang with Tommy for three years, 1940–42

jazz. Jimmy and Tommy each had a small jazz band within the big band. And the soloists were still there.

With Tommy's band, a new phase began late in 1939. The radio sponsorship ran out. Money was tight. Salary cuts were imposed. Edythe Wright had departed. Jack Leonard left, and Frank Sinatra joined. Regardless of overhead, Tommy hired the Pied Pipers—this time, just four of the original eight, and they included Jo Stafford. Paul Weston left for California, Sy Oliver joined. Buddy Rich was hired, and Connie Haines.

And so began a new direction. An outpouring of great recordings resulted throughout 1940 and 1941. The pace-setter, as we know, was *I'll Never Smile Again*, recorded in the spring of 1940. In January, 1941, there were the expansive *For You*, sung by Jo Stafford, a Sy Oliver arrangement; *Without a Song*, sung with a beat by Frank Sinatra, arranged by Sy Oliver; and *Oh, Look at Me Now*, sung by Connie Haines, Frank Sinatra, and the Pied Pipers. The next month brought a Sy Oliver original, *Yes, Indeed!*, and an Oliver arrangement of *Deep River*. In the same month, there were *Everything Happens to Me*, sung by Sinatra; *Let's Get Away from It All*, sung by Connie Haines, Frank Sinatra, and the Pied Pipers; and *Will You Still Be Mine?*, sung by Connie Haines.

The band had some outstanding soloists during this period, including, beside Buddy Rich, Ziggy Elman. There were veterans, too. The lead saxist, Freddie Stulce, had been with Tommy since early in 1936. One of the trombonists, Dave Jacobs, was in Tommy's original band, when it was organized in the fall of 1935.

Amapola was the big event with Jimmy's band. It was one of the "three-in-one-tempoed" arrangements figured out by Tutti Camarata for the Twenty Grand radio show during the previous summer. The arrangement was in three parts—with Bob Eberly singing the number in ballad style, Jimmy playing a jazz solo with the band, and Helen O'Connell singing a final chorus.

Amapola was recorded in February, 1941. It was an immediate hit. Ninety thousand records were sold in the first week after its release. It caused national attention to be focused on the band. With *Donna Maria* on the other side, *Amapola* was the first of a cycle. *Green Eyes*, the biggest hit of them all, was recorded the next month. Later in the year came *Tangerine*. Other hit records at this same time were *When the Sun Comes Out*, sung by Helen O'Connell, and *Maria Elena*, sung by Bob Eberly. The stir created by *Amapola* is one more example of the importance of a hit record. In 1937, when *Marie* was doing so much for Tommy, Jimmy had no recording that was comparable. Now, in 1941, there was *Green Eyes*, and it wasn't too late.

This all happened during the period when ASCAP music (American Society of Composers, Authors, and Publishers) was withdrawn from use on the radio networks, because of the failure of ASCAP and the networks to reach an agreement on performance fees. The networks organized BMI (Broadcast Music, Inc.) for publication of music outside the ASCAP catalogues. Tutti Camarata comments: "The BMI-ASCAP feud was a blessing in disguise for the Jimmy Dorsey band. Because of the ASCAP strike, Latin material was substituted from the BMI catalogue, resulting in *Yours, Amapola, Green Eyes*, and so on."

From an overall musical standpoint, the bands of Tommy and Jimmy in the forties were probably the best they ever had. They didn't stand still. They made the changes which circumstances required, and continued to move ahead and develop.

At the same time, much of the old clubby atmosphere had vanished. Jack Egan remembers Bunny Berigan, when he was back with Tommy for a while, saying, "The sections don't even know each other any more." There were no longer little groups hanging around together between sets. "In the old band," Jacks says, "everybody knew everybody's business." The different atmosphere was undoubtedly a natural progression. The old bands were closer to the pioneering days. But the bands did swing—more than ever.

In 1941, Tommy decided to do his own booking. The guerrilla warfare between Tommy and M.C.A. ended with the organizing of Tommy Dorsey, Inc. I can't help remembering a comment made by Billy Goodheart, second in command at M.C.A. in 1936. In an effort to promote the radio show, I was suggesting some moves I thought should be made in Tommy's direction. Said Goodheart, "Don't you worry about him. He knows what time it is."

That same year, 1941, Cork O'Keefe ended his association with Rockwell-O'Keefe, and devoted himself to projects of his own. Rockwell-O'Keefe became General Artists, inheriting a long-term management contract with Jimmy Dorsey, which Cork had negotiated. Today Cork is head of a multi-faceted music publishing enterprise.

In 1942, arranger Bill Finegan joined Tommy. Several years before, in 1939, Glenn Miller had asked Tommy if he knew of a good arranger. Tommy said he did. He was thinking of Bill Finegan, who

Jimmy greets former boss Paul Whiteman

Miss Turner wishes Jimmy well . . .

. . . as does Miss Lamour

Scenes from Jimmy Dorsey Palladium opening in October 1941

Jimmy chats with Victor Schertzinger, director of "The Fleet's In,"
Mrs. Schertzinger, Helen and Bob

Jimmy Gardner with Jimmy and Jane Dorsey

Bob Hope

Tommy joins Jimmy for latter's September 29, 1942 opening at the Palladium

Sister Mary and Mother join the brothers at the Palladium in September 1942

Buddy Rich and Ziggy Elman stirred up a storm on TD screamers like
Swing High, Blue Blazes and *Well, Git It*

Dick Haymes replaced Frank Sinatra with Tommy

had just done Tommy's arrangement of *Lonesome Road*. Finegan went to work for Glenn, and remained with him until Glenn joined the Air Corps.

Early in 1939, Glenn was going through a rough period, and Tommy knew it. Jack Egan remembers Tommy handing Glenn a check for five thousand dollars to help out. The events which immediately followed proved Tommy's faith to be well founded. Glenn was booked that spring at Frank Dailey's Meadowbrook, where the band was a big success, and the following summer at Glen Island was a triumph.

The early forties were great years for bands, including those of Tommy and Jimmy Dorsey. But the war was on. There were changes and there were departures. Frank Sinatra departed to work independently. Soon afterward, Axel Stordahl left to become musical director for Sinatra. Frank's place was filled for a short time by Dick Haymes, a truly fine singer, one of the best of them all. Jo Stafford went back home to California. Her husband-to-be, Paul Weston, was already there. Buddy Rich joined the Marines. Bob Eberly joined the Army. Helen O'Connell left to get married.

There were some sad notes. One was Bunny Berigan's death. Another occurred when Tommy and his wife, Toots, came to a parting. Jimmy and Jane had been separated intermittently for most of the time since the first trip to California.

The bands played on—through the forties and into the fifties.

33

...And the Bands Played On

THE war brought changes in the world of the big bands. The armed forces pulled away both band personnel and customers. The Stage Door Canteen in New York and USO centers everywhere entertained former customers who were now servicemen stationed at nearby bases before shipping out. Fewer spots were available to the large number of bands that had been built up. Maintaining a big band with top personnel and steady bookings was not easy.

The bands played on, played the swing music of the thirties right on through the forties, on the home scene and in the theatres of war. The European Theatre had Glenn Miller with a band that included Ray McKinley, Carmen Mastren, Trigger Alpert, and Peanuts Hucko. Artie Shaw led a band in the South Pacific, with Claude Thornhill, Max Kaminsky, Dave Tough, and Sam Donahue. Benny Goodman, Tommy Dorsey, Jimmy Dorsey, and many others made V-discs and played at Army and Navy bases around the country.

Bobby Byrne, who had taken Tommy's place in the Dorsey Broth-

Part of the Jimmy Dorsey powerhouse blowing up a storm at New York's Strand, January 1943. Top: Jack Ryan, Buddy Schutz, Billy Oblock, Mario Saratella, Steve Lipkin, Nate Kazebier, Shorty Solomon. Bottom: Chuck Gentry, Charlie Frazier, Sonny Lee, Billy Prichard, Phil Washburn, Andy Russo

Jimmy's band appeared in MGM's Abbott & Costello epic, "Lost in a Harem," in May 1944

At Jimmy's Palladium opener on June 13, 1944: (front) Lou Costello,
Marilyn Maxwell, John Conti; (rear) Bud Abbott, Jimmy, Charlie
Frazier

Bing, radio announcer and Jimmy at the Palladium, June 1944

Gene Krupa was a surprise addition to TD's band in late 1943

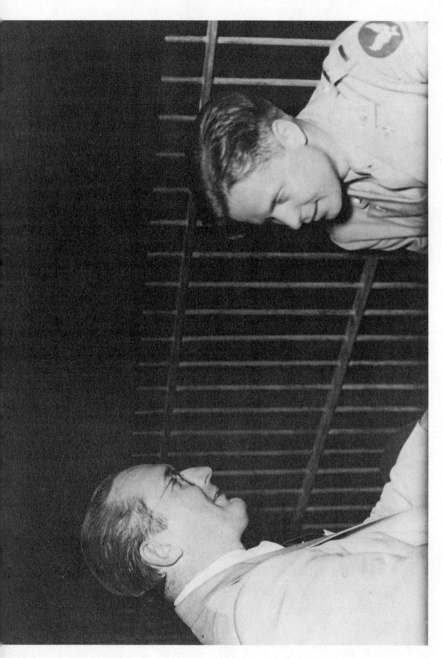

Austin, Texas, 1944: Tommy meets with his successor of nine years earlier in the Jimmy Dorsey trombone section, Bobby Byrne

Bobby Byrne sits in with Tommy's band at a University of Texas prom in mid-1944. Gene Krupa is on drums

After the ball was over, Tommy, Gene and Bobby pose with one of the girl singers and vocalist Bob Allen

ers band when it became the Jimmy Dorsey band, and who launched his own band in 1940, was commissioned a lieutenant in the Army Air Corps in 1943 at the age of 24. This was not what Bobby had in mind when he began his flying lessons seven years earlier in California. At that time, he just liked flying and wanted to learn how; he became an expert pilot. The Army assigned him as instructor at Eagle Pass Army Airfield in Texas, where he was also bandleader with the Sixteenth Army Air Corps.

In the summer of 1944, Bobby flew to Austin to see Tommy Dorsey and his band, who were playing a dance at the University of Texas. Besides seeing old friends, including Gene Krupa and Pee Wee Erwin, who were then with Tommy, Bobby received a warm welcome from the bandleader who had spotted him at the high school auditorium in Detroit nine years before. Instead of being invited to sit in and play with Tommy's band, Bobby was invited to play his trombone in front and *lead* the band while Tommy sat in and played.

It developed that Tommy was planning to go by train to see friends in Houston the next day. Bobby offered to fly him there. Tommy accepted immediately: it was a fine idea, a short flight instead of a long and tedious train trip. Then Tommy began thinking it over. He thought maybe it would be more sensible to stick to his plan, go by train, and not bother Bobby to fly him.

Bobby reiterated that the flight was short and simple, not really out of the way, no trouble at all. Detecting that Tommy might have doubts about safety, Bobby said, "Look, I'm just as concerned about my own safety as anyone else's."

Tommy disclaimed any thought about safety. No, no, it was just that he had planned to go by train and could relax. The question was discussed again, later in the evening, and it looked as if Tommy would fly. In the end, he went by train. There was no stated reason. It just might be that he involuntarily found himself unable quite to believe that the sixteen-year-old trombone player he and Jimmy had discovered in Detroit nine years before was actually a commissioned officer in the Army Air Corps, an accredited pilot and flying instructor.

After the war, Bobby reactivated his band for a time, conducted the orchestra on the Steve Allen television show, and was a top executive at Command Records. Today he devotes himself to the business world—in electronic manufacturing, sales brokerage, and educational production and manufacturing. If this seems odd for a trombone player, remember that, back at Glen Island, Bobby was a camera buff, practiced fencing, rode a motorcycle, and was about to take flying lessons.

Later in that same summer, during an engagement at the Palladium in Los Angeles, Tommy revealed his newest project. The method chosen for its announcement was Tommy's own. He and the Palladium management were miles away from an agreement on the proper compensation for a band with top drawing power. One night, Tommy simply announced to a capacity crowd that he would thenceforth be appearing at his own ballroom in nearby Ocean Park and they were all invited to be there. Years of feuding with M.C.A. had made Tommy a healthy skeptic and had put him on guard when dealing with management. And if a good idea came to him, his way was to set it in motion without pondering it. This had just the right Dorsey touch.

With two partners—Harry James and brother Jimmy—Tommy had bought Casino Gardens, a few miles west in Ocean Park, adjoining Santa Monica. It was a vast place, rivalling the enormous White City Ballroom on Chicago's South Side. There were enough customers to fill it; the war boom was on; aircraft companies in the vicinity were operating around the clock. Business was great.

When the war was over, it wasn't as easy. Tommy bought out his partners and was alone as owner and proprietor. The giant ballroom could be a lonely place with only a hundred or so people. Tommy searched for ways to bring in more business. He sent for Jack Egan, who came out from New York in July 1946 to handle publicity. It was arranged for both Tommy's and Jimmy's bands to appear on the same night for a gala battle of music. Both were in town for the filming of "The Fabulous Dorseys." It was a swinging affair and drew a large, responsive crowd. But there were more slow nights to deal with.

Tommy asked the ballroom manager for the mailing list. He had an idea. It is interesting to speculate on what Tommy might have chosen for a career if he had not been a musician. He might have wanted to be a baseball player; anyone who ever played in his band knows that. He would have been a raconteur along with whatever else he did. He might have become an idea man with projects for sales promotion. The latter was his role when he asked the manager for the mailing list.

A car contest was organized and set in motion. Chances were sold at the ballroom. Jack Egan, as publicist, got the word around: the

TD band manager Bobby Burns joins TD graduates Jo Stafford, Connie Haines, Frank Sinatra and Chuck Lowrey of the Pied Pipers. Scene: Cock and Bull Restaurant, Hollywood. Time: 1945

Charlie Shavers was Tommy's star trumpeter in the postwar era

point was stressed that the holder of the winning ticket had to be present at the drawing in order to win the car. The capacity of Casino Gardens was about four thousand. On the night of the drawing, the place was packed to overflowing. The bar business was prodigious.

Promotions involving a lottery with a drawing at a stated time and place more often state that a ticket holder need not be present in order to win. The object, in such a case, is to sell more tickets. Tommy's thinking, in his case, was right. The underlying purpose was to get more people into the ballroom and let the word of capacity business get around.

Bobby Burns recalls another facet of the Casino Gardens venture. "Tommy brought a guy, a pizza baker, all the way from New York to Santa Monica, California, and installed a pizza oven and kitchen, primarily because he liked this fellow's pizzas." This will be no surprise to those who knew Tommy and remember the fatal fascination which good Italian restaurants held for him. "Of course, very few of the patrons were interested in pizzas between dances," says Bobby. "It was a noble but costly experiment. Most of the pizzas were consumed, gratis, by the musicians after the final theme."

From a financial standpoint, Tommy would have been better off if he had accepted the Palladium's offer. But that would not have been Dorsey. He wanted to show them how he felt about it, and he did.

About a year before, in 1945, Jack Egan was in New York one Sunday afternoon and stopped in Kelly's (the same one—remember? —there's always a Kelly's) near the Pennsylvania Hotel, where Jimmy Dorsey was staying. The band was playing at the hotel, and Sunday was the night off. Jack telephoned Jimmy. "Come right up," said Jimmy. "I've got a case of Haig & Haig. We'll hear some records." This was wartime; good scotch was rare. It was characteristic of Jimmy that he would have on hand both good scotch and good records.

Jack went to Jimmy's room and found Squirrel Ashcraft among those present. Squirrel, then in the Navy, was on his way from Washington to New London, Connecticut, and to go direct from the Pennsylvania Station to Grand Central without calling Jimmy would have been unthinkable. Jimmy lamented the fact that his date for that evening had fallen through. Jack recalls someone making the hilarious suggestion that they call Roy Rogers, who was in town for a rodeo, and ask if Trigger was doing anything. This was one of those pleasant chance meetings that kept the threads securely tied.

The war ended and Eddie Condon opened his jazz club. It seemed a logical sequence, as if Eddie had been vamping with jazz concerts and was proclaiming that jazz was to be pursued vigorously, that now was the time and this was the place. Right on through the forties and fifties, while Fifty-second Street endured the stripper phase and made way for office buildings, Eddie Condon's was a general head-quarters for jazz.

The club was located on West Third Street, in New York's Green-wich Village, a block south of Washington Square. It was a spacious place, formerly occupied by the Howdy Club, with a balcony sur-rounding the main room and a stage large enough to allow the band uncramped working space. Pete Pesci, co-owner of Julius's, was manager; Eddie was bandleader and entrepreneur.

For the opening in December 1945 Eddie assembled Wild Bill Davison on cornet; Joe Marsala, clarinet; Brad Gowans, valve trom-bone; Dave Tough, drums; Gene Schroeder, piano; Bob Casey, bass. Over a period, the musicians who played there constitute a roster of stars. For many of us, just the mention of Condon's brings to mind, by the process of instant association, the name of Bill Davison, not only because he played there so much of the time, but because he played such good notes.

Joe Sullivan played solo piano between sets. It was a big attraction. As a result, the featured piano between sets became a fixed policy. Later on, this spot was filled by Ralph Sutton, now pianist in the World's Greatest Jazz Band.

Among those who often dropped in were Jack Bland (who, with Eddie, was one of the Mound City Blue Blowers), Max Kaminsky, George Wettling, and Tommy Dorsey. At that time, Tommy was shuttling between New York and California, where he still had Casino Gardens to keep going, and where he was then married to the Hollywood actress, Pat Dane. In New York, he was chosen to play the new 400 Club, which was becoming another popular band spot at Fifth Avenue and Forty-third Street. Tommy's band was in fine form. Buddy Rich was back. Charlie Shavers was a valuable addition, both for his swinging trumpet and for the arrangements he wrote, includ-ing *I've Got a Crush on You, Sweet Georgia Brown,* and an original, *Shavers Shivers. Sy Oliver's Opus No. 1,* recorded the year before, was becoming a Tommy Dorsey milestone.

Among the returning servicemen was trumpeter Jimmy McPart-

Fabian Sevitzky, conductor of the Indianapolis Symphony, in a 1947 pose with the brothers and Virginia Mayo

Sevitzky runs JD's band through *Stardust* as Tommy sits in

land. He did not return alone. With him was the English pianist he had met and married in Belgium. We were to hear much more of Marian McPartland. They arrived in New York, checked in at the Victoria Hotel, stopped briefly at the Chinese restaurant next door, and sped downtown, straight to Eddie Condon's. Having just docked, Jimmy didn't know who was playing there, but it didn't matter. There would be old friends and the music was sure to be right.

1947 was a sort of hiatus year. A number of prominent bands had closed down, including those of Benny Goodman, Woody Herman, and Tommy Dorsey. Anyone who is aware of what's going on today knows that Woody's closing in 1946 didn't take. And anyone who knew Tommy knew he would be back in business. I saw Tommy in California that year, and I knew he would be back.

One thing that marked 1947 as the Year of the Gap was the release of the film, "The Fabulous Dorseys." With few exceptions, Hollywood has mishandled musical-biographical pictures. "The Fabulous Dorseys" was not one of the exceptions. Bill Priestley recalls Eddie Condon's comment when he first heard that Hollywood was planning to produce a film about the Dorseys. Eddie remarked, "Of course they'll have Tommy play the part of Jimmy and Jimmy play the part of Tommy."

Back in business in the fall of 1947, Tommy was appearing at the Circle Theatre in Indianapolis while Jimmy was playing at the Indiana Roof Ballroom. The Dorseys were scheduled to appear with the Indianapolis Symphony Orchestra, conducted by Fabien Sevitzky, the following January. Tommy and Jimmy being in town at the same time was fortuitous; it furnished an opportunity for them together to meet with Sevitzky and others concerned with the forthcoming event.

One of those concerned was Henry Butler, Indianapolis journalist whose column appears today in the *Indianapolis News*; he was then music critic on the *Indianapolis Times*. This is the same Henry Butler whose home town was Mauch Chunk, Pennsylvania, and who played in a local combo with Tommy and Jimmy when they were all three teenage kids.

The meeting with Sevitzky was set for an evening at the Indiana Roof, where Jimmy was playing. Tommy came over from the Circle Theatre after his last show. Details of the January concert were agreed upon and the plans were sealed with a performance by Sevitzky and the two Dorseys. Tommy sat in with Jimmy's band, Jimmy remained in the sax section, and Sevitzky conducted *Stardust*. A picture was taken of Sevitzky conducting. Henry Butler's print, shown here, is probably the only one extant. The negative was destroyed, at Sevitzky's urgent request, because, according to Henry, Sevitzky "was having some of his perennial difficulties with his Board of Directors and he thought publication of that shot might injure him in their eyes."

The concert, on January 29, 1948, was a benefit performance for the Indianapolis Symphony Pension Fund. Tommy and Jimmy donated their services, and Tommy donated those of his band. Roy Harris, the noted contemporary symphony composer, took part in the concert, conducting his new composition, *The Quest*. For Tommy, this was another reunion, in addition to that with Henry Butler. Roy Harris had become an admirer of Tommy's work ten years before, was a frequent guest at the Pennsylvania Roof, and wrote and scored a composition especially for Tommy's band.

The big number in the program was *Dorsey Concerto*, by Leo Shuken, with Tommy playing solo trombone and Jimmy on solo sax and clarinet. Henry Butler says, "I remember Jimmy making the amusingly pious gesture of blessing himself when the composition started."

Henry Butler's review of the program in the *Indianapolis Times* on January 30 included this paragraph: "It was a great musical show, concluding with a total-war version of Tschaikovsky's *1812 Overture* and a *Stars and Stripes Forever* encore by both orchestras."

III

REFLECTIONS

34

Swing...Jazz...Music

NOSTALGIA is always with us. In recent years, it has come on strong. "No, No, Nanette," the hit musical of 1925, was revived in January of 1971 and was still playing to capacity houses more than a year later. Film festivals perennially attract crowds to see stars such as Joan Crawford, Humphrey Bogart, W. C. Fields, and the Marx Brothers. "Gone With the Wind" was revived yet again, and once more was the biggest all-time grosser, running neck-and-neck with "The Sound of Music." *The Saturday Evening Post* and *Liberty* reappeared. And the big bands of the thirties, never forgotten, are enjoying a renewed popularity that seems destined to continue. Collections of the recordings of Benny Goodman, Tommy Dorsey, Glenn Miller, Artie Shaw, and others are finding increasingly wide circulation.

It is revealing to observe the reaction of people as they listen to these recordings. They enjoy what they hear; they enjoy it *now*— without reservation and without relating to history. This music strikes a sympathetic vibration in both those who remember the bands in their heyday and young people who are hearing them for

223

the first time. Older people are reassured; younger people, some of them surprised, are interested. The swing music played by the big bands in the thirties is not dated, except by the calendar.

The Paul Whiteman music of the early twenties was universally popular in its time. Those early Whiteman recordings are delightful to hear today, but we are aware that they belong to a bygone era. The Original Dixieland Jazz Band recordings sound primitive today, but we know that these five musicians made history in 1916 when they burst through and made the public aware of basic jazz. Ragtime, called forth from the archives, is entertaining Americana. No such indulgence is needed in order to appreciate the big band music of the Swing Era. Although pushing forty, it stays young.

Ballroom dancing has always been an avenue for the developing of music. Along with the one-step and fox trot came popular tunes in two-four and four-four that were suitable for jazz. The prodigious development of jazz in the twenties revealed itself to the public through the dance bands. And in the thirties, it was dance music that ushered in the jazz we called swing.

But there was a new aspect. Swing was also for *listening*. Only aficionados *listened* to jazz in the twenties. *Everybody* listened to swing in the thirties. Sometimes an entire floor of dancers stopped, moved toward the bandstand, and listened. They bought quantities of records in order to listen at home. There were those who gravitated to the band spots solely to listen. Benny Goodman's *King Porter Stomp*, Duke Ellington's *Showboat Shuffle*, Glenn Miller's *Tuxedo Junction*, Artie Shaw's *Carioca*, and Tommy Dorsey's *Boogie Woogie* all made mighty good listening.

The emergence of swing in the big bands of the thirties was the culmination of a logical sequence. Early in the century, jazz began developing a kind of language, a jazz idiom that would later characterize much composition. In the twenties, the bands grew bigger. Consequently, arrangers became a necessity. Among instrumentalists, the number of competent musicians increased. Talented arrangers could give vent to creative ideas, knowing that they had bands and musicians who could perform them. Bandleaders were playing musicians, some of them virtuosos. It all exploded in the swing of the Big Band Era. The jazz was organized, but there still was improvisation, the essential quality which makes jazz preeminently a performing art. The arranged backgrounds often *inspired* improvisation on the part of performers.

There was something more: the time was right. The creative force of the twenties in art, literature, and music had had a lasting effect. Radio had exposed more people to more music and more kinds of music than ever before. The Depression was ending. The public was ready, and Benny Goodman came along and raised the curtain in 1935. Then, with Duke Ellington, who had been there all along, Tommy Dorsey, Artie Shaw, Glenn Miller, Count Basie, Jimmy Dorsey, Harry James, Jimmie Lunceford, Claude Thornhill, and many others, jazz became universally accepted and gained musical standing.

The public's ear for jazz was something that had to be acquired over a period of years. In 1923, George Gershwin was working on the *Rhapsody in Blue*. He was twenty-four, still living with his family. One day, his father looked into the room where George was fingering some of the themes on the piano.

"That's strange-sounding music, Georgie. What are you going to call it?"

"Oh, I don't know, Father. . . . *Jazz Symphony*, maybe."

(Pause) "Better make it *good*, Georgie. It *might* be *important*."

Rhapsody in Blue is not jazz in the strict sense. It is a composition in the jazz idiom, making use of blues and jazz themes. Its popularity and influence in composition helped condition the public. It was commissioned by Paul Whiteman and introduced in his concert at New York's Aeolian Hall in February, 1924. This was more than a decade before swing, but Whiteman evidently believed that jazz was for listening. Included in the program was *Livery Stable Blues*.

Swing is jazz, and jazz is music. Categories are useful as reference points, but they sometimes get in the way if they are considered as having rigid boundaries. Duke Ellington, when being interviewed, has always tried to avoid being labelled specifically a jazz composer. There is no doubt that Ellington does compose in the jazz idiom, and certainly he is responsible for some of the finest of jazz performances, but he prefers to think of his compositions as his kind of *music*. Jazz is a personal thing. It is the way some of us hear and feel music.

There is a future for jazz, because young people like it when they hear it. Willis Conover, producer of "Music U.S.A." for the Voice of America, was interviewed for an article in *Variety* in September, 1971. He had recently produced a series of jazz concerts at New York's Town Hall. In one of them, the fine guitar duo, George Barnes and Bucky Pizzarelli, appeared. "When George Barnes and Bucky

Pizzarelli were playing, I was looking at the youngsters out in front," Conover said. "I was waiting for a look which might have said, 'Who are those two old guys?' or 'What kind of music is this?' But instead, the youngsters, long hair and all, were appreciating the genuine musicianship of George and Bucky."

There are still big bands to be heard today, such as those of Duke Ellington, Count Basie, Woody Herman, Buddy Rich, Warren Covington playing some of the old Tommy Dorsey book, Lee Castle playing some of the old Jimmy Dorsey book, and the World's Greatest Jazz Band. But there are not enough of them to provide anything like the saturated circulation of the many bands that were playing in the thirties. Jazz recordings, of course, are available—new ones and reissues of the classics—for young people to hear.

But to increase exposure and give more young people the opportunity to listen to jazz and to develop new talent, it is desirable to find ways of providing personal contact and participation. This is taking place in the schools. In that same *Variety* interview, Mr. Conover states, "Today there are some five hundred big bands in universities playing jazz. The music they play is even more adventurous than most professional bands play today." There are many thousands of bands on the high school level. "I can't believe," Mr. Conover continues, "that when all these youngsters graduate they are not going to continue their interest in playing or listening to good music."

There are clinics, collegiate jazz festivals, and workshops being held all over the country, with jazz musicians participating in them. Marian McPartland is one who devotes considerable time to appearances at schools, where she not only plays, but conducts informal discussions with students. "This is really a beautiful experience," Marian says. "I think we all have one hope, one thought, one ideal in common—to see an appreciation of jazz passed on to the young people, so that they can add *their* voices, *their* ideas, *their* styles to what has gone before, and find the joy and excitement and sheer pleasure in it which I myself have found."

Buddy Rich appears now and then on a television talk show. His continuing devotion to jazz is evident. He has been playing steadily since 1937, and he says he will never retire. "There are a lot of good young players," affirms Buddy. In an appearance in the Johnny Carson Show in January, 1972, at which Artie Shaw was also present, Buddy stated his admiration for Shaw's musicianship and hoped

Shaw would come back and play again, so that young people could hear him in person.

There is a thread of permanence in the creative work of the swing bands that will be long and affectionately remembered. The contemporary acceptance and continuing vitality of their music point toward a bright future.

Marian McPartland

35

Genus Species: Jazz Musician

I met Yank Lawson late one afternoon at Hurley's, the little restaurant-and-bar nestled on the northeast corner of Sixth Avenue and Forty-ninth Street, surrounded by the tall buildings of Rockefeller Center. It had been there for generations. Hurley, who owned the small three-story building, refused to sell when Rockefeller Center was built. Hurley's remained to become a kind of annex for actors and musicians working upstairs at NBC.

Yank had just come from an all-day recording session. The music recorded at the session was not swing, pop, or show music. It was an original score for a motion picture soundtrack. I asked Yank what his trumpet part was like.

"It looked exactly as if someone had thrown ink all over the page."

I could see that the score had plenty of sixteenth notes. Sightreading, too. It had been some time since Yank had been confronted with this kind of sightreading, but he managed it with no difficulty.

After a few minutes at Hurley's, he left to go upstairs for a rehearsal and taping of the Johnny Carson Show. Later in the evening, he would be at Eddie Condon's jazz club, where he was leader and trumpeter in a six-piece jazz band. For this there was no music to read.

Yank's calendar that day was representative of that of a large number of jazz musicians, whose modus vivendi demands training, discipline, stamina, and a sense of humor—besides talent. This was not the stereotype of the song-and-story jazz musician, who leads a bohemian life punctuated with melodramatic incident. Yank had given up playing in the big bands years before, in favor of studio work, in order to be with his family. Today he is traveling again—in many parts of the world—as co-leader, with Bob Haggart, of the World's Greatest Jazz Band.

Kay Weber, recalling some of the people who came to the Dorsey Brothers opening at Glen Island Casino, mentioned Jerry Colonna, remarking that he "had not yet embarked on his career as a comic. He was still a *working musician.*" The emphasis is Kay's, and she added, with a smile, "Please tell me, what's *that?*" Kay knows the answer. She was married to one—the late Ward Sillaway, who played trombone with the Crosby band and with Tommy Dorsey.

But there is a kinship between the jazz musician and the legendary song-and-story musician of olden times. The wandering minstrel of ancient days travelled about with his instrument, playing one-nighters. He played pubs, wayside inns, and castles. He improvised freely. He performed indigenous music and sang the songs of the people. The jazz musician does all of these things.

The jazz musician is essentially a creative musician with an intuitive feeling for jazz and a talent for improvising. It is pleasant to call forth, in one's mind, an auditory montage of jazz improvisations . . . the distinctive approaches displayed in *Stop, Look and Listen* by Pee Wee Erwin's trumpet, Johnny Mince's clarinet, Tommy Dorsey's trombone, and Bud Freeman's tenor, punctuated and shaded by Dave Tough's drumming . . . the sound of Bix's cornet on *Singin' the Blues, Clementine, I'm Coming, Virginia* . . . Bud Freeman's solo on Tommy's record of *Smoke Gets in Your Eyes* . . . the design in all of Bunny Berigan's playing . . . Louis Armstrong's treatment of *La Vie en Rose*, close around the melody, but with Louis' own phrasing . . . Jimmy Dorsey's variations on *So Rare* . . . Bix's break in *Riverboat Shuffle* . . . Tommy Dorsey's spellbinding variations at the finish of his recording of *Washboard Blues* . . . Earl Hines playing *Fifty-Seven*

Varieties . . . Louis playing *Darling Nellie Gray* . . . Joe Venuti and
Eddie Lang, *Goin' Places* and *Doin' Things* . . . Yank Lawson adding
a touch of the blues to *Hawaiian War Chant* . . . Jack Teagarden on
I Cover the Waterfront and all of the blues. Duke Ellington's instrument is his orchestra. *Creole Love Call, Echoes of Harlem, Showboat
Shuffle, Clarinet Lament* are Ellington improvisations, extended by
his soloists.

One night at Eddie Condon's, a customer learned, sadly, that there
is a basic requirement for improvising with a group. The customer
brought his sax with him and asked if he could sit in and play with
the band. Sitting in was something that happened when a pro
stopped in and was invited to play. But Yank and Eddie were agreeable. They knew the customer; he was a magazine writer, a nice guy.

The band launched into a number that was a standard in the jazz
repertoire. The guest saxophone player took a solo and displayed
astonishing facility with notes, but his notes were not in the right
chords. His notes were not in any chords; they were just notes. This
put the piano and guitar in limbo and signalled disaster in the last
chorus.

Cutty Cutshall, who played trombone in the band, was the one
who set the customer straight. Cutty, in addition to being a fine
musician, was a gentleman. In all the years I knew him, I never heard
him raise his voice. In this case, he did not make a scene on the stand,
but, when they stepped down, he commanded, emphatically, "Never
do that again. If you don't know chords, you don't play jazz."

Improvising can lead to composition. Improvising is, in fact, a
process of composing. Many good tunes have been written by jazz
musicians. *What's New?* is by the bassist-arranger-bandleader, Bob
Haggart. *Tenderly*, one of the most requested numbers in all piano
rooms, was composed by the pianist, Walter Gross. *Misty* began as
an improvisation of Errol Garner. *Old Folks* is by Willard Robison,
pianist and leader of the Deep River Orchestra, once so popular on
New York's WOR. *I'll Be Around* is Alec Wilder's composition. *I'll
Never Be the Same* is by the Paul Whiteman violinist, Matty Malneck.
Tommy Dorsey arrangers Paul Weston and Axel Stordahl col-
laborated on *Day by Day* and *I Should Care*.

Among the foremost song composers are bandleader Duke Ellington (*Sophisticated Lady*), jazz pianist Fats Waller (*Ain't Misbehavin'*),
and arranger-conductor Victor Young (*Street of Dreams*); Hoagy Carmichael has given us a whole library. The great stride pianist, James

P. Johnson, a jazz immortal, composed the music for a 1923 all-Negro Broadway revue, "Running Wild," which included *Old-Fashioned Love* and *Charleston*. Another great stride pianist, Jelly Roll Morton, composed instrumental jazz numbers, including *King Porter Stomp* and *Milenberg Joys*.

An intuitive feeling for jazz can be present in a sensitive musician who is not a jazz musician per se. This was proven one night in the twenties at the White City Ballroom on Chicago's South Side, where Jimmy McPartland and his band were playing. Bix Beiderbecke, Frank Trumbauer, and Pee Wee Russell were playing at Hudson Lake, Indiana. On their night off, they drove to Chicago to hear Jimmy and his group, which included Bud Freeman, Dave Tough, and Frank Teschmaker. When Jimmy finished for the night at White City, the whole gang moved to the Sunset Cafe, where Louis Armstrong was playing and which stayed open later. When Louis closed, the entire bunch went to the Apex Club, where Jimmy Noone was playing and which stayed open still later.

On one of these nights, Maurice Ravel, composer of the world-famous *Bolero*, dropped in at White City Ballroom to hear Jimmy McPartland and his group. Bix, Pee Wee, and Trumbauer were already there. When the group migration began, Ravel went along and did the whole bit, picking up Louis at the Sunset Cafe and winding up at the Apex Club.

There is no rigid line. After writing his first song, *Sweet Sue*, Victor Young wrote jazz arrangements, conducted every kind of radio orchestra, and composed motion picture scores, including one for "For Whom the Bell Tolls" which he conducted in the Hollywood Bowl with a symphony orchestra. Don Voorhees was equally successful conducting "Earl Carroll's Vanities" and the Bell Telephone Concert Orchestra. Duke Ellington was at home at the Cotton Club and is at home in a church conducting his religious music.

Rossini, one of the great composers of opera in the nineteenth century, might have been a jazz composer in the twentieth century. Arthur Fiedler, Boston Pops conductor, in a television interview last year, quoted Rossini: "All music is good, except the boring kind." Although he didn't know it, Rossini was writing the theme music for the Lone Ranger when he was composing the *William Tell Overture*.

Anyone who has ever heard musicians engage in a discussion of other musicians, past or present, has surely heard the remark, "He's the greatest." It will be repeated and applied to more than one

musician. Everybody is "the greatest." It is not meant literally. It is
a term of admiration or recognition. It may be an appraisal of a style,
or an appreciation of a particular chorus on a recording, or a recollection of an inspired bit of playing at a jam session.

As between the great ones, comparison is idle. Aside from a personal preference, the tagging of one as better or best is misdirected.
It is like trying to decide whether George Gershwin's music is better
than Jerome Kern's. What is interesting and important are how they
differ, what the individual characteristics are, what one has that the
other does not have.

Hoagy Carmichael, speaking of his many friends among the jazz
greats, said just recently, "There is this that they were probably born
with, and probably acquired more of in association with other good
musicians—that very distinctive sense of 'knowing'—knowing a good
note from a bad one—knowing a good or bad personality either on
sight or after a few words. Even knowing he is a bit better in his work
than some contemporary. He will never tell anybody that, and actually he couldn't quite tell you why, because he can't even tell you
where that 'knowing' came from."

In his first book, *Stardust Road*, Hoagy said that the jazz fraternity
was shocked at Don Murray's death. The statement was true, and
Hoagy was right in using the term "jazz fraternity." The feeling of
fraternity is very real with jazz musicians. It was this that caused
Jimmy Dorsey to take his whole band to California to play on Bing
Crosby's radio show, when he could have taken only key men and
filled in with local replacements.

One time, when Tommy was playing at New York's Pennsylvania
Hotel and Glenn Miller was appearing at the Paramount Theatre,
Bobby Burns awakened Tommy at 8:00 A.M. with word that Glenn
was ill and couldn't make it to the theatre. Tommy sped immediately
to the Paramount and did the shows with the Miller band, playing
Glenn's trombone parts. One week, during the summer of 1938 in
Hollywood, Tommy was down with a virus and couldn't make one
of the radio shows. It was Victor Young who came over and conducted the show for us.

All of us who made the pilgrimage to Squirrel Ashcraft's house in
Evanston in the thirties were drawn by this feeling of fraternity. It
was implicit in every gathering. Early in 1969, Hank O'Neal called
Pee Wee Russell about participating in a recording that was being
put together to recall some of those sessions at Squirrel's. Pee Wee's

response was, "Good, we'll be going back to Evanston." It is sad that we lost Pee Wee that year.

The jazz musician is also a family man. Gene Traxler was bassist in Tommy Dorsey's original band in September of 1935. Married and the father of a son and daughter, Gene left in the spring of 1940 to engage in non-travelling studio work and stay with the family. Today Gene and the family, including seven grandchildren, are doing fine. In April 1972 Gene completed twenty-seven years with the Arthur Godfrey radio show. "I joined him for thirteen weeks," Gene says, "and it went on and on and on."

Sometimes the jazz musician is a talented painter, as demonstrated by Pee Wee Russell, George Wettling, and Pee Wee Erwin. Pee Wee Russell's paintings are abstracts of high quality. Bob Haggart, Yank Lawson, and I stopped at Pee Wee's apartment one day to see a collection that was being put together by his wife Mary for a showing at one of the galleries. We were much impressed. I remember Bob remarking that one of the paintings seemed to him to be an expression of a Pee Wee clarinet solo. Before we left, Yank had earmarked one of the paintings, which he later purchased and which now hangs in his apartment.

The jazz musician gets around a lot in the music he listens to in his off hours. Axel Stordahl got lost in another world listening to Ravel's *Daphnis and Chloe*. Bud Freeman likes Richard Strauss. Yank Lawson played Gunther Schuler's *Music for Brass* one evening at his apartment, then Artur Rubinstein's recording of the Brahms *Intermezzi*, and followed this with Bix Beiderbecke playing *Ostrich Walk*. I think all jazz musicians like Delius. And I have yet to meet one who did not like Victor Young's *Stella by Starlight*.

I asked Hoagy Carmichael what he thought about the genus species. He responded with the "unhappy realization that musicians never really communicated except over a drink and, unless you lived with one for a while, there was so little you remember of what was said or done. The outsider saw and heard more than we the intimates ever saw or heard. We were all so interested in ourselves and what we were going to play next that, outside of exchanging a dirty joke or two, we never took the patience to explore the character of the man or even inquire about the background of his life, his tastes, and/or dislikes." Hoagy recalls that "eventually little circles were drawn together to go eat pizza pie or try out one of the wives' spaghetti. And about these girls—nice girls in the background who loved not only the mellow tones of the husband but those of the fellow musician as well. I wonder what has become of them, because I loved them all. And the men, as well as the women in their lives, held a claim to something else besides good musicianship: that is, an innate sense of good behavior toward his fellow man."

Following are a few stray quotes from various members of the genus species, recalled at random:

EDDIE CONDON:	(addressing the audience at a jazz concert) ". . . and when we come to the last chorus, everybody run for cover."
PAUL WESTON:	(commenting on a derivative ballad which was enjoying a fleeting vogue due to Tommy's trombone and Jack Leonard's voice) "Yes, but it's been written so many times before."
WILLIE "THE LION" SMITH:	(opening exit door, facing blizzard, quickly closing door) "Man, it's like a stampede out there!"
SQUIRREL ASHCRAFT:	". . . the complicated things, so much easier for lesser musicians than originality . . ."
BOB HAGGART:	(written on Pee Wee Russell's part in a music chart) "Pee Wee—go wild, eight bars."
YANK LAWSON:	(listening to Lou McGarity on a record) "When Lou takes a solo, he goes for broke."
EDDIE CONDON:	(to taxi driver, who is weaving perilously close to pillars supporting the Sixth Avenue el) "Hey, fellow, stick to the melody."
HOAGY CARMICHAEL:	"We were a small flock of people who were drawn together by the forces of sound and tone."
ANY OF THEM:	"He was the greatest."

36

The Writers

IN the early thirties, I was director of a radio program featuring a large orchestra conducted by Victor Young. On one occasion, immediately before going on the air, we discovered a mistake in the timing. We needed a cut—a sizable one—or we would be in trouble. There was a convenient cut in the closing number, a passage next to the ending. But the ending did not logically follow what preceded the cut. We needed a new ending in a hurry; otherwise, we would be suspended in mid-air. Or we might be forced to play a chord in G, as in a minstrel show.

Victor called out to the orchestra. "Strings! Hold the E flat. Brass! (pointing to each instrument) D flat, A flat, F. Next bar, B natural, F sharp, D sharp . . ." The musicians quickly marked the notes on their parts. In a few seconds, we were on the air without having had time to try it.

The new ending worked fine. It was simply a sequence of unrelated basic chords, making a dramatic finish. It sounded written and rehearsed. There might have been some other cut that would have led, acceptably if not ideally, to the original ending. But Victor knew that the original ending was written expressly to follow the cut portion. And he knew that, given the cut, the improvised ending was right. There was no time to ponder.

Actually, it was not as much of a feat as it may have seemed to an onlooker. Victor Young was a talented and experienced arranger.

He was much in demand in radio; he could deliver any kind of music and interpret it with sympathy and understanding. In his orchestras were musicians who were soon to become leaders of the great swing bands. The Pond's Program is especially memorable for its theme, composed by Victor, sung by Lee Wiley, then a new discovery, and played on solo trombone by Tommy Dorsey.

Arrangers are a band's writers. They supply the script for the show. In the beginning, when free-wheeling jazz was played entirely by small groups, arrangers were not needed. The soloist was on his own and the ensemble knew the chords.

It was the increasing size of the bands that made arrangers necessary. Once on the scene, arrangers not only did what was necessary, they helped create individual band styles. Among the early jazz groups, style was pretty much the same; individuality came from performances of soloists. In the big bands, free-wheeling jazz was still there, enhanced by the arranged background. In the organized swing of the thirties, arrangers were all-important. They provided design, layout, direction. As the individual soloist had his personal style, so did the arranger, and he contributed to the style of the band as a whole.

As the writing of arrangements developed, arrangers came from the ranks of the bands in which they played. Throughout the history of bands, most of the arrangers have been playing musicians. Naturally, their special capabilities and leanings were felt in the style and character of the bands for which they arranged. An outstanding example is that of Sy Oliver, who both played trumpet and arranged in the Jimmie Lunceford band (later joining Tommy as arranger only).

In some cases, the leader has also been arranger—Fletcher Henderson, Duke Ellington, Glenn Miller, Claude Thornhill. Whether or not the leader is arranger, he is editor. He chooses arrangers whose capabilities will produce the characteristics he wants to emphasize in the band. Tommy Dorsey did this expertly.

To some of those who remember the California Ramblers or who have heard their recordings, it comes as a surprise to learn that they

Victor Young

used no specially-written arrangements. Emerging before the mid-twenties, the Ramblers came early in the procession of bands, but they were a large enough band to benefit from arrangements. Ed Kirkeby notes that, while the Ramblers were still in their heyday, Adrian Rollini wrote a few arrangements, which indicates that regular writing of arrangements was on the way.

At this same time, throughout the twenties, Fletcher Henderson and Duke Ellington were writing their own arrangements, creating patterns that would have a far-reaching and lasting effect on bands as they developed ten years later. It is interesting and revealing to hear some of the earliest Ellington recordings today. One of these is *Black Beauty*, made under the name of the Washingtonians, that being the name of the Duke's first band in his home town of Washington in the early twenties. It is primitive Ellington, but it *is* Ellington, revealing what became recognizable characteristics.

The public was not yet aware of what Henderson and Ellington were doing. The big attraction was Paul Whiteman and his orchestra. Whiteman was not presenting jazz, but he was doing much for popular music. A few years hence, he would introduce some fine jazz artists to his large following. One thing he did, as early as 1920, was make the public aware of the "special arrangement": *Whispering, Japanese Sandman, Avalon.*

A milestone in the writing of arrangements for bands featuring jazz came with Bill Challis and his work with the historic Jean Goldkette band. Paul Mertz, a key member of the original Goldkette band in the mid-twenties, tells of an incident which serves as a preface to Bill's entrance a couple of years later.

Paul traces what he calls "concerted sectional playing of jazz" to the time when Frank Trumbauer was with the Benson Orchestra, before joining Goldkette. In the Benson recording of *I'll Never Miss the Sunshine*, there was an outstanding solo chorus by Trumbauer. Jimmy Dorsey, in the Goldkette band, listened to the Benson recording. He liked Trumbauer's chorus so much that he learned it and played it at the Greystone Ballroom in Detroit, home base for the Goldkette band. When Jimmy played it again, Don Murray played along in harmony. Then Murray wrote a third part for Doc Ryker and the three of them played a harmonized version of Trumbauer's jazz chorus.

Bill Challis joined the Goldkette band, in the summer of 1926, as sax player and arranger. He soon abandoned the sax in favor of full-time arranging, and it proved good territory for Bill. Bix and Trumbauer had joined. It was a fortuitous meeting of musical minds. Bix and Tram each inspired the other. Bill was catalyst for both of them. Bix's playing prompted Bill to think of ideas for arrangements. Bill's arrangements gave Bix the perfect settings for his playing. They had the same musical viewpoint.

Jimmy and Tommy Dorsey were in and out of the Goldkette band, on the way to the California Ramblers and back again, continuing to return for Goldkette recordings. Bill Challis' recorded arrangements of *Sunday, Hoosier Sweetheart*, and *My Pretty Girl* are as good examples of ensemble arranging for a jazz-playing band as can be found.

A year later, they were together again—Tommy, Jimmy, Bix, Tram, and Bill—in Paul Whiteman's organization. Among Bill's many arrangements during this period were the classics, *Washboard Blues* and *Changes*, and *Louisiana*, memorable also for Bix's solo with the hat and Bing's vocal riff, ". . . I do-do-declare . . ."

As the twenties closed out to make way for the Depression and the rise of radio, there were two great bands playing great jazz: Ben Pollack and Casa Loma. They were heralds of the approaching Big Band Era. Pollack had a galaxy of star performers, including Glenn Miller as arranger. Casa Loma was edging up with Gene Gifford's swing arrangements, such as *Black Jazz, White Jazz*, and *Casa Loma Stomp*.

The Dorsey Brothers threw out the cue in 1934 with Glenn Miller as arranger. Benny Goodman raised the curtain in 1935 with Fletcher Henderson as arranger. It seems almost according to script. Goldkette, Pollack, Casa Loma, and the Dorsey Brothers all played swing, all with fine arrangers, two of them with Glenn Miller. Goodman firmly established swing with its character set by a veteran arranger, Fletcher Henderson. While all this was going on, Duke Ellington continued to go his own way, a way that has always been, and continues to be, productive of fine, distinguished music. ·

Tommy Dorsey was keenly aware of the importance of arranging. What is most important in his case is that he handled the problem in exactly the way that was right for the kind of band he wanted to have. During the early years, Tommy used around six arrangers regularly, and several more on an occasional basis. Paul Weston and Axel Stordahl were mainstays. They did everything. Axel had a way with a ballad. He could make it pretty and give it just enough of a swing. Paul, in addition to every kind of writing for the band, was available to supply material needed for the radio show, and he contributed a great deal. Deane Kincaide delivered his meticulously designed arrangements of dixieland and other categories, and he also played tenor sax. Three other players arranged steadily—guitarist Carmen Mastren, saxist Freddie Stulce, and pianist Howard Smith, as did Dick Jones, who preceded Howard. The book included the work of various non-staff arrangers, including Benny Carter, Jimmy Mundy, and Edgar Sampson. After a few years, Tommy's library was enriched by the arrangements of Sy Oliver and Bill Finegan.

Drawing from these varied sources, there was no single approach that was dominant in Tommy's library. This policy was consistent with Tommy's desire to maintain a wide-ranging repertoire, and it helps explain why his band was probably the best *all-around* band of the period.

It was inevitable that Glenn Miller would organize his own band and set the pace and style with his own arrangements. Arranging help came from Jerry Gray, who had written for Artie Shaw, and from Bill Finegan, who also wrote for Tommy Dorsey.

Tutti Camarata was the arranger who helped the Jimmy Dorsey band find itself. Jimmy, after the Dorsey Brothers period, was heading in no definite direction. Jimmy always had excellent arrangers, such as Fud Livingston, Freddie Slack, Don Redman, and Joe Lipman. But it was Camarata who pulled various tangents together and helped develop a definite character for the band.

One of the most original of arrangers is bassist Bob Haggart, who created most of the distinctive book of the Bob Crosby band. He is now writing the arrangements for the World's Greatest Jazz Band. One of the most creative of all the arrangers was Claude Thornhill, a true artist.

Arranging, like the improvising of the musicians, requires a degree of composing talent. Some of the "originals," composed by arrangers, were impressive, and they performed an important function in repertoire. These compositions supplemented the popular and standard tunes, adding variety and change of pace. Originals could also provide a band with something of its own, which, if not exclusive, became associated with it in the public's mind.

The mention of Benny Goodman automatically calls to mind *Stompin' at the Savoy*, by Edgar Sampson, and *Christopher Columbus*, by Fletcher Henderson. Mention Glenn Miller and the likely association is *In the Mood*, by Joe Garland.

Jo Stafford and Paul Weston on the Jo Stafford Show on CBS Television, c.1954. Paul's band included six musicians formerly with Tommy Dorsey: trumpeters Zeke Zarchy, George Seaburg, Clyde Hurley; Freddie Stulce (alto sax), Babe Russin (tenor sax), Paul Smith (piano). Also present: Matty Matlock, clarinetist formerly with Bob Crosby; Jack Ryan, bassist formerly with Jimmy Dorsey; Nick Fatool, drummer formerly with Benny Goodman; George Van Eps, guitarist formerly with Ray Noble

Some of the most serviceable arrangements in the Tommy Dorsey book were two Benny Carter originals, *Symphony in Riffs* and *Devil's Holiday; Satan Takes a Holiday*, by Larry Clinton; and the succession of Sy Oliver originals, including the definitive *Opus No. 1*. Bob Haggart composed *South Rampart Street Parade* when he was with the Bob Crosby band. It is a hardy perennial, much requested today at appearances of the World's Greatest Jazz Band.

The story of Duke Ellington's band is, to an appreciable extent, a procession of Ellington originals, *Creole Love Call*, *Warm Valley*, *Mood Indigo*, and many more, supplemented by those of his protege, Billy Strayhorn, such as *Chelsea Bridge*.

The writing of originals opens the way for experimentation, an area in which Stan Kenton has been a leader. This search for new horizons is worthwhile, even if some of the sounds produced along the way are unfamiliar. Deems Taylor was once approached by a self-appointed critic for an opinion on a certain "modern" composition considered by the questioner to be "incorrect." Deems replied, "If the composer likes it, it's correct."

Deems's statement, certainly, was correct. Music, the most subjective of the arts, is a personal thing. Jazz is a personal thing. It comes to life in the performance of individual musicians. It is inherent in the jazz arrangement or composition; it is recognized and interpreted by the musicians. Ideally, the writer of a jazz arrangement has in mind the individual musicians who will play it. He makes use of their strong points and avoids their limitations. The aim is to draw out the best possible performance and achieve the best interpretation of the writing.

It has always been Duke Ellington's custom to write parts for the individuals who will interpret them. The notation at the top of a part, instead of indicating the instrument, would be marked "Rex" or "Harry" or "Johnny." The melody of the popular Ellington song, *Do Nothing Till You Hear from Me*, was originally composed for trumpeter Cootie Williams and entitled *Concerto for Cootie*.

In the original version of *Come Sunday*, from Ellington's orchestral suite, *Black, Brown, and Beige*, the melody is carried throughout by Johnny Hodges on the alto sax. It is a glorious melody, heightened by the harmonic structure of the background. A lengthy, unhurried introduction, with Ray Nance on violin in the foreground, settles the listener in a reflective mood. Hodges enunciates the melody articulately, prayerfully, soaring midway to an expansive height, returning once more to philosophic calm. It all fits together: a heroic melody, interpreted with understanding over a background which sustains the mood in every nuance.

Ellington introduced the suite in a concert at Carnegie Hall in 1943. Johnny Hodges fairly sang *Come Sunday* on his alto, making the melody cry for words. Some years later, Ellington wrote words, and it was sung by Mahalia Jackson in a revised version.

The song settings provided for Maxine Sullivan at the Onyx Club in the thirties made a deep and lasting impression. Created by Claude Thornhill and played by the John Kirby band, they were wonderfully sympathetic to both the singer and the song. We can think back and hear *The Folks Who Live on the Hill* . . . the clarinet introduction, played by Buster Bailey, which recurs and returns at the finish, forming a perfect design. I have often wondered if Oscar Hammerstein ever heard it. The melody was Jerome Kern's, and, for Oscar, it was the favorite of all the Kern songs for which he wrote lyrics.

In the arrangement of *You're a Sweetheart* for Tommy Dorsey and Edythe Wright, Axel Stordahl used a blues figure in the background, tucked in the first two beats of the third bar (between "You're a sweetheart . . ." and ". . . if there ever was one . . ."). The figure is repeated in the appropriate places and forms the ending. It is impossible to think of this song without recalling that figure; it has permanently attached itself to the tune. The figure does not get in the way of the tune or lyric; in fact, each time it is heard, it seems to cue the words and music which immediately follow.

The Deane Kincaide arrangement of *Boogie Woogie* for Tommy Dorsey is a remarkable piece of writing. The material is the original composition of Pinetop Smith, the pioneer jazz pianist. The composition created a pianistic pattern, with repetitive rhythm in the bass, widely used thereafter. The title, *Pinetop's Boogie*, resulted in the generic term, "boogie woogie." Howard Smith played the piano passages in the arrangement. The problem for the arranger was how to write the band passages without making them lumbering repetitions of what the piano could do better. Trombones added emphasis to the rhythmic figure in the bass, clarinets played the treble piano notes, the brass came in with punctuating chords at the end of phrases. The ensemble was pianistic in character and the whole thing was homogeneous. It could not have come off without the expertise of Tommy and the band. And it was played with a light touch, always so important with Tommy.

Some years ago, Yank Lawson and Bob Haggart recorded a series of jazz albums, several of which were versions of Broadway show scores, including "Porgy and Bess" and "South Pacific." The voicing and spacing in Bob's arrangements give an impression of size and scope equal to that of the large orchestras in the original productions, yet the recordings were made by a nine-man jazz band. And the magnificence of the ensemble in no way inhibits the assurance of the soloists.

Paul Weston's orchestral suite, *Crescent City*, reveals a talented composer and the hand of an experienced arranger. Creole folk melodies are interwoven with original themes in a series of tonal sketches, including *Storyville, Esplanade at Sunset*, and *Mardi Gras*. A small jazz band within the orchestra is part of the scene, playing *Riverfront Blues* in traditional New Orleans style. The mood varies from the gaiety of *Mardi Gras* to the sweet sadness of *Miss Lucy*, sensitively conveyed by Eddie Miller on tenor sax. The opening theme keynotes the feeling, turning the calendar back to the days of old New Orleans, the "Crescent City."

The creative writing of the arrangers, as well as the creative playing of the musicians, helped produce the quality of permanence inherent in the jazz played by the swing bands in the thirties.

37

Horn and Singer

IT is pleasant to recall those Sunday afternoon jam sessions at the Famous Door on Fifty-second Street, back in the swinging thirties. Everything was informal. Nothing was planned or rehearsed. Musicians came because it was sure to be congenial and because there was sure to be good music. They could play what they felt, and that might be blues, jazz standards, or free improvisation.

The musicians played, and a special kind of singer sang with them. One such singer was Lee Wiley, and there were times when she chanced to be there with such as Bunny Berigan, Jack Teagarden, Pee Wee Russell, Eddie Condon, and Joe Bushkin. Lee would just naturally sing with them *as one of them*. The song might have been *I'm Coming, Virginia, A Hundred Years from Today,* or maybe just the blues. They all understood one another.

Mildred Bailey is remembered today with fervor and loyalty, both by those who heard her in person and those who know her only from her recordings, for how she could captivate an audience with her way of doing a song. Ella Fitzgerald is universally loved today, as she has been for years, for her ability to sing just about anything with charm and grace. Bing Crosby still reigns in his enduring position at the top, a position he earned years ago by doing what came naturally. Frank Sinatra is second to none in his intuitive talent for interpreting a song, both words and music, drawing out all of its meaning.

These singers, of course, are outstanding, but they are representative of a larger number who have something in common. It is not only excellence. It is that they phrase a song the way a good jazz musician does. There is a relationship, a certain shared approach.

In the thirties and forties, the big bands were the natural habitat of popular singers. Surrounded by working musicians, and with many different songs to sing and new arrangements to learn, the singer found there was much to be learned by listening to the musicians. When Tommy Dorsey played the melody of a song on solo trombone, he virtually sang it. His phrasing was exactly right for the lyric. One has only to think of the first chorus of *Once in a While, All the Things You Are, I'll Never Smile Again.* His breathing was a model for both musician and singer.

I remember Jack Leonard saying that he learned his songs by listening closely to Tommy's trombone. Frank Sinatra has stated that he learned much from the way Tommy breathed and phrased on the trombone. Bob Eberly recalls that, when he first joined the Dorsey Brothers, he discovered how helpful it was to observe Tommy's breathing. To this day Lee Wiley, who sang with Tommy in radio and on recordings, mentions how much she learned from Tommy in this respect.

Some singers have a special feeling for jazz, and, like jazz musicians, they have a talent for improvisation. When Ella Fitzgerald sang *Stairway to the Stars* with Chick Webb's band, she used a variation in the last chorus which was delightfully appropriate to the written melody and could well have been the creation of a jazz soloist. It was equally impressive to hear her sing *Skylark* in a television variety show. She sang the melody, sensitively phrased—and with that special touch that could only come from an accomplished jazz artist.

The prototype for this rapport between singer and jazz musician is Ethel Waters. Singers, musicians, critics, and aficionados seem to agree on this. When Lee Wiley was new in New York, meeting people in the music field and learning her way around, Tommy Dorsey invited her to come out to his house in Freeport, on Long Island, expressly to listen to some Ethel Waters records. According

Frank in 1945

Chanteuse Lee Wiley

to Jimmy McPartland, Bix Beiderbecke never missed an Ethel Waters appearance if he was near enough to get to it. Whether it was in her early records in the twenties, or her performance of *Supper Time* in the Irving Berlin revue, "As Thousands Cheer," or in her introduction of *Stormy Weather* with Duke Ellington at the Cotton Club in 1933, she has always been a model of the right way to deliver a song.

Louis Armstrong was a prototype for both musician and singer. In his case, the rapport between singer and musician was a built-in relationship. Only Louis could sing like Louis; it was always a delight to hear his matchless phrasing in the vocal, as well as on trumpet. Bix was an early student of Louis' playing, but so was everybody. Ella and Louis did some wonderful things together. Two recordings that come to mind are *Dream a Little Dream of Me* and *A Kiss to Build a Dream On.* They are memorable particularly for the reciprocal use of counter melody and the way each side builds with joyous abandon. There is, demonstrably, complete understanding between them.

Mildred Bailey's ear was always tuned to the sound of the musicians working with her—in Paul Whiteman's orchestra, in her recordings with the Dorseys, and in Red Norvo's band. They worked together understandingly, the musicians responding sympathetically to the mood Mildred created for a song. This is evident in her classic recordings of *Washboard Blues, 'Round My Old Deserted Farm*, and *More Than You Know.*

We mentioned Maxine Sullivan and the arrangements Claude Thornhill made for her performance at the Onyx Club. What made everything complete was bassist John Kirby's band, with Charlie Shavers on trumpet and Buster Bailey on clarinet. There was just the right blend of reticence and swing. They all fit together.

Lee Wiley has always been surrounded with leading jazz musicians. In radio, there was Victor Young, Tommy Dorsey, Bunny Berigan, and Willard Robison and his Deep River Orchestra. Lee's first record album was of a selection of Gershwin songs. Not surprisingly, Bud Freeman, Max Kaminsky, Pee Wee Russell, and Joe Bushkin were with her. On one track, *Someone to Watch Over Me*, she was accompanied on organ by "Maurice," who actually was Fats Waller; his name could not be used because of a contract with another label. Bobby Hackett worked side by side with Lee in one of her most popular albums, "Night in Manhattan."

Hoagy Carmichael is another who has always been surrounded by the best jazz musicians. In fact, he made it a point to collect them, so that he could be surrounded by them. Hoagy, of course, is mainly a composer and songwriter, but he does sing. He sings in a fashion all his own, and it belongs with the horns—like Bix, the Dorseys, Benny Goodman, Joe Venuti, and the whole bunch—who were usually there when he sang. He played piano with them, too, and the horns always liked to play what he wrote. Bud Freeman enjoys *Stardust* because, as he says, the improvisation is "built in." The same could be said for *Skylark*, which was written after Bix's style. Some of Louis Armstrong's great recordings are of Hoagy's tunes—*Rockin' Chair, Georgia on My Mind, Eventide.*

Frank Sinatra's rapport with musicians is well known, and is apparent in all his work, whether it is an up-tempo number such as *You Make Me Feel So Young* or a sentimental ballad such as *All the Way.* He is equally at home with a swing band or a large concert orchestra. On many of his recordings using large orchestra, the conductor-arranger was another Tommy Dorsey alumnus, Axel Stordahl, who filled the assignment for ten years.

The bands produced some excellent singers, and the public took them to heart. Some of the graduates are a welcome part of today's scene—Kay Starr, Peggy Lee, Helen O'Connell, Sarah Vaughan. A band singer fondly remembered is Helen Ward, who was the first vocalist in Benny Goodman's original band. She retired from the business at the height of her popularity. I recall hearing her during Benny's first engagement at the Madhattan Room in New York's Pennsylvania Hotel. Singing with the band, she was part of it. Randy Hall still believes she was the best of all the band singers. In a letter mailed from Disney World, in Florida, Deane Kincaide writes: "Did a jazz concert last Saturday and Sunday in Manassas, Virginia. Saw Helen Ward, and it was a ball. She still has that lovely face and figure."

Mel Torme is another of those rare ones who have a built-in relationship of musician and singer. In his recordings, the arrangements —either his own or those of a talented arranger such as Marty Paich —are worked out so that the vocal line is an integral part of the whole effect. Mel's vocal treatment of *Lullaby of Broadway* is a tour de force that could only be done by a singer who is a musician.

Bing Crosby started as a partner in the west coast singing duo, Crosby and Rinker. Al Rinker was also pianist. When Paul Whiteman hired them, Harry Barris was added for a New York-Tin Pan Alley

Mature Frank

Ginger and Johnny Mercer at home in Los Angeles, 1972

injection, and they became the Rhythm Boys. There had been singing trios before, but not one like this. They were a whole band. To
be convinced, one has only to listen to *There Ain't No Sweet Man
That's Worth the Salt of My Tears*, featuring Bix Beiderbecke, Frank
Trumbauer, Bing Crosby and the Rhythm Boys.

When Bing went out on his own, he was accompanied on records
by Tommy and Jimmy Dorsey and the bands they assembled for the
purpose. By the time the Dorsey Brothers band was launched, Bing
was settled in Hollywood. As it turned out, it was Jimmy who worked
the radio show, but Bing remained close to both Tommy and Jimmy
right to the end.

Johnny Mercer is considered the foremost lyricist of our time, but
he really should have a classification of his own. As a singer with Paul
Whiteman around 1933 and 1934, he was a leading spirit in the
"Swing Wing," with Jack and Charlie Teagarden. In addition to fine
jazz, the Swing Wing delivered some very special vocal duets by
Mercer and Teagarden. Johnny was also starting to write songs. His
first big hit was *Lazy Bones*, in which he wrote the lyric for Hoagy
Carmichael's tune. Moving on to Hollywood in 1935, he wrote *I'm
an Old Cowhand*, both words and music. Bing liked it and arranged
to put it in his picture, "Rhythm on the Range."

At this point, Johnny was a singer-writer-composer who saw eye-
to-eye with jazz musicians, singers, and composers. There were more
songs with Hoagy, *Skylark* among them; lots with Harold Arlen,
including *Blues in the Night;* the lyric for Duke Ellington's *Satin
Doll;* and a Sinatra hit, *Something's Gotta Give*, for which Johnny
wrote both words and music. The list of Johnny's song hits seems
endless—*Jeepers Creepers, You Must Have Been a Beautiful Baby,
And the Angels Sing . . . Moon River . . .*

Johnny is still a singer. This was impressively brought to mind at
the first annual awards dinner of the Songwriters Hall of Fame in
March of 1971. Johnny was named president by acclamation. His
function that night was that of master of ceremonies and singer.
Present to sing the songs of writers and composers receiving awards
were several singers whose appearance, as noted by John S. Wilson
in the *New York Times*, "evoked memories equal to those associated
with the songs they sang." Lee Wiley sang *I've Got a Crush on You*,
by George and Ira Gershwin, and *A Hundred Years from Today*, by
Victor Young and Ned Washington, "still projecting," according to
Mr. Wilson, "the smoky, intimate, sweet-and-sour sound that made

her one of the most distinctive singers of the nineteen-thirties."
Other singers were Lanny Ross, Allan Jones, Al Hibbler, Anita Gil-
lette, Gordon MacRae, Celeste Holm, Oscar Brand, and Margaret
Whiting. One of the songs heard that night was *Too Marvelous for
Words*, composed by Margaret's father, Richard A. Whiting, with the
lyric by Johnny Mercer and sung by—Johnny Mercer.

Present at the Songwriters Hall of Fame dinner were others who
figured prominently in the Dorsey Years, among them Hoagy Carmichael, Cork O'Keefe, Eddie Condon, and Frank Sinatra. Frank didn't
sing—he didn't have time, because he was on his way to the Joe
Frazier-Muhammed Ali fight—but he remarked, addressing the writers, "Without you, I would have been selling ties."

I remember hearing some of Tommy's musicians—I think it was
in 1938—say, "There's a gal over at WNEW—you should hear her.
She's good." It was the first time I had ever heard of Dinah Shore.
Naturally enough, the word came from the guys in the band. They
didn't miss. Dinah made it without being a regular member of a
band, but she has always been one of them. Jazz musicians have
always had an intuitive sense about singers. When Jo Stafford was first
with Tommy Dorsey, as one of the Pied Pipers, she was a voice in the
ensemble, but the musicians knew then that she was someone they
would hear more of.

Maybe it's what Hoagy Carmichael calls "that very distinctive
sense of 'knowing'—knowing a good note from a bad one . . ."

38

Bix: Recurring Theme

THREE of us went to Roseland one night in September of 1927. It was the farewell engagement of the Goldkette band. We didn't want to miss it, and we especially wanted to see and hear Bix. Two of us, Bill Priestley and Dick Turner, were college trumpet players. Bill was mainly a guitarist at the time, but, inspired by Bix, was learning trumpet.

Roseland Ballroom was then located on Broadway, between Fifty-first and Fifty-second. Downstairs was Upmann's Cigar Store, which did not sell cigars. We were right in the middle of Prohibition, and what Upmann's dispensed was important. Bix and others in the band joined us at Upmann's between every set.

After the last set, over what was presumably a nightcap, Bix, who had not missed a between-sets rendezvous, decided we should have more music. We would continue. But where? Ferde Grofe, who had joined us, provided the answer. Paul Whiteman's office was around the corner on Seventh Avenue, and Ferde had a key. Fortified with a couple of bottles and an enormous pail of ice, the five of us trans-

ferred the action to Whiteman's office. Without delay, Bix sat down
and began playing the piano.

Grofe was, of course, familiar with Bix's trumpet playing, but he
had never heard him play piano. Ferde was transfixed. So were the
rest of us. Bix was not only playing piano, he was making music,
wonderful music.

At intervals—partly to give Bix a rest, and propelled by the time-
honored piano player's compulsion to get on the stool—Ferde relieved Bix. Ferde also improvised, playing some beautiful Grofe
chord sequences. Then Bix again. There was no intermission. Con-
tinuous show was the policy of the house.

All too soon, it was eight o'clock in the morning. We departed, still
under the spell of the music.

It had been a great night. There was no talk. We just wanted to
listen to Bix play the piano. Refills were widely spaced and accomplished quietly. The drinks only made us more attentive. It was
absorbing music. Bix was improvising and developing a design with
each successive theme. It was intuitive, but there was a design.

It was daylight as we left the Whiteman office and went our separate ways. The music stayed with me. I am sure it stayed with the
others. I kept on hearing those chord progressions, the accented
rhythms, relieved by an occasional poignant melody . . . gentle, but
strong.

The Beiderbecke legend was taking shape at this time. It had
begun building four years earlier, when Bix joined the Wolverines in
Chicago at the age of twenty. The cast of characters in the Bix story
could not have been more appropriate if it had been planned in
advance. In Chicago, there were Bud Freeman, Eddie Condon, Dave
Tough, Benny Goodman, Jimmy McPartland. In Bloomington, Indiana, Hoagy Carmichael began his permanent role in the story. In
Detroit, with Frank Trumbauer, Bix joined Goldkette and became
allied with Tommy and Jimmy Dorsey and Bill Challis.

We were aware of most of this as we listened that night at Roseland. And there was more to come. With some steering from Jimmy
Dorsey, Bix joined Paul Whiteman with Trumbauer and Challis at
about the same time as Bing Crosby and the Rhythm Boys.

Then, only four years later, Bix was dead at twenty-eight.

Bix had already become a reference point with musicians. If one
remarked, "He plays like Bix," it did not mean he copies Bix; it meant
playing with a similar approach—after the manner of Bix. As young

From the original sheet music, autographed by Bix for Bill Priestley

as Bix was at the time of his death, the music he left with us and the memory both of his playing and of Bix himself were enough to form a permanent chapter in American jazz.

Bix was a fine cornet player, but more important was the music he created. His improvisations were thoughtful; there was design. He had an intuitive sense of the right interval and the salient note. There was simplicity, the kind that goes with excellence.

It seems reasonable to believe that these qualities in Bix's music belonged to a remarkable person. This was certainly true. Bix was a sensitive, perceptive individual. He was natural, with no pretense. He was preoccupied with music, in another world much of the time. His drinking has been overemphasized in the legend. He drank, sure, more than was good for him, but it was incidental; it was a release. Life to Bix was music and friends.

Professional excellence and likability do not always equate. But with Bix, there was a quality of sympathy which showed in both his music and his personality. This quality communicated itself to musicians and friends. It is the welding of music and human being that make the Bix story so memorable.

Hoagy Carmichael, in his book, *Sometimes I Wonder,* speaks of Bix and remarks, "It is his gentleness that is lost in the legends, his ability to charm, to hold friends, to make one feel that it was still possible to know and need—and be known and needed by—another human being."

Bix was an idol of the college crowd, including our group of jazz musicians at Princeton. One of them, Bill Priestley, who was with us that night in Whiteman's office, got to know Bix well, became a close friend. Bill reminisces, recalling what it was like to know Bix: ". . . talking about everything with that wonderful, sensitive, intelligent, interesting guy . . . in seventh heaven listening to countless hours of his piano, in which he never played things exactly the same twice, would mix in a theme from one composition with any of the others, show me lots of little things on the horn I'd never have found for myself . . ."

When Bill was in New York in the fall of 1971, he brought along his trumpet and played some of those wonderful Bix choruses. Reflecting on what might have happened if Bix could have lived on and stayed well, Bill said, "I know one thing—Bix would have kept developing." We would surely have more compositions like *In a Mist* and *Candlelights,* which grew out of the improvisations we heard that night in Whiteman's office. These piano compositions, fortunately, were annotated by Bill Challis. Bill Priestley went on to imagine Bix and Challis still working together: "I'll hazard a guess that what they'd be playing today would be so far ahead of the most far-out modernists it would be silly to compare them."

I was with Yank Lawson, about ten years ago, when he took a band to Columbus, Ohio, for a month's engagement at the Grandview Inn. With Yank were two other Tommy Dorsey alumni—Deane Kincaide and Cliff Leeman. Others were Cutty Cutshall, Dill Jones, and Joe Williams. The customers included people of all ages. Many of them were students at Ohio State. Rock music was popular, but these students came to hear Yank play jazz. They knew all about Bix and his music. They collected his records. They were amazed to learn that we had known Bix. "You mean you actually *saw* Bix? You *knew* him?"

That same year, Yank and I put together a television special about Bix. We wrote to Paul Whiteman, asking him if he would participate. In his reply he said, "I'm always more than delighted to do anything for Bix."

A group in Long Valley, New Jersey, celebrates the memory of Bix annually in what is called the Bix Beiderbecke Memorial Stomp. In the *New York Times* of May 24, 1971, John S. Wilson reported the sixth running of the event, held at the home of E. William Donahoe, "a Beiderbecke enthusiast who keeps his kitchen clock permanently stopped at 9:30, the time when Mr. Beiderbecke died on August 6, 1931 . . ." More than two hundred musicians and guests stayed from 4:00 P.M. until midnight. The musicians, "playing in groups of seven or eight, performed on a platform against Mr. Donahoe's garage, on the side of which were a large portrait of Mr. Beiderbecke and a red banner that proclaimed, 'Bix Lives.' "

Another tribute to Bix was reported in the *New York Times* on August 7, 1971, with a dateline of Davenport, Iowa: "Jazz buffs and musicians wearing 'Bix Lives' buttons toasted the jazz immortal, Bix Beiderbecke, with early morning champagne and the *Davenport Blues*—the song he wrote for his hometown—over his grave here today. More than 1,500 people gathered before the simple headstone in the Beiderbecke family plot to honor the trumpeter and composer on the fortieth anniversary of his death at age twenty-eight on August 6, 1931 . . . Shirtless youths with beards and shoulder-length hair and white-haired men and women listened in silence as the Rev. C.

H. Meyer, pastor of St. Mark Lutheran Church, eulogized Mr. Beiderbecke while the eight-piece band made up of those who revere
his memory, as well as professional musicians, played *Davenport
Blues.*"

Especially interesting is the observation of Esten Spurrier, one of
the musicians who was present and who had played with Bix: "What
is exciting is the second generation of Bix devotees. A lot of them
aren't old enough to remember him in his prime but they still love
his music."

Like a motif in a symphony, Bix is a recurring theme, running
permanently through the continuing story of jazz.

IV

DENOUEMENT

39

Sessions at Priestley's: Tommy Tells Stories

IN the fifties, it was a different scene. There were fewer big bands. Bop had left its mark and given way to "progressive." Rhythm-and-blues was going public, becoming known as rock-and-roll. Television was becoming the message; Eddie Condon was doing a weekly jazz roundup on CBS-TV. Duke Ellington, Count Basie, and both Dorseys were making wonderful music. There were new sounds from Stan Kenton, Woody Herman, and Dizzy Gillespie. Gerry Mulligan, who began his creative work writing for the bands of Gene Krupa and Claude Thornhill, was creating some great new sounds for his jazz quartet.

In New York, Marian McPartland was at her post in the Hickory House, where discriminating lovers of jazz came night after night to listen. Red Nichols, with an eight-piece band including Joe Rushton and his bass sax, was playing classic jazz at the Roundtable.

In Chicago, an old custom was revived. The jazz gatherings remembered as "Sessions at Squirrel's" in the thirties were resumed at the home of Crickie and Bill Priestley in Lake Forest, near Chicago.

The sessions at Squirrel's were interrupted by the war. Everybody cut out in all directions. After the war, Squirrel moved to Washington. Joe Rushton travelled with Red Nichols. For a time, not much happened in the way of sessions. Crickie Priestley was the one who got things moving. As a regular at Squirrel's sessions, she had been thoroughly indoctrinated. Crickie issued the call, and people came from all over for the first session "which we all agreed," says Bill, "had to become an annual event. We decided the appropriate title was The Annual Bix Festival, believing Bix deserved one as much as J. S. Bach." There were four or five of these annual festivals—or sessions—on Sunday afternoons at the Priestleys'.

Tommy Dorsey attended one of the sessions, arriving without his trombone. He borrowed one belonging to Park Burgess, headmaster of the Lake Forest Country Day School, who was one of those assembled. Tommy started playing the blues and was joined on bass sax by Spencer Clark, who had followed Adrian Rollini in the California Ramblers; on guitar by Howard Kennedy, who had played with Tommy in the Goldkette days; by Jack Howe on clarinet, George Kenyon on mellophone, Squirrel on piano, and Bill on cornet.

After the first set, Tommy thanked Park Burgess for the use of the horn, and added, "This is a great horn, Park. What do you use on the slide—muselage?" According to Bill and Squirrel, Park's trombone was not in the best of shape, but it worked.

The session was taped by John Steiner. A recording, one of the Paramount Chicago Jazz Series, was issued in 1952 entitled "The Third Squirrel." On the label Tommy is identified as "Dorsey Burgess," with a bow to the trombone's owner. A clue to the identity of the trombonist was the blues title, *TD's DT's*.

Present at the session was Jack Gardner, whom Squirrel calls "one of the very greatest of the 'full' pianists. Arthur Schutt was one of his heroes, and Teddy Wilson told me that his first real conception of tenths bass came to him from listening on radio when Jack was playing with Maurie Sherman at the College Inn in Chicago." The record label identifies Jack as "Jarvis Fernsworth."

A tape was made of Spence Clark playing *Somebody Loves Me* on five different instruments in sequence—piano, clarinet, bass sax, drums, and bass. The result was a remarkable one-man band.

Tommy was the big hit of the afternoon—not on trombone, as one might expect, but as story-teller. He began to reminisce. One anecdote followed another, going from speakeasy days right on through to the present. Listening to the tape, it is as if Tommy is in the room, with all of his idiosyncrasies of speech. Tommy had a way of making a mirthful sound in his throat and sustaining it in the pauses. It had the effect of keeping the listener hanging on. As we listen, we could be back in Bernardsville. Or even further back, in Plunkett's.

Most of the anecdotes, of course, had to do with musicians. No music session, such as this one, could escape mention of Dave Tough, whom so many consider the greatest drummer of them all, and who is certainly one of the most affectionately remembered of all people. Tommy received a phone call one night . . .

"I got this call from the Forest Bar. They said Dave was there and wanted to talk with me. When he got on the phone, I could see what was wrong. I went over to the Forest and there was Dave—after two years on the wagon, he'd fallen off—way off. I could see this demanded special attention, so I took him out to the house, out in Bernardsville, so he could get some rest, take it easy—then I figured he'd be okay. The idea was do it gradually—give him a few drinks each day and *gradually* dilute them with water—get him sober, so we can talk to him. Days went by and we didn't notice any improvement. I said, 'This thing isn't working out—he's not responding.' We couldn't figure out what was wrong. We kept the liquor locked up. Then I remembered. I was collecting miniatures as a hobby, those little bottles you get in the dining car. I must have had a hundred of them. They were put away in a closet on the top shelf. We took a look—GONE!"

It was inevitable that someone would mention Jimmy Plunkett, proprietor of the bar which had been General Headquarters back in the studio days . . .

"Plunkett? Sure—I knew the son. The old man was a lush. He was corked out every night. Jimmy—the son—was a real character. He was living out at the house for a while. Wanted to get out of the city, get some of that good country air. I used to keep a pretty good stock of liquor at the bar, so a guest could get anything he asked for. One time, someone wanted Mount Vernon rye. No one ever asked for it—there must have been a case on hand. We opened a bottle, poured a drink—WATER! So we tried another bottle—*that* was water. We must have opened seven or eight bottles. All water. I didn't even know he was drinking . . ."

A 1939 session with jazz aficionados Bill Priestley and Squirrel Ashcraft

Jimmy and Marian McPartland

Joe Rushton on clarinet, Bill Priestley on cornet, Jumbo Jack Gardner (ex-Harry James) on piano

Miff Mole, first giant of the jazz trombone and a key influence on Tommy's style

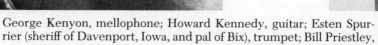

George Kenyon, mellophone; Howard Kennedy, guitar; Esten Spurrier (sheriff of Davenport, Iowa, and pal of Bix), trumpet; Bill Priestley, cornet; Spencer Clark (formerly with the California Ramblers), bass sax

Someone asked about Charlie Shavers, who had played trumpet with Tommy in recent years . . .

". . . we were at the Edgewater Beach. We had an afternoon rehearsal. We were trying out things—placing mikes, balancing the band, so it would sound good that night on the air. It was a bright, sunshiny day. During a break, we sent Charlie outside to play. The sun was blinding. He came running back inside, with his head covered, eyes closed. We said, 'Char-lie, that's sun-shine.' He said, 'Why don't they spotlight it?' "

There were other stories, kaleidoscopic mentions of people and places . . . the Everglades Club, the Speakeasy where the guy woke up, saw the palm trees on the oilcloth walls, and thought he had gone South . . . the place across the street, where the band finished "kind of early, around four" . . . the plush joint where the tariff was twenty-five or thirty dollars a bottle for "applejack with baking soda" . . . the bandleader who told the night club owner, "If you're going to complain about the music, go put your show on some place else."

But the best story of the day—one of the best ever—was Tommy's account of the drafting of Pee Wee Russell. Tommy embarked on the story with relish:

"Pee Wee arrived home on payday, very late, well sluiced, and with very little of the week's take remaining. The bar bill had been impressive. The first Mrs. Russell—the one Condon referred to as 'the strike breaker'—flew into a towering rage, and Pee Wee ran for his life, followed by pots, pans, and anything else handy she could throw. He stayed with friends for a couple of days to allow her to cool off. When he returned, she *forgot* to tell him that, during his absence, a notice had arrived from Washington informing him he was drafted—and she had torn it up. So he continued to play at Nick's, blissfully unaware that he was AWOL. The Army, instead of going to the address where they had sent the draft notice, to find out why they hadn't heard from him, naturally did it the hard way. They first went to his birthplace, where his mother, a delightful lady, still lived. She told them all about Pee Wee's boyhood, showed them a picture of Pee Wee at the age of fifteen, in his military academy uniform, at which the man from Washington nodded wisely, and one said to the other, 'Hm-m, officer material.' They followed a trail of saloons and night clubs through Oklahoma, Texas, St. Louis, Detroit—and finally arrived at Nick's, where Pee Wee was taking a chorus. They remembered the picture they saw at his mother's, looked carefully at Pee Wee, and asked, 'What happened?' Then they took him off the stand at Nick's and went up to the Grand Central office building, where the physical exams were being given. Pee Wee was told to strip, and the first exercise was to stand on one foot and jump off the floor on the one foot forty times. In exactly thirty seconds, he was classified 4F, and he was back on the stand at Nick's in time to finish the set."

Recalling Tommy telling the story, Bill Priestley says, "Tommy was in rare form, and his asides and embellishments had us helpless, with tears streaming down our cheeks." Bill was a close friend of Pee Wee and, like many of us, a great admirer: "his style continued to develop so that he was one of the few of his contemporaries whom the young musicians, two generations younger, loved to play with."

On that Sunday afternoon, beside musicians, the assembled group included a lawyer, an architect, a teacher, a business man, an engineer—and they, too, were musicians. Music was the common denominator. It was communication.

The choice spot on a variety bill, traditionally, has always been next-to-closing. On that Sunday afternoon at the Priestleys', Tommy Dorsey the raconteur came on in the next-to-closing spot. There were encores and audience participation. For the closing spot, Tommy Dorsey the trombone man picked up his horn and joined the group for a real good jam session.

40

The Lyric Revisted

TOMMY played the Lyric Theatre in Indianapolis for the last time in November of 1952. It was like meeting up with an old friend. A lot had happened thereabouts. The Lyric is gone now. It lasted into 1969, when it was shuttered and marked for demolition. Gene Gladson, Indianapolis author and publisher, tried his best to save it, but the Lyric's time, like that of so many theatres, had come.

The Lyric was one of the country's leading vaudeville houses, founded by a champion wrestler, Charles M. Olson. It had several things in common with the prototype of vaudeville houses, the Palace in New York. They were about the same age; the Lyric, dating from 1912, was one year older. The two were close in seating capacity; the Lyric, seating 1,892, was actually ninety-two seats larger. The Palace had almost twice as much room on stage. They both played stage shows, in addition to films, right through the Depression years.

For Tommy, it wasn't just playing the Lyric that brought on a wave of memories. It was being in Indiana. Besides contributing George Ade, Booth Tarkington, and Cole Porter, Indiana had delivered Hoagy Carmichael—Hoagy, who kept the jazz piano going at the

Book Nook in Bloomington, and who drove Bix to Richmond, Indiana, on that winter's day in January 1925 for that recording session at the Gennett studios, where Bix's *Davenport Blues* was born and named by Tommy for Bix's home town . . .

The stage of the Lyric was where, in March of 1939, Tommy introduced a guest pianist, Mrs. Howard Carmichael, who played *Maple Leaf Rag* and stole the show away from Hoagy and Tommy. The very next year, Tommy played the Lyric with a new singer making his first apperance with the band. The theatre took a six-inch ad in the paper with Tommy's name in one-inch letters and the singer's name in one-eighth-inch letters. The billing was small, but the singer broke it up. The ad billed him as "Frank Sinatra, Romantic Virtuoso."

Another thing: right next to the theatre ad in the *Indianapolis Star* was an ad for the St. Moritz restaurant: "Dinner served—Popular Mixed Drinks—Old-fashioned, Tom Collins, Whiskey Sour, Manhattan, Martini, Gin Fizz—twenty cents."

The Lyric played "The Fabulous Dorseys" in June of 1947. Tommy wasn't there. If he had been on hand, he could have done nothing to alleviate the pain or atone for what Hollywood had wrought. The picture was one of a double-feature bill, sharing time with "Abie's Irish Rose" and competing with "Perils of Pauline" at the Indiana and "Blaze of Noon" at the Circle.

The next year, in 1948, the Dorseys, Tommy and Jimmy, appeared in person, not at the Lyric this time, but as soloists with the Indianapolis Symphony, Fabien Sevitzky conducting. The walls almost came tumbling down with the *1812 Overture.*

In 1952 at the Lyric, admission prices were higher. Matinee and evening performances, instead of forty cents and sixty cents, cost seventy-five cents and a dollar. This was Tommy's third time at the Lyric, but he was outdistanced: the record for a musical act was held by the Ezra Buzzington Rube Band with eight times on stage.

On October 12, 1969, the *Indianapolis Star* reported that the Lyric was scheduled for demolition "to make way for another parking lot." Demolition expert Ed Zebrowski was given the assignment. Gene Gladson, who had been conducting a "Save the Lyric" campaign, was quoted in the *Star:* "I predict that Zebrowski will make a big hit, and bring down the house." Lowell Nussbaum, columnist on the *Star,* visited the Lyric after the wreckers began their work and observed: "Aside from the trash which littered the place, my most vivid impression was of rope—miles and miles of it. I never realized how much rope it takes to operate a theatre with its many stage curtains and other drops."

In a letter to the *Star*, Gladson wrote: "I think this town needs a theatre like the Lyric, which is equipped for both stage shows and movies. Indianapolis will not be the same without the Lyric."

There have been other campaigns to save time-honored structures. One that worked was the drive to save Carnegie Hall in New York. The outcome was good for everybody. Carnegie still has the best acoustics. The Lyric's New York counterpart, the Paramount, is gone. A giant complex is rising on the site where once were heard the sounds of Goodman, Dorsey, Shaw, Miller, and the rest. Contained inside this complex, along with acres of office space, will be a large theatre, not directly accessible from the street. In 1972, the site where the Lyric once stood is still a parking lot.

After his 1952 appearance at the Lyric, Tommy returned to New York. There was much to be done, and the first item on the list of things to do involved both himself and the brother.

41

Reunited: Mac and Lad

IT was rough going in the band business. Like so many bandleaders, Jimmy had to close down. He joined Tommy's band. In the barnstorming days, when they were young musicians, just beginning to get around in the field, their moves seemed to follow a pattern: Tommy joined the band where Jimmy was playing. It was that way in the California Ramblers, the Goldkette band, and the Whiteman band. Now it was Jimmy who was joining the band where Tommy was playing. The brothers were reunited in 1953. Although it was Tommy's band, they were once again known as the Dorsey Brothers.

The band played in the Cafe Rouge at New York's Statler Hilton Hotel. We knew it as the Pennsylvania, when it was the scene of those early triumphs for both Tommy and Jimmy. The Big Apple was forgotten, and it was not yet time for the Twist. The music was the thing, and the Dorsey brothers programmed it well. They took turns leading the band. Each featured his own book and introduced the other as soloist. The audience heard the numbers associated with each one in his rise to fame. It was a band for all seasons. Classic jazz,

distinguished treatments of standard and current popular songs—
and swing, too.

It was good to see Lee Castle in the band, and hear him play
trumpet. Lee joined Tommy's band in 1937. He played with Teagarden for a time, also with Benny Goodman, and he led his own band
for a while, but he was associated with the Dorseys most of the time.
In this latter-day Dorsey Brothers band, he played solos in the big
band, and he was in the front line with Tommy and Jimmy in the
small jazz band. He was also assistant conductor and the line of
communication between the brothers.

Lee conducted the band during the dinner set from 7:00 to 8:00.
Jimmy conducted from 8:00 to 9:00. Tommy came on at 9:00, and
then, according to Lee, "Everybody straightened up and started to
play." Tommy was the leader. He knew just what had been played,
and how it sounded, during the dinner set; he had been listening,
upstairs in his room, where he had had the band piped in.

Carmen Mastren comments, "When Tommy took Jimmy with
him, toward the end, Tommy was the boss. Jimmy needed help, and
Tommy gave it to him. Jimmy told me this at the table in the Statler-
Hilton. He was happy to be back in action again. But he was much
happier leading his own band."

Jackie Gleason was an old friend of Tommy and Jimmy. Their
friendship went back to the Club 18, where Gleason appeared occasionally in the forties. The Dorseys enjoyed the humor at the Club
18 where the master of ceremonies, Jack White, heckled the customers and was heckled by his henchmen, Frankie Hyers and Pat Harrington. White emceed the floor show from a spot next to the ladies'
room. When it was time to start the show, White watched for one or
more ladies to disappear inside. Then, when the door opened and the
gals emerged to return to their seats, White signalled a quick drum
roll and hollered, "Everybody out of the can—show's on!" The spotlight and the customers' eyes followed the ladies across the floor.
White usually withstood the heckling of Hyers and Harrington un-
daunted. One time, however, he broke up when a series of interrup-
tions was climaxed by Hyers shouting, "Turkey, they're gonna *roast*
you!"

Gleason loves good jazz. Whenever his television troupe entrained
for Florida (before settling there permanently), it was always accompanied by a personally selected group of jazz musicians whose playing matched the unquenchable enthusiasm of the troupe. Yank Law-

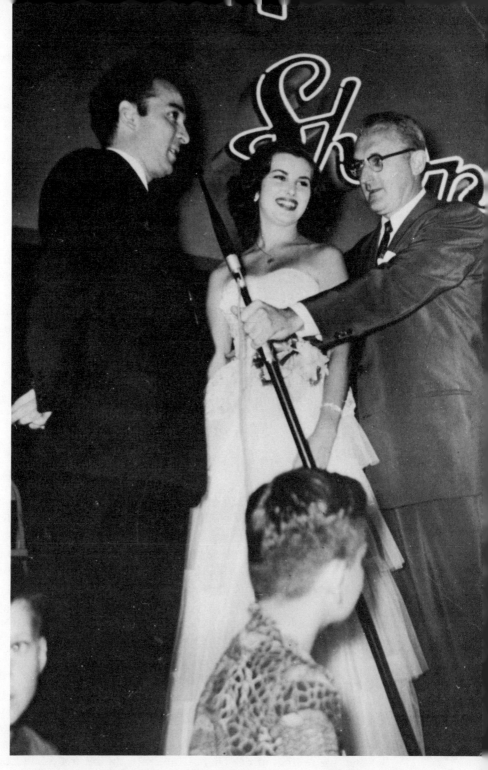

Tommy opens a Stockton, California department store in 1954, aided by Miss Universe. But since Miss Universe speaks only Italian, Tommy calls on trumpeter-assistant conductor Lee Castle (*né* Castaldo) for help with the translating

son remembers the day when ground was broken for Toots Shor's new place on Fifty-second Street. Gleason recruited Yank and some other jazz stars to enliven the ceremony. It was a cold, wet day, but the band played, and there was good cheer to pass around.

Gleason showed his regard for the Dorseys and their kind of music by installing them as summer replacement for his variety show on CBS. The contract specified that if Tommy was present and Jimmy was not, the agreement remained in effect; but that if Jimmy was present and Tommy was not, the agreement was not valid.

When the contract arrived and Tommy spotted this provision, he showed it to Lee Castle. "Look at this," he said. "When the brother sees it, he's going to think I put them up to it. I knew nothing about it."

The summer series, "Stage Show," introduced guests, one of whom was an item of new talent, Elvis Presley, and featured band numbers associated with both bands. There was a weekly meeting of the production staff, after rehearsal on the day before the show. In one of the meetings, at which Jimmy was not present, a cut was made in *Amapola*. Running down the routine, before going on the air the next evening, Jimmy discovered the cut and was infuriated. He looked at Lee.

"What's this? Who made this cut in *Amapola?*"

"We needed a cut, and that was the logical one."

"I didn't know anything about this. Why *Amapola?*"

"Don't ask me. Speak to your brother."

Jimmy spoke to Tommy and got a short answer. "Next time, show up at the meeting."

Evidently, there was still something left of the old Mac and Lad. It would have been incredible if it had been any other way. But it wasn't serious. There was more room now.

The Swing Era was well represented in Garry Moore's daily television show, which I was then producing for Garry. The pianist and musical director was a Tommy Dorsey alumnus, Howard Smith. Carl Kress, Joe Helbock's associate at the Onyx Club in 1935, played guitar. Bassist Trigger Alpert and clarinetist Ernie Caceres had played with Glenn Miller. Eddie Shaughnessy, the drummer, was younger than the others, but there was no age gap. He had played with George Auld after the war.

Many of Garry's guests were from the jazz world. For Maxine Sullivan we recreated the Onyx Club, with the intimate bandstand

and the pin spot. Some of the others were Louis Armstrong, Jonah Jones, Jack Teagarden, Yank Lawson, Wild Bill Davison, Eddie Condon, Gene Krupa, Cozy Cole, Marian McPartland, Erroll Garner, and Mary Lou Williams. Teagarden did a ten-minute spot, including *Aunt Hagar's Blues.* After rehearsal, we had to make a small cut, or risk having the commercial cut short by the quarter-hour station break. There appeared to be a few bars in *Aunt Hagar's Blues* which could be snipped without hurting the number. Jack looked pained and said, "Oh, man, don't cut my blues." We left it alone.

Randy Hall was another of Garry's guests. Randy is an accomplished player of jazz on the tin whistle. He used to carry the whistle in his pocket, like a fountain pen, in order to be equipped when Marian McPartland, Red Nichols, Tommy or Jimmy Dorsey asked him to sit in. In 1953, Dick Rodgers and Oscar Hammerstein wrote an extra scene in their Broadway musical, "Me and Juliet," in which Randy played the whistle. Randy and Wild Bill Davison were two of the program's guests included in Garry's Columbia record album, "My Kind of Music." Bill did *Yesterdays* and *Ain't Misbehavin'*, backed by forty strings. Randy did *Lady Be Good* and *After You've Gone,* backed by a jazz band.

"I was on the west coast," says Randy, "when I got a telegram from Garry. I had the choice of waiting until I returned to New York or doing it out there." Randy learned that in Hollywood he would be backed by the Rampart Street Paraders, including Eddie Miller (tenor sax), Matty Matlock (clarinet), Charlie Teagarden (trumpet), Abe Lincoln (trombone), Nick Fatool (drums), and Stan Wrightsman (piano). "That was it!" proclaims Randy. His part in the album was recorded "out there."

The idea of assembling this particular group of musicians came from another Tommy Dorsey alumnus, Paul Weston, then a conductor at Columbia Records.

A year or so later, Randy was owner and proprietor of a restaurant in Boynton Beach, Florida, called the Whistle Stop. There were two reasons for its name: Randy played the whistle, and it *was* a whistle stop, midway between Delray and Palm Beach. It was a refueling stop for musicians who were in that part of the country or driving through.

While Garry's show was in Winterhaven, Florida, for two weeks, Garry, his wife Nell, and several others of us drove to the Whistle Stop for a good dinner and some music. In the course of the evening

A selection of 18-century French prints from Randy Hall's "Whistle Stop" home, Boynton Beach, Florida. Prints are inscribed to Randy and autographed by famous friends

"To Randy—We all wore these costumes during the 'bop' days.— Benny Goodman"

"Randy—It was good seeing you again, of course. I've put on considerable weight since this was taken. Sincerely, Tommy Dorsey"

"To Randy—May the spirit of music reign forever!!!—Wild Bill Davison"

"Randy—This is the instrument I
mastered while a member of
Husk O'Hare's fine outfit.
You remember! Lots of good luck
and happiness.
—Sincerely, Jimmy Dorsey"

"To my pal, Randy—Best always—
Jimmy McPartland"

"Randy—Whee! for the Whistle Stop—
Eddie Condon"

"To Randy—in great admiration—
Garry Moore"

Teagarden combo featured Kass Malone, bass; Kenny Davern, clarinet; Ray Bauduc, drums

Jack blows Tommy's part in the Dorsey book

Tommy, Jimmy and their band pay a surprise visit to Jack Teagarden at the Bali Key Club, Brentwood, Pa. in 1954

Tommy always felt Jack Teagarden was the better jazz trombonist, said so at the first *Metronome* All-Star session

Tommy, Lee Castle on trumpet, Buddy Rich on drums, Mr. Tea

Randy Hall playing the tin whistle at a 1962 jazz musicale. Originally a sax player, Randy gets a lot of jazz out of the whistle. Author Sanford on piano

we looked around the place and noticed some old prints, framed and hung on the wall among autographed pictures of friends and performers.

On closer inspection, we saw that they were eighteenth-century French prints. Each one was a stylized representation of a musician of the period. All of them were autographed, each with a personal inscription. The print of the French horn player was autographed by Wild Bill Davison; the guitar player was autographed by Eddie Condon; the reed-instrument player by Benny Goodman; the trombone player by Tommy Dorsey; the bassoon player by Jimmy Dorsey; and the cornet player by Jimmy McPartland. There was one more, a print of the conductor, autographed by Garry Moore.

The Dorsey Brothers did some travelling in the mid-fifties. One night, during an engagement in Pittsburgh, around Christmas time of 1954, the entire band piled into the bus with instruments and music, and rode to suburban Brentwood. The bus stopped at the Bali Key Club. Tommy announced, "We're going in to hear the master." The master was Jack Teagarden, and the visit from Tommy and Jimmy and the band was a big surprise.

The band filed into the Bali Key, set up music stands, and started tuning up, just as if it were playing a date. In a moment or two the Dorsey band, augmented by the Teagarden group, was making music. Jackson T. and his group got over the initial shock and had a fine time. So did the manager and the customers. Jack's group included Ray Bauduc on drums, Kenny Davern on clarinet, Fred Greenleaf on trumpet, Norma Teagrden on piano, and Kass Malone on bass. Teagarden and Dorsey played a trombone duet on the blues, the way they had played it at the first *Metronome* All-Star record date fifteen years before. Both Lee Castle and Kenny Davern have mentioned the incident recently, in 1972.

Lee Castle, besides being next in command, was a close friend of both Tommy and Jimmy. Tommy was living in Greenwich, Connecticut, with his third wife Janie and their two children. It was the custom for Lee to drive with Tommy as far as the Bronx, where Lee then lived. Tommy wanted Lee to buy a piece of property next to his, and build a house. Lee demurred, realizing that the cost would be considerable. "Don't worry about it," Tommy said. "I'll take care of the down payment." He was still the same Dorsey; if there was a project in view, nothing must stand in the way.

On one occasion, setting out in Tommy's car for a playing date in

Boston, Tommy wanted to make up some sleep. He asked Lee to drive. Before dropping off to sleep, Tommy insisted on a turn which Lee felt certain was in the wrong direction. When Lee noticed a sign, "This way to New York," he turned around and headed for Boston. Tommy was asleep. They were the last to arrive. This was embarrassing; Tommy liked to be first. Of course it was Lee's fault. "You let the bus get here ahead of us. Even the brother got here first."

Lots of old friends came to see Tommy and Jimmy at the Cafe Rouge. Jack Egan and Joe Helbock checked in, bringing "Mom" Dorsey with them. During the fall of 1956, I spent an evening at the Cafe Rouge, talking with Tommy and Jimmy and enjoying the music. Tommy asked if I had read *Auntie Mame.* I had to confess that I had not yet got around to it. I really should have got to it sooner; it was a best-seller—deservedly so, as I later discovered. Everyone was talking about it.

Tommy looked at me in amazement. "You mean you haven't read *Auntie Mame?*"

"No, but I will. I know it's great."

Tommy spoke to his manager and whispered a few words. The manager disappeared and returned a moment later with a copy of *Auntie Mame,* which Tommy handed to me.

"Here, take it. It's yours."

I objected that I didn't want to take his copy. I promised I would get it and read it without further delay.

"No, no, it's an extra copy. It's for you. It's the funniest thing I've ever read in my life. You'll love it. Take it. Read it."

I learned that Tommy had so fallen in love with *Auntie Mame* that he kept a supply of copies in his room at the hotel. When he discovered a friend who was so remiss that he had not yet read *Auntie Mame,* he saw to it that the friend did not depart without a copy. It was another Tommy Dorsey project.

"My Fair Lady" opened that year and was playing nightly to a capacity house. It was next to impossible for anybody to get tickets. The show and the difficulty encountered in obtaining tickets were the subject of conversation everywhere.

"Have you seen it yet?" Tommy asked.

"Not yet—it's impossible to get tickets."

"You've *got* to see it."

"I will, for sure, later on." I knew there was no chance of "My Fair Lady" closing in the foreseeable future. I figured I would wait. Someday it would be possible simply to *buy* tickets without having to negotiate for them.

"Nothing doing. You'll have tickets tomorrow."

This was building up. First, a copy of *Auntie Mame*. And now theatre tickets? And for "My Fair Lady?"

After the closing theme, it was time to depart. I thanked Tommy for the copy of *Auntie Mame* and said I'd be seeing him soon.

The next afternoon, a messenger delivered two tickets for "My Fair Lady" to my office at CBS. I was grateful, but not really surprised. It was so characteristic of Tommy.

The next week, on the Wednesday before Thanksgiving, Randy Hall stopped in at the Statler Hilton with Lyda Barclay (now Mrs. Randy Hall) to see Tommy and Jimmy. Tommy appeared to be in a cheerful mood. Actually, he was anything but happy; there was trouble at home, an impending divorce with all its unsettling effects. But Tommy didn't let on.

"Tommy and Jimmy sat with Lyda and myself during dinner," Randy recalls. "Tommy confided that never in his life had things gone so well. Even an old stock he had thought worthless had come to life after ten years. Had a hard time finding the certificates in a trunk . . ."

42

Journey's End

ON the Monday following Thanksgiving, 1956, Cork O'Keefe's telephone rang. It was Jimmy. He sounded far away.

"Did you hear about Mac?"

"No, what?"

"He's dead."

Cork hurried to the Statler Hilton and got to Jimmy's side. Tommy had died in bed the night before at his home in Greenwich. Apparently he had choked while asleep, and died without awakening.

Jimmy was numb with grief, trying his best to face the fact that Tommy was dead. And there was an ordeal ahead: he must tell Mom. Following her husband's death in 1942, Mrs. Dorsey had come to New York and made her home in an apartment Tommy and Jimmy found for her in the East Eighties.

Word of Tommy's death had not reached Mom when Jimmy and Cork got there. Jimmy could not bring himself to tell her immediately. Lee Castle and other friends began arriving. Mrs. Dorsey remarked it was a coincidence that some of them happened to drop in on the same afternoon. All the while, Jimmy was pacing, staying close to Cork, trying to muster up the courage to tell his mother that Tommy had died. He simply could not do it. It was Tino Barzie, Tommy's personal manager, who finally told her.

It was dark when Jimmy and Cork left Mrs. Dorsey's apartment. As they walked down the block, Jimmy started to cry. They stopped by a lamppost, while Jimmy gained strength to move on. Jimmy looked at Cork and said:

"I don't think I'll last out the year."

News of Tommy's death travelled fast. Shock and disbelief. Then sadness settled in. Word reached Jack Egan at Ratazzi's, a midtown New York restaurant frequented by writers and publicity people. Jack left and went to the Spotlight, a pub across town on Broadway which was, and still is, a meeting place for musicians. It was quiet there. They had heard the news.

Next morning, newspapers confirmed the report that Tommy had choked to death in his sleep the night before. Tommy had always driven himself, propelled by great energy and stamina, often sleeping only in short stretches. On the night of his death, he was tired. After a big dinner, he slept soundly. When he choked in his sleep, he was unable to awaken and recover.

Jackie Gleason organized a television tribute to Tommy, broadcast over the CBS Television Network later that same week. Some of those who had been with Tommy in his band twenty years earlier participated—Bud Freeman, Max Kaminsky, Carmen Mastren, Pee Wee Erwin, Howard Smith, Jack Leonard, Paul Weston, and Axel Stordahl. Bob Crosby, who sang with the original Dorsey Brothers band, took part; and Bobby Byrne; and Jo Stafford. Jimmy was there, along with Joe Venuti, Eddie Condon, and Russ Morgan. Paul Whiteman delivered an affectionate and moving tribute.

They played and sang some of the songs that were permanently associated with Tommy. The music was just right. It sounded an "up" note. It was the way Tommy would have wanted it. It was the way those present wanted to remember Tommy.

Tommy Dorsey dead at fifty-one. It was hard to believe.

Now there was only one Dorsey brother. Jimmy's heart was broken. He did his best to carry on, but he said to Lee Castle, "It's your band now. I'll be gone in six months." A month or so after Tommy's death, Jimmy was operated on; a lung was removed. He didn't know there was cancer.

Mom kept track of Jimmy. She was worried. She called Cork

Fall, 1956: a party at Tommy's Connecticut estate, and one of the last pictures ever taken of the Sentimental Gentleman. Lee Castle is second from left, Bert Parks smiles on Tommy's right, Charlie Shavers squats in front of the boss

O'Keefe. And she called Bobby Byrne, saying, in that brogue every-one loved, "I don't like the way he's lookin'." The band continued to play, but Jimmy stayed in his room most of the time. Lee led the band, and looked after Jimmy. I remember seeing Jimmy in his room. At his side was the record player he always kept handy. As always, there was a record he wanted a friend to hear. This time it was a new arrangement sung by the Hi-lo's. "Isn't that *beautiful* music?" he smiled.

The doctor advised a change of scene. Jimmy went to Miami Beach and put in at the Bell Harbor Hotel. Cork O'Keefe telephoned him there in March. "Come on up," Jimmy said. Cork found Jimmy in bad shape. Walking was difficult, and Jimmy's condition was obviously getting worse.

"We've got to get you home," Cork told Jimmy.

"Home," replied Jimmy. "Where's home? The Statler Hotel?"

Cork wasn't thinking of any hotel. He managed to get Jimmy lodged on a plane bound for New York, where he was transferred direct to Doctors Hospital. Jimmy never left the hospital.

Bob Eberly, Jimmy's close friend through all the years, was with him much of the time through those last days. Bob remembers a day when Jimmy spent considerable time adjusting the pads on his clarinet, then tried to play. He couldn't make it. He burst into tears. "He knew the end was coming, but he would not accept the thought," remarks Bob.

The end came on June 12, 1957, three months after entering the hospital, six months after Tommy's death. Only a few days before, Lee Castle had presented Jimmy with his gold record for *So Rare*. It had been recorded the previous November and had sold more than a million copies.

43

The Dorsey Years

THE Dorsey Years began in the twenties, along with Scott Fitzgerald's Jazz Age. The Dorseys' kind of jazz was music. Tommy and Jimmy loved to make music—as kids in the coal-mining region of Pennsylvania, as barnstorming musicians, as headliners across the country, as veteran bandleaders. They grew up with jazz, and they helped steer the course of jazz in its formative years. They matured with big-band jazz, advancing through the Depression and the rise of radio. They weathered the step from Plunkett's under the el to the Onyx on Fifty-second Street. They helped point the way all through the time of the big bands, with its swing concerts, jam sessions and hit records. They saw jazz become universally accepted and take its place as a permanent art form.

The lives of the brothers were intertwined, whether they were together or apart. When they worked together, they fought—though each continued to display a protective attitude toward the other. This dual attitude prevailed to the point of each insisting on the right to fight, and making this position clear to anyone who attempted to interfere. Jimmy started most of the fights, and Tommy made most of the noise. There was no professional jealousy; each greatly admired the work of the other. When they worked separately, each was a booster for the other. They really loved each other very much.

Jimmy never completely grew up. Their mother once reflected, "The strong one was the first to go."

There was a drive, some kind of inner voice, that kept the Dorseys going in the face of any circumstance, whether it was the break-up of a band, a feud with a booking office, or a terminal illness. Tommy was never without a project of some kind to answer an existing need: now a ballroom, then a booking office. At the time of his death, he was looking forward to forming a giant recording company. Jimmy tried to go on leading the band after his operation; he wouldn't quit. One night he had to call upon Lee Castle, while playing, to take over.

The Dorsey reaction to a person, or in a situation, was mobile, and not always predictable. A musician who decided to leave either band, even for a compelling reason, could be sure that Tommy or Jimmy would be piqued. But he wouldn't know whether to expect a threat of blacklisting, a recommendation, or maybe an unsolicited offer of financial aid. There was always help for a friend. Tommy's place in Bernardsville was a convalescing home for any friend who was ailing.

Tommy could denounce, and in most emphatic terms, anyone who stood in his path. Often he was right, but not always. He could also show humility. One time, when he learned he was to be part of a group which was to include Pat O'Brien, he asked Lee Castle, "Do you think he'll know me?"

Tommy also had a memory. A prominent music publisher was a regular visitor at Tommy's playing engagements. The publisher once remarked, "Tommy always treats me fine, but I never can get him to play any of my tunes." What the publisher didn't remember was that, when Tommy was struggling with the original Dorsey Brothers band, he asked the publisher for a professional copy of the stock orchestration of one of the publisher's numbers, and was charged seventy-five cents.

The Dorsey sense of humor was an important part of their equipment, along with that "inner voice." Whatever the situation, there was room for a laugh, and the laugh was usually found. Tommy and Jimmy each made a lot of money, but the important thing was not money. It was music, excellence in music. In relations with their fellow men, they could hold their own anywhere, in any company. Theirs were big souls. They travelled first class all the way.

Whenever two or more of us who were associated with Tommy or Jimmy get together, we speak of the Dorseys and the Dorsey Years. The talk is of things clearly remembered, and we seem to be there with them once again. There are laughs, and heart-throb too. Those were great days. And that music! It was wonderful.

Appendix I

DORSEY HONOR ROLL

A listing of outstanding musicians, singers and arrangers who worked with the Dorseys over the years.

DORSEY BROTHERS ORCHESTRA

The Early Years, 1928–35

Trumpet:	Bunny Berigan, Mickey Bloom, Frank Guarente, Manny Klein, Charlie Margulis, Bill Moore, Phil Napoleon, Nat Natoli, Muggsy Spanier, Charlie Spivak, George Thow
Trombone:	Glenn Miller, Jack Teagarden, Joe Yukl
Saxophone:	Larry Binyon, Bud Freeman, Skeets Herfurt, Adrian Rollini, Babe Russin, Jack Stacey
Clarinet:	Frank Teschmaker
Piano:	Fulton McGrath, Arthur Schutt, Frank Signorelli, Bob Van Eps
Guitar:	Perry Botkin, Roc Hillman, Carl Kress, Eddie Lang, Dick McDonough
Bass:	Artie Bernstein, Delmar Kaplan, Joe Tarto
Drums:	Ray Bauduc, Ray McKinley
Violin:	Joe Venuti
Female vocalist:	Mildred Bailey, Boswell Sisters, Connee Boswell, Kay Weber
Male vocalist:	Smith Ballew, Chick Bullock, Bing Crosby, Bob Crosby, Bob Eberly, Seger Ellis, Skinnay Ennis, Skeets Herfurt, Ray McKinley, Johnny Mercer
Arranger:	Glenn Miller, Herbie Spencer

JIMMY DORSEY ORCHESTRA

Trumpet: Ray Anthony, Cy Baker, Lee Castle, Maynard Ferguson, Conrad Gozzo, Bobby Hackett, Nate Kazebier, Ray Linn, Ralph Muzzillo, Phil Napoleon, Al Porcino, Red Rodney, Shorty Sherock, Shorty Solomon, Charlie Teagarden, George Thow, Nick Travis

Trombone: Will Bradley, Bobby Byrne, Cutty Cutshall, Brad Gowans, Sonny Lee, Don Matteson, Buddy Morrow, Frank Rehak, Andy Russo, Bruce Squires, Earl Swope, Joe Yukl, Si Zentner

Saxophone: Danny Bank, Serge Chaloff, Bob Dukoff, Charlie Frazier, Stan Getz, Jimmy Giuffre, Herbie Haymer, Skeets Herfurt, Fud Livingston, Dave Matthews, Frank Maynes, Ted Nash, Babe Russin, Jack Stacey, Phil Urso, Milt Yaner

Piano: Lou Carter, Dick Cary, Johnny Guarnieri, Al Haig, Joe Lipman, Arnold Ross, Freddie Slack, Bob Van Eps

Guitar: Herb Ellis, Roc Hillman, Steve Jordan, Tommy Kay, Nappy Lamare, Allan Reuss, Guy Smith (Zeb Julian), Hy White

Bass: Joe Mondragon, Jack Ryan, Barney Spieler

Drums: Ray Bauduc, Barrett Deems, Karl Kiffe, Ray McKinley, Buddy Schutz, Terry Snyder

Female vocalist: Anita Boyer, Claire Hogan, Kitty Kallen, Helen O'Connell, Dee Parker, June Richmond, Kay Weber

Male vocalist: Bob Eberly, Skeets Herfurt, Nappy Lamare, Ray McKinley, Andy Roberts, Terry Shand, Teddy Walters

Arranger: Sonny Burke, Toots Camarata, Larry Clinton, Howard Gibeling, Dizzy Gillespie, Joe Lipman, Fud Livingston, Pat McCarthy, Don Redman, Len Whitney

TOMMY DORSEY ORCHESTRA

Trumpet: Bunny Berigan, Sonny Berman, Jimmy Blake, Mickey Bloom, Sterling Bose, Billy Butterfield, Lee Castle, Ziggy Elman, Pee Wee Erwin, Andy Ferretti, Bobby

Hackett, Clyde Hurley, Max Kaminsky, Yank Lawson, Ray Linn, Doug Mettome, Bobby Nichols, Chuck Peterson, Doc Severinsen, Charlie Shavers, Shorty Sherock, Charlie Spivak, Ray Wetzel, Jimmy Zito

Trombone: George Arus, Will Bradley, Warren Covington, Earle Hagen, Dave Jacobs, Les Jenkins, Walter Mercurio, Buddy Morrow, Tommy Pederson, Sonny Russo, Ward Sillaway, Elmer Smithers

Saxophone: Noni Bernardi, Sid Block, Ernie Caceres, Nick Chiazza, Corky Corcoran, Sam Donahue, Bud Freeman, Dave Harris, Skeets Herfurt, Deane Kincaide, Al Klink, Walt Levinsky, Don Lodice, Vido Musso, Boomie Richman, Les Robinson, Art Rollini, Babe Russin, Hymie Schertzer, Bill Shine, Freddie Stulce, Johnny Van Eps, Tony Zimmers

Clarinet: Heinie Beau, Gus Bivona, Buddy DeFranco, Joe Dixon, Peanuts Hucko, Slats Long, Johnny Mince, Abe Most, Sid Stoneburn

Piano: Joe Bushkin, Bob Carter, Johnny Guarnieri, Dick Jones, Bob Kitsis, Dodo Marmarosa, Milt Raskin, Billy Rowland, Jimmy Rowles, Jack Russin, Gene Schroeder, Howard Smith, Paul Smith

Guitar: Barry Galbraith, Carmen Mastren, Tony Rizzi

Bass: Jack Lesberg, Ed Mihelich, Artie Shapiro, Phil Stephens, Gene Traxler, Sid Weiss

Drums: Louis Bellson, Buzzy Drootin, Gene Krupa, Cliff Leeman, Jackie Mills, Moe Purtill, Buddy Rich, Alvin Stoller, Dave Tough

Vibes: Terry Gibbs

Female vocalist: Anita Boyer, Connie Haines, Peggy Mann, Lucy Ann Polk, Lynn Roberts, Jo Stafford, Edythe Wright

Male vocalist: Bob Allen, Don Cherry, Stuart Foster, Dick Haymes, Skeets Herfurt, Jack Leonard, Tommy Mercer, Sy Oliver, Gordon Polk, Charlie Shavers, Frank Sinatra

Arranger: Benny Carter, Larry Clinton, Bill Finegan, Neal Hefti, Dick Jones, Deane Kincaide, Carmen Mastren, Fred Norman, Sy Oliver, Howard Smith, Axel Stordahl, Freddie Stulce, Paul Weston

Appendix II

1935 DORSEY BROTHERS BAND ITINERARY

Being the remains of a murderous schedule issued to band members in April 1935. Contributed by Kay Weber Sillaway.

APRIL 12   Toronto, Can.—Silver Slipper
13   Erie, Pa.
14   Cleveland—Trianon
     To New York for suits, apts., etc.

18   transcriptions
19   "
20   Pottstown, Pa.
21   New London, Conn.
22   Waltham, Mass.—Nuttings
28   Bristol, Conn.—Lake Compounce
29   Troy, N.Y.
30   Deerfield, Mass.—Gables

MAY 1   Scranton, Pa.
2   Mahanoy City, Pa.
3   Union College—Schenectady, N.Y.
4   Dartmouth—Hanover, N.H.
5   Passaic, N.J.—Kantor's Hall
6   Harrisburg, Pa.—Madrid
7   Pittsfield, Mass.
8   Waterbury, Conn.—Hamilton Park
9   Rhode Island State College—Providence
10   Loyola College—Baltimore
11   Allentown, Pa.—Mealy's Ballroom
     Band must immediately come to New York for uniforms, balance, tests, etc.
16   Glen Island Casino

INDEX

Page numbers in italics represent photographs.